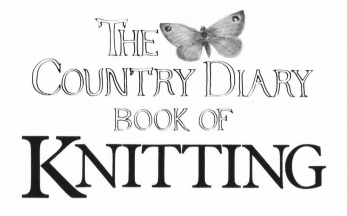

THE
COUNTRY DIARY
BOOK OF
KNITTING

The Country Diary
Book of
KNITTING

Annette Mitchell

Henry Holt and Company
New York

DEDICATION
To my friends and family with love.

Copyright © 1987 by Annette Mitchell

The publishers would like to thank Rowena Stott,
Edith Holden's great-niece and the owner of the original work,
who has made the publication of this
book possible.

Published in the United States by
Henry Holt and Company, Inc., 115 West 18th Street,
New York, New York 10011.

Originally published in Great Britain by
Webb & Bower (Publishers) Limited
9 Colleton Crescent, Exeter, Devon EX2 4BY
in association with Michael Joseph Limited
27 Wright's Lane, London W8 5TZ

Library of Congress Cataloging in Publication Data
Mitchell, Annette.
The country diary book of knitting.
1. Knitting.   I. Title.
TT820.M58   1987   746.43′2   87-8587
ISBN: 0-8050-0516-1

Henry Holt books are available at special discounts
for bulk purchases for sales promotions, premiums,
fund raising, or educational use. Special editions
or book excerpts can also be created to specification.

For details contact:

Special Sales Director
Henry Holt and Company, Inc.
115 West 18th Street
New York, New York 10011

Designed by Ron Pickless

Technical Editor Marilyn Wilson

Production by Nick Facer/Rob Kendrew

Typeset in Great Britain by P&M Typesetting, Exeter, Devon
Colour origination by Peninsular Repro Services, Exeter, Devon

Printed and bound in Hong Kong

10 9 8 7 6 5 4 3 2

CONTENTS

AUTUMN

WINTER

INTRODUCTION

The Country Diary Book of Knitting follows the success and popularity of *The Country Diary Book of Crafts* (Webb & Bower, 1985).

It was clear that many people were delighted to be given the opportunity to make things for the home and for themselves from designs inspired by the wonderful illustrations contained in *The Country Diary of an Edwardian Lady*. *The Country Diary Book of Knitting* is, as the name implies, a collection of knitting patterns which has also been inspired by Edith Holden's enchanting watercolours of the English countryside.

Due to the very nature of knitting techniques however, and in an effort to provide a wide range of patterns, the designs contained in *The Country Diary Book of Knitting* are not such direct replicas as many of those which can be found in *The Country Diary Book of Crafts*. Instead, the designs in this book echo the rich atmospheric and seasonal themes of the countryside strongly portrayed throughout the pages of *The Country Diary of an Edwardian Lady*. The exquisite shading of Edith Holden's watercolours, coupled with the different textures she so cleverly captured on paper, have provided a wealth of inspiration which has been used and interpreted through a wide variety of knitting techniques and a carefully selected range of yarns and colours.

The Country Diary Book of Knitting has been divided into four major thematic sections to represent country life as it progresses through the four seasons. Within each season is a choice of knitting patterns suitable for all the family and for all levels of knitting ability. In short, it is hoped that *The Country Diary Book of Knitting* includes something for everyone!

Spring
Delicate pastels gently mingle with soft neutrals to introduce the first signs of spring. 'Fair Maids of February' combines subtle pastels with texture and Fair Isle designs in the production of a delightful set of children's and toys' outfits, inspired by snowdrops and primroses.

'Song Thrush and Young' uses soft neutral and brown tones, worked in a simple basket stitch representing a bird's nest, for an easy-to-knit set of useful family sweaters.

A glance at the middle pages of the section leaves little doubt as to which of nature's small creatures inspired this fun-to-wear collection of children's hand-knitwear for spring.

Summer
The warmth of summer light brings sharper pastels and shades of deeper hue, producing strength of contrast and design as well as the continuation of romantic looks.

'May' is a lady's 4 ply lace sweater in white, inspired by the texture and colour of the abundance of hawthorn at this time of year. Lace is further applied to children's wear in 'Honeysuckle', where feminine pastels, simple lace pattern-repeats and satin bows have been cleverly combined to produce a charming matching sweater and cardigan. This use of bows is a good example of how ribbons can be applied to knitwear to give an exclusive finishing touch to a fairly plain garment.

'Willow Herb' could not be easier to make and is therefore an ideal first garment for the beginner. Here, the application of simple cross-stitch embroidered flowers adds special interest.

More vibrant shades of summertime have inspired several designs including: 'Kingfisher' — a lady's stocking-stitch cardigan; 'Wild Hyacinths' — a child's lacy cotton-look sweater; 'Butterfly — a stunning lady's mohair jacket worked in Fair Isle; and 'Ladybirds' — a matching ribbed sweater and cardigan highlighted by ladybird buttons, with useful matching 'bug-bag' as well as a spotty ladybird sweater for Teddy!

Autumn
Rich, red tones introduce the magic of autumn. Fair Isle techniques are applied to wonderful poppy designs for both ladies and children. Further autumn treasures are unearthed in the form of intricately textured designs depicting ears of corn, thistles, berries and leaves.

Toadstools and hedgehogs inspire a brightly coloured sweater and cardigan set for children and an enviable hedgehog sweater accompanied by an irresistible little knitted companion!

Winter
As the sun sets, the sombre November shades of seed-vessels invite designs of a more subtle and subdued nature, both in texture and colour.

The cold air and colours of winter are quickly dispersed however with the celebrations of Christmas and the presence of holly, ivy and mistletoe. These have produced a host of designs decorated with lace and enhanced by a full use of texture and colour, and which make delightful Christmas gifts.

The theme of ice and snow is captured wholeheartedly in 'Snowbirds', 'Snowflakes', 'Frost and Ice' and 'Robins'. This section is full of the fun and excitement radiated by children playing in the first snow and it provides the greatest possible encouragement to get out the knitting needles on a cold winter's evening.

In recognition of its great source of inspiration, the designs and the illustrations of *The Country Diary Book of Knitting* have been styled in keeping with Edwardian times. It is hoped that this has given the book added interest to all who appreciate both the craft of knitting and the beauty of the countryside.

Finally, *The Country Diary Book of Knitting* is the culmination of the work of many who are involved with knitting, either as a hobby or professionally or indeed both. Their common interest has brought them together to participate in the production of this special book of knitting in a sincere endeavour to encourage knitting to continue for as long again as Edith Holden's 'Nature Notes' of 1906 have done to date.

SUBSTITUTING YARNS AND KNITTING TO TENSION

The knitting patterns included in this book have been knitted and photographed in the brand and quality of yarn stated at the beginning of each set of instructions. Should there be any difficulty in obtaining the yarns (or any other products) do not hesitate to contact the company involved, by referring to the lists of addresses given at the back of the book.

No responsibility can be taken by either the publisher or the author for any yarn which has been discontinued by the manufacturer. *Do not be discouraged* however, if this is the case. It is highly likely that a substitute yarn can easily be found with the help of a reputable wool shop. Great care must be taken to ensure that an alternative yarn can be knitted to correspond with the tension clearly printed at the beginning of the pattern.

Before starting to knit any design, *check the tension* of your knitting by working a small *tension square.* Do not forget that the correct tension can often be obtained by merely *altering the needle size.* If the tension is *too loose* (making the sample square too big) try a *smaller needle.* If the tension is *too tight* (making the sample too small) try a *larger needle.*

ABBREVIATIONS

K – knit
P – purl
st(s) – stitch(es)
st st – stocking stitch (US stockinette stitch) 1 row K, 1 row P
rev st st – reverse stocking stitch (US reverse stockinette stitch) 1 row P, 1 row K
alt – alternate
beg – beginning
cont – continu(e) (ing)
dec – decreas(e) (ing)
inc – increas(e) (ing)
foll – follow(s) (ing)
patt – pattern
rem – remain(s) (ing)

rep – repeat
RS – right side of work
WS – wrong side of work
sl – slip
psso – pass slipped stitch over
tog – together
tbl – through back of loop(s)
yfwd – yarn forward (US yarn over)
yon – yarn over needle (US yarn over)
yrn – yarn round needle (US yarn over)
ybk – yarn back
ch – chain
dc – double crochet (US single crochet)
tr – treble crochet (US double crochet)
cm – centimetre(s)
in(s) – inch(es)

mm – millimetres
g – gramme(s)
K up – pick up and knit
g st – garter stitch (every row K)
M1 – pick up bar that lies between needles and K tbl.
□ on chart keys refers to blue squares on charts
Instructions are given for the smallest size. Larger sizes are given in the following square brackets. Where only one set of figures is given, this will apply to all sizes.
Yarn amounts are based on average requirements and are, therefore, approximate.

SPRING

Fair Maids of February *Children's Sweater, Cardigan and Berets*

Sizes

Cardigan and sweater
To fit chest 51[56:61:66]cm,
20[22:24:26]ins
Actual chest 56[61:66:71]cm,
22[24:26:28]ins
Length 36[39:43:48]cm,
14¼[15½:17:19]ins
Sleeve seam 28[31:33:37]cm,
11[12¼:13:14½]ins

Berets
All round head approximately
37.5[42]cm, 14¾[16½]ins

Materials

Cardigan OR sweater
2[2:2:2] × 50g balls of Wendy Dolce in main colour (A)
1[1:2:2] balls in contrast colour (B)
1[1:1:1] ball each in contrast colours (C and D)
Cartwheel beret
1 × 50g ball each of Wendy Dolce in main colour (A) and contrast colour (B)
Patterned beret
1 × 50g ball each of Wendy Dolce in main colour (A) and contrast colour (B)
Oddments (odds and ends) in contrast colours (C and D)
One pair each 3¼mm (US3) and 4mm (US6) knitting needles
4mm (US6) circular needle
6[6:7:8] buttons for cardigan
4 buttons for sweater

Tension/Gauge

24 sts and 34 rows to 10cm, 4ins over stripe patt using 4mm (US6) needles

STRIPE PATT

1st–2nd rows: With B, K.
3rd–8th rows: Beg with a K row, work 6 rows st st in C.
9th–10th rows: With A, K.
11th–16th rows: Beg with a K row, work 6 rows st st in B.
17th–18th rows: With C, K.
19th–24th rows: Beg with a K row, work 6 rows st st in B.
25th–26th rows: With A, K.
27th–32nd rows: Beg with a K row, work 6 rows st st in B.
33rd–34th rows: With A, K.
35th–40th rows: Beg with a K row, work 6 rows st st in C.
41st–42nd rows: With A, K.
43rd–48th rows: Beg with a K row, work

6 rows st st in B.
49th–50th rows: With C, K.
51st–56th rows: Beg with a K row, work 6 rows st st in A.
57th–58th rows: With B, K.
59th–64th rows: Beg with a K row, work 6 rows st st in A.
65th–66th rows: With B, K.
67th–72nd rows: Beg with a K row, work 6 rows st st in C.
73rd–74th rows: With A, K.
75th–80th rows: Beg with a K row, work 6 rows st st in B.
81st–82nd rows: With A, K.
These 82 rows form the stripe patt.

CARDIGAN

BACK

Using 3¼mm (US3) needles and A, cast on 66[72:78:84] sts. Cont in K1, P1 rib for 5[5:5:6]cm, 2[2:2:2½]ins ending with a WS row, inc 1 st at end of last row. 67[73:79:85] sts.
☆☆Change to 4mm (US6) needles and beg with 33rd[25th:17th:9th] patt row cont in stripe patt until 82nd patt row has been worked.
Cont in A only.
Beg with a K row, work 6 rows st st.☆☆
Commence motif
1st row: K4[5:6:7]A, (1D, 1A) 5 times, ☆1A, 1D, 2A, (1D, 1A) 7[8:9:10] times, rep from ☆ once more, 1A, 1D, 2A, (1D, 1A) 5 times, K3[4:5:6]A.
2nd row: P7[8:9:10]A, ☆1D, 3A, (1D, 1A) 5 times, 2A, 1D, 1[3:5:7]A, rep from ☆ twice more, P6[5:4:3]A.
Commence working from chart, reading odd numbered rows (K) from right to left and even numbered rows (P) from left to right. Use small separate balls of yarn for each area of colour and twist yarns tog on WS of work when changing colour to avoid a hole.
3rd row: K11[12:13:14]A, ☆work 1st row of chart, K9[11:13:15]A, rep from ☆ once more, work 1st row of chart, K11[12:13:14]A.
4th row: P11[12:13:14]A, ☆work 2nd row of chart, P9[11:13:15]A, rep from ☆ once more, work 2nd row of chart, P11[12:13:14]A.
These 2 rows establish the position of the chart. Keeping chart correct until completed cont in this way then cont in A only, work 2 rows.
Shape armholes
Cast off 2 sts at beg of next 2 rows.

63[69:75:81] sts.
Dec 1 st at each end of next and every foll alt row until 51[57:63:69] sts rem, ending with a P row. Leave sts on a spare needle.

LEFT FRONT

☆☆☆Using 3¼mm (US3) needles and A, cast on 32[36:38:42] sts. Cont in K1, P1 rib for 5[5:5:6]cm, 2[2:2:2½]ins ending with a WS row, inc 1 st at side edge of last row. 33[37:39:43] sts.
Work as given for back from ☆☆ to ☆☆.
Commence motif
1st row: K5[5:6:6]A, (1D, 1A) 6[6:7:7] times, 1A, 1D, 2A, (1D 1A) 5[6:6:8] times, K2[4:3:3]A.
2nd row: P3[3:2:6]A, (3A, 1D) 2[3:3:3] times, (1A, 1D) 4 times, (3A, 1D) twice, P6[6:9:9]A.
Commence working from chart.
3rd row: K14[14:17:17]A, work 1st row of chart, K10[14:13:17]A.
4th row: P10[14:13:17]A, work 2nd row of chart, P14[14:17:17]A.
These 2 rows establish the position of the chart. Keeping chart correct until completed, cont in this way then cont in A only. ☆☆☆
Work 2 rows.
Shape armhole
Cast off 2 sts at beg of next row. Work 1 row. ☆☆☆☆Dec 1 st at armhole edge on next and every foll alt row until 25[29:31:35] sts rem, ending with a P row.
Leave sts on a spare needle.

RIGHT FRONT

Work as given for left front from ☆☆☆ to ☆☆☆.
Work 3 rows.
Shape armhole
Cast off 2 sts at beg of next row.
Complete as given for left front from ☆☆☆☆ to end.

SLEEVES

Using 3¼mm (US3) needles and A, cast on 30[32:36:38] sts. Cont in K1, P1 rib for 6[6:6:8]cm, 2½[2½:2½:3]ins, ending with a RS row.
Inc row: Rib 2[0:2:2], ☆work twice into next st, rep from ☆ to last st, rib 1. 57[63:69:73] sts.
Change to 4mm (US6) needles and beg with 25th [17th:9th:1st] patt row cont in stripe patt until 82nd patt row has been worked.

* on page 14

FAIR MAIDS OF FEBRUARY

Cont in A only.

Beg with a K row, work 6 rows st st.

Commence motif

1st row: K2[4:6:7]A, (1D, 1A) 7 times, 1A, 1D, 2A, (1D, 1A) 9[10:11:12] times, 1A, 1D, 2A, (1D, 1A) 7 times, K1[3:5:6]A.

2nd row: P5[7:9:6]A, (1D, 3A) 2[2:2:3] times, (1D, 1A) 4 times, (1D, 3A) 3[4:4:5] times, (1D, 1A) 5[4:5:4] times, (1D, 3A) 3[3:3:4] times, P2[4:6:3].

Commence working from chart page 14.

3rd row: K13[15:17:18]A, work 1st row of chart, K13[15:17:19]A, work 1st row of chart, K13[15:17:18]A.

4th row: P13[15:17:18]A, work 2nd row of chart, P13[15:17:19]A, work 2nd row of chart, P13[15:17:18]A.

These 2 rows establish the position of the chart. Keeping chart correct until completed, cont in this way then cont in A only, work 2 rows.

Shape sleeve top

Cast off 2 sts at beg of next 2 rows. Dec 1 st at each end of next and every foll alt row until 41[47:53:57] sts rem, ending with a P row.

Leave these sts on a spare needle.

YOKE

With RS of work facing, using 4mm (US6) circular needle and B, K across 25[29:31:35] sts of right front, 41[47:53:57] sts of sleeve, 51[57:63:69] sts of back, 41[47:53:57] sts of sleeve and 25[29:31:35] sts of left front. 183[209:231:253] sts.

Work in rows.

1st row: K.

2nd row: K5[11:6:5], (K2 tog, K8[6:6:6]) 17[23:27:30] times, K2 tog, K6[12:7:6]. 165[185:203:222] sts.

3rd row: K.

4th row: K5[11:6:5], (K2 tog, K7[5:5:5]) 17[23:27:30] times, K2 tog, K5[11:6:5]. 147[161:175:191] sts.

5th row: K.

6th row: K5[11:6:5], (K2 tog, K6[4:4:4]) 17[23:27:30] times, K2 tog, K4[10:5:4]. 129[137:147:160] sts.

7th row: K.

Change to A.

8th row: K to end dec 2[0:0:3] sts evenly. 127[137:147:157] sts.

9th row: P2, ☆K3, P2, rep from ☆ to end.

10th row: K2, ☆P3, K2, rep from ☆ to end.

Rep 9th and 10th rows 2[3:4:5] times more, then work 9th row again.

Next row: K2, ☆P2 tog, P1, K2, rep from ☆ to end. 102[110:118:126] sts.

Next row: P2, ☆K2, P2, rep from ☆ to end.

Next row: K2, ☆P2, K2, rep from ☆ to end.

Rep last 2 rows 1[1:2:3] times more, then the first of them again.

Next row: K2, ☆P2 tog, K2, rep from ☆ to end. 77[83:89:95] sts.

Next row: P2, ☆K1, P2, rep from ☆ to end.

Next row: K2, ☆P1, K2, rep from ☆ to end.

Cast off in patt.

TO MAKE UP/TO FINISH

Join underarm seams.

BUTTONBAND

Using 3¼mm (US3) needles and A, cast on 5 sts.

1st row: (RS) K1, ☆P1, K1, rep from ☆ to end.

2nd row: P1, ☆K1, P1, rep from ☆ to end.

Rep these 2 rows until band is long enough, when slightly stretched, to fit up front edge to neck, ending with a WS row.

Leave sts on a safety pin.

Sew button band in place. Mark the positions of 5[5:6:7] buttons, the first to come 1cm, ½in above cast on edge, the last at 4th row of yoke, with the others evenly spaced between.

BUTTONHOLE BAND

Work as given for buttonband, making buttonholes opposite markers as foll:

Buttonhole row: (RS) K1, P1, yrn, P2 tog, K1.

Sew buttonhole band in place.

NECKBAND

With RS of work facing, using 3¼mm (US3) needles and A, rib 5 sts of buttonhole band, K up 75[81:87:93] sts evenly around neck edge, rib across 5 sts of buttonband. 85[91:97:103] sts.

Next row: (P1, K1) twice, ☆P2, K1, rep from ☆ to last 3 sts, P1, K1, P1.

Next row: (K1, P1) twice, ☆K2, P1, rep from ☆ to last 3 sts, K1, P1, K1.

Rep these 2 rows 3 times more, working a buttonhole as before on foll 2nd row.

Cast off in rib.

With C, embroider primroses to motifs using French Knots as shown.

Join side and sleeve seams. Sew on buttons.

SWEATER

BACK

Work as given for cardigan back, using B instead of A for welt and varying stripe patt sequence as desired.

FRONT

Work as given for back.

SLEEVES

Work as given for cardigan, using B instead of A for cuffs and varying stripe patt sequence as desired.

TO MAKE UP/TO FINISH

Join underarm seams, leaving left back seam open.

YOKE

With RS of work facing, using 4mm (US6) circular needle and B, K across 41[47:53:57] sts of left sleeve, 51[57:63:69] sts of front, 41[47:53:57] sts of sleeve and 51[57:63:69] sts of back. 184[208:232:252] sts.

Work in rows.

Next row: K to end, dec[inc:dec:inc] 1 st at end of row. 183[209:231:253] sts.

Beg with 2nd row, complete as given for yoke of cardigan.

NECKBAND

Using 3¼mm (US3) needles and A, with RS of work facing, K up 75[81:87:93] sts evenly around neck edge.

Work 4 rows in K2, P1 rib. Cast off in rib.

BUTTONBAND

Using 3¼mm (US3) needles and A, with RS of work facing, K up 21[24:25:29] sts evenly from 8th row of yoke on left sleeve back opening edge to top of neckband.

Next row: K.

Next row: K2[2:3:3], ☆yfwd, K2 tog, K3[4:4:5], rep from ☆ to last 4[4:4:5] sts, yfwd, K2 tog, K to end.

Next row: K.

Cast off.

Complete as given for cardigan.

SNOWDROPS

CARTWHEEL BERET

☆☆Using 3¼mm (US3) needles and A, cast on 90[100] sts. Work 6 rows in K1, P1 rib.

Inc row: ☆K twice into next st, K1, rep from ☆ to end. 135[150] sts.

Change to 4mm (US6) needles. Beg with a P row, cont in st st, work 9[11] rows.

Change to B and K 14 rows. ☆☆

Change to A and K 1 row.

Next row: ☆K3, P2, rep from ☆ to end.

Next row: ☆K2, P3, rep from ☆ to end.

Rep the last 2 rows 3[4] times more, then the first of them again.

Next row: ☆K2, P2 tog, P1, rep from ☆ to end. 108[120] sts.

Next row: ☆K2, P2, rep from ☆ to end.

Rep the last row 4[6] times more.

Next row: ☆K2, P2 tog, rep from ☆ to end. 81[90] sts.

Next row: ☆K1, P2, rep from ☆ to end.

Next row: ☆K2, P1, rep from ☆ to end.

Next row: ☆K1, P2, rep from ☆ to end.

Change to 3¼mm (US3) needles.

Next row: ☆K2 tog, P1, rep from ☆ to end. 54[60] sts.

Next row: ☆P2 tog, rep from ☆ to end. 27[30] sts.

Next row: ☆K2 tog, rep from ☆ to last 1[0] sts, K1[0]. 14[15] sts.

Cut off yarn, thread through rem sts, draw up and fasten off securely.

TO MAKE UP/TO FINISH

Join back seam. Using B, make a tassel approximately 20cm, 8 ins long and attach to crown.

PATTERNED BERET

Work as given for cartwheel beret from ☆☆ to ☆☆.

Change to A.

Next row: K12[8], (K2 tog, K20) 5[6] times, K2 tog, K11[8]. 129[143] sts.

Beg with a P row, work 3[5] rows st st.

Next row: K1D, ☆1A, 1D, rep from ☆ to end.

Next row: P3A, ☆(1D, 1A) 7 times, 4[6]A, rep from ☆ to end.

Next row: K8[10]A, ☆(1D, 1A) 3 times, 12[14]A, rep from ☆ to last 13 sts, (1D, 1A) 3 times, 7A.

Cont in A only.

Beg with a P row, work 5[7] rows st st.

Change to 3¼mm (US3) needles and B.

Next row: ☆K3, K2 tog, rep from ☆ to last 4[3] sts, K4[3]. 104[115] sts.

K 5 rows.

Next row: ☆K2, K2 tog, rep from ☆ to last 0[3] sts, K0[3]. 78[87] sts.

K 5 rows.

Next row: ☆K1, K2 tog, rep from ☆ to end. 52[58] sts.

K 5 rows.

Next row: ☆K2 tog, rep from ☆ to end. 26[29] sts.

Next row: K0[1], ☆K2 tog, rep from ☆ to end. 13[15] sts.

Cut off yarn, thread through rem sts, draw up and fasten off securely.

TO MAKE UP/TO FINISH

Using C, embroider primroses using French Knots as shown. Join back seam. Using B, make a pom-pon approximately 12cm, 4¾ins in diameter and sew to crown.

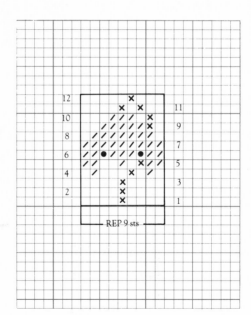

Key
A □
B /
C ●
D ×

SNOWDROPS
Lady's Jacket

Sizes

To fit bust 76 – 81[86 – 91:97 – 102]cm, 30 – 32[34 – 36:38 – 40]ins

Actual bust 96[105:113]cm, 37¾[41¼:44½]ins

Length 61[62:63]cm, 24[24½:24¾]ins

Sleeve seam 43cm, 17ins.

Materials

17[18:19] × 50g balls of Phildar Shoot in main colour (A)

1[1:1] × 50g ball each of Phildar Sagitaire in contrast colours (B, C and D)

One pair each 4mm (US6) and 5mm (US8) knitting needles

Cable needle

7 'Pikaby' buttons

Pair of shoulder pads

Tension/Gauge

24 sts and 26 rows to 10cm, 4ins over patt using 5mm (US8) needles

CABLE PANEL

(worked over 8 sts)

1st row: (RS) K.

2nd row: P.

3rd–6th rows: Rep 1st and 2nd rows twice more.

7th row: Sl next 4 sts onto a cable needle and hold at front of work, K4 then K4 from cable needle.

8th row: P.

These 8 rows form the cable panel.

FLOWER PANEL

(worked over 15[17:19] sts but sts are made and lost within the patt)

1st row: (RS) P1[2:3], P2 tog, P4, pick up the bar that lies between st just worked and next st and K tbl – called M1, K1, M1, P4, P2 tog, P1[2:3].

2nd row: K6[7:8], P3, K6[7:8].

3rd row: P1[2:3], P2 tog, P3, (K1, yfwd) twice, K1, P3, P2 tog, P1[2:3].

4th row: K5[6:7], P5, K5[6:7].

5th row: P1[2:3], P2 tog, P2, K2, yfwd, K1, yfwd, K2, P2, P2 tog, P1[2:3].

6th row: K4[5:6], P7, K4[5:6].

7th row: P1[2:3], P2 tog, P1, K3, yfwd, K1, yfwd, K3, P1, P2 tog, P1[2:3].

8th row: K3[4:5], P9, K3[4:5].

9th row: P1[2:3], P2 tog, K4, yfwd, K1, yfwd, K4, P2 tog, P1[2:3].

10th row: K2[3:4], P11, K2[3:4].

11th row: P2[3:4], K11, P2[3:4].

12th row: As 10th row.

13th row: P1[2:3], P twice into next st, K4, sl 1, K2 tog, psso, K4, P twice into next st, P1[2:3].

14th row: As 8th row.

15th row: P1[2:3], P twice into next st, P1, K3, sl 1, K2 tog, psso, K3, P1, P twice into next st, P1[2:3].

16th row: As 6th row.

17th row: P1[2:3], P twice into next st, P2, K2, sl 1, K2 tog, psso, K2, P2, P twice into next st, P1[2:3].

18th row: As 4th row.

19th row: P1[2:3], P twice into next st, P3, K2 tog tbl, K1, K2 tog, P3, P twice into next st, P1[2:3].

20th row: As 2nd row.

21st row: P1[2:3], P twice into next st, P4, sl 1, K2 tog, psso, P4, P twice into next st, P1[2:3].

22nd row: K7[8:9], P1, K7[8:9].

23rd row: P7[8:9], P into front and back of next st twice, turn K4, turn P4, turn K4, turn pass 2nd, 3rd and 4th sts over 1st st, sl 1st st onto right hand needle, P7[8:9].

24th row: K.

These 24 rows form the flower panel.

BACK

Using 4mm (US6) needles and A, cast on 92[104:112] sts.

Cont in K2, P2 rib for 8cm, 3 ins ending with a RS row.

Inc row: Rib 8[9:8], ☆inc in next st, rib 3[4:4], rep from ☆ to last 8[10:9] sts, inc in next st, rib to end. 112[122:132] sts.

Change to 5mm (US8) needles and commence patt.

1st row: (RS) P6[7:8], ☆work 1st row of cable panel, work 1st row of flower panel, rep from ☆ to last 14[15:16] sts, work 1st row of cable panel, P6[7:8].

2nd row: K6[7:8], ☆work 2nd row of cable panel, work 2nd row of flower panel, rep from ☆ to last 14[15:16] sts, work 2nd row of cable panel, K6[7:8].

These 2 rows establish the position of the cable and flower panels with rev st st at each edge. Keeping panels correct cont as set until work measures 38cm, 15ins from beg, ending with a WS row.

Shape armholes

Keeping patt correct, cast off 3 sts at beg of next 2 rows. Dec 1 st at each end of foll 2[3:4] alt rows. 102[110:118] sts.

Cont without further shaping until work measures 61[62:63]cm, 24[24½:24¾]ins from beg, ending with a WS row.

Shape shoulders

Cast off 33[35:37] sts at beg of next 2 rows. Leave rem 36[40:44] sts on a spare needle.

LEFT FRONT

Using 4mm (US6) needles and A, cast on 48[52:56] sts. Cont in K2, P2 rib as foll:

1st row: (RS) P1, ☆K2, P2, rep from ☆ to last 3 sts, K3.

2nd row: P3, ☆K2, P2, rep from ☆ to last st, K1.

These 2 rows form the rib. Cont in rib for 8cm, 3ins ending with a RS row.

Inc row: Rib 3, ☆inc in next st, rib 5[5:4], rep from ☆ to last 9[7:13] sts, inc in next st, rib 8[6:12]. 55[60:65] sts.

Change to 5mm (US8) needles and commence patt.

1st row: (RS) P6[7:8], ☆work 1st row of cable panel, work 1st row of flower panel, rep from ☆ to last 3 sts, K3.

2nd row: P3, ☆work 2nd row of flower panel, work 2nd row of cable panel, rep from ☆ to last 6[7:8] sts, K6[7:8].

These 2 rows establish the position of the cable and flower panels with rev st st at side and st st at front edge. Cont in patt as set, keeping panels correct, until work measures 38cm, 15ins from beg ending with a WS row.

Shape armhole

Cast off 3 sts at beg of next row. Dec 1 st at armhole edge on foll 2[3:4] alt rows. 50[54:58] sts.

Cont without further shaping until work measures 53cm, 21ins from beg, ending with a RS row.

Shape neck

Cast off 6[8:10] sts at beg of next row. Dec 1 st at neck edge on foll 11 rows. 33[35:37] sts.

Cont without further shaping until front measures same as back to shoulder shaping, ending with a WS row.

Shape shoulder

Cast off rem sts.

RIGHT FRONT

Using 4mm (US6) needles and A, cast on 48[52:56] sts.

Cont in K2, P2 rib as foll:

1st row: (RS) K3, ☆P2, K2, rep from ☆ to last st, P1.

2nd row: K1, ☆P2, K2, rep from ☆ to last 3 sts, P3.

These 2 rows form the rib. Cont in rib for 8cm, 3ins ending with a RS row.

Inc row: Rib 8[6:12], ☆inc in next st, rib 5[5:4], rep from ☆ to last 4 sts, inc in next st, rib 3. 55[60:65] sts.

Change to 5mm (US8) needles and commence patt.

1st row: (RS) K3, ☆work 1st row of flower panel, work 1st row of cable panel, rep from ☆ to last 6[7:8] sts, P6[7:8].

2nd row: K6[7:8], ☆work 2nd row of cable panel, work 2nd row of flower panel, rep from ☆ to last 3 sts, P3.

These 2 rows establish the position of the cable and flower panels with rev st st at side and st st at front edge.

Complete to match left front, reversing all shapings.

SLEEVES

Using 4mm (US6) needles and A, cast on 52[56:60] sts. Cont in K2, P2 rib for 8cm, 3ins ending with a RS row.

Inc row: Rib 6[5:4], ☆inc in next st, rib 2, rep from ☆ to last 7[6:5] sts, inc in next st, rib to end. 66[72:78] sts.

Change to 5mm (US8) needles and cont in patt as given for back, *at the same time*, inc and work into patt 1 st at each end of every 3rd row until there are 118[124:130] sts.

Cont without further shaping until work measures 43cm, 17ins from beg, ending with a WS row.

Shape top

Cast off 3 sts at beg of next 2 rows. Dec 1 st at each end of next 20 rows. Cast off 8 sts at beg of foll 6 rows. 24[30:36] sts.

Cast off.

SWALLOWS *His & Her Sweaters*

POCKET LININGS
(make 2)
Mark a position on side edge of back 10cm, 4ins above rib.
With RS of work facing, using 5mm (US8) needles and A, K up 20 sts between marker and top of rib.
Beg with a K row, work in rev st st for 10cm, 4ins. Cast off.

POCKET EDGINGS
(make 2)
Mark a position on side edge of each front 10cm, 4ins above rib. With RS of work facing, using 4mm (US6) needles and A, K up 20 sts between marker and top of rib. Cast off.

TO MAKE UP/TO FINISH
Join shoulder seams.

NECKBAND
With RS of work facing, using 4mm (US6) needles and A, K up 28[30:32] sts from right front neck, K across 36[40:44] sts on back neck, then K up 28[30:32] sts from left front. 92[100:108] sts.
Work 9 rows K2, P2 rib. Cast off in rib.

BUTTONBAND
With RS of work facing, using 4mm (US6) needles and A, K up 140 sts across edge of neckband and down left front.
Work 9 rows K2, P2 rib. Cast off in rib.

BUTTONHOLE BAND
With RS of work facing, using 4mm (US6) needles and A, K up 140 sts up right front and across neckband edge.
Work 4 rows K2, P2 rib.
Buttonhole row: Rib 3, ☆yfwd, K2 tog, rib 20, rep from ☆ to last 5 sts, yfwd, K2 tog, rib 3.
Rib 4 rows, cast off in rib.

Set in sleeves. Join sleeve seams and side seams above and below pocket opening. Catch pocket linings in place. Sew on buttons.
Using B, C and D embroider petal shapes on flower panels as shown, using Lazy Daisy and French Knot stitches. Sew in shoulder pads.

Sizes
To fit chest/bust 76 – 81[86 – 91: 97 – 102:107 – 112]cm, 30 – 32[34 – 36:38 – 40:42 – 44]ins
Actual chest/bust 84[95:105:115.5]cm, 33[37½:41¼:45½]ins
Length 55[59:64:69]cm, 21¾[23¼:25¼:27¼]ins
Sleeve seam 42[44:46:48]cm, 16½[17¼:18¼:19]ins

Materials
5[5:6:6] × 100g hanks of Rowan Aran in main colour (A)
3[3:4:4] hanks in contrast colour (B)
One pair each 4mm (US6) and 5mm (US68) knitting needles
4mm (US6) and 5mm (US8) circular knitting needles

Tension/Gauge
23 sts and 32 rows to 10cm, 4ins over patt using 5mm (US8) needles

BACK AND FRONT
– worked in one piece to armholes
Using 4mm (US6) circular needle and A, cast on 165[177:193:209] sts.
Work in rows in K1, P1 rib as foll:
1st row: K1, ☆P1, K1, rep from ☆ to end.
2nd row: P1, ☆K1, P1, rep from ☆ to end.
Rep these 2 rows for 10cm, 4ins ending with a 2nd row.
Inc row: Rib 12[8:24:20], ☆inc in next st, rib 4[3:2:2], rep from ☆ to last 13[9:25:21] sts, inc in next st, rib to end. 194[218:242:266] sts.
Change to 5mm (US8) circular needle and P 1 row.
Now cont in patt, sl all sts P-wise with yarn on the WS of work.
1st row: (RS) With B, K1, ☆sl 1, K2, rep from ☆ to last st, K1.
2nd row: With B, K1, ☆P2, sl 1, rep from ☆ to last st, K1.
3rd row: With A, K1, ☆K1, sl 1, (K2, sl 1) 3 times, K3, (sl 1, K2) 3 times, sl 1, rep from ☆ to last st, K1.
4th row: With A, K1, ☆sl 1, (P2, sl 1) 3 times, P3, (sl 1, P2) 3 times, sl 1, P1, rep from ☆ to last st, K1.
5th row: With B, K1, ☆K2, (sl 1, K2) 3 times, sl 1, K1, sl 1, (K2, sl 1) 3 times, K1, rep from ☆ to last st, K1.
6th row: With B, K1, ☆P1, (sl 1, P2) 3 times, sl 1, P1, sl 1, (P2, sl 1) 3 times,

P2, rep from ☆ to last st, K1.
7th–8th rows: Rep 1st–2nd rows using A instead of B.
9th–10th rows: Rep 3rd–4th rows using B instead of A.
11th–12th rows: Rep 5th–6th rows using A instead of B.
These 12 rows form the patt. Cont in patt until work measures 28[32:37:42]cm, 11[12½:14½:16½]ins from beg, ending with a WS row.
Divide for armholes
Next row: Cast off 22 sts, patt 74[86:98:110] sts including st used to cast off, turn leaving rem sts on a spare needle.
Work on these sts for back. Cont in patt until work measures 55[59:64:69]cm, 21¾[23¼:25¼:27¼]ins from beg, ending with a WS row.
Shape shoulders
Cast off 18[22:24:28] sts at beg of next 2 rows. Leave rem 38[42:50:54] sts on a spare needle.
With RS of work facing, return to sts on first spare needle. Rejoin yarn, cast off 22 sts, patt to end. 74[86:98:110] sts.
Work on these sts for front. Cont in patt until work measures 47[51:56:61]cm, 18½[20:22:24]ins from beg, ending with a WS row.
Shape neck
Next row: Patt 30[35:40:45] and turn, leaving rem sts on a spare needle.
Complete left side of neck first.
Cast off 4[4:6:6] sts at beg of next row, 3[4:5:5] sts at beg of next alt row, 3[3:3:4] sts at beg of foll alt row, then 2 sts at beg of next alt row. 18[22:24:28] sts.
Cont without further shaping until front measures same as back to shoulder shaping, ending at armhole edge.
Shape shoulder
Cast off rem sts.
With RS of work facing return to sts on spare needle, sl centre 14[16:18:20] sts onto a holder, rejoin yarn at neck edge, patt to end.
Patt 1 row. Complete as given for first side of neck.

SLEEVES
Using 4mm (US6) needles and A, cast on 41[45:49:53] sts.
Work in K1, P1 rib as given for back and front for 8cm, 3ins ending with a 2nd row.
Inc row: Rib 4[8:12:6], ☆inc in next st,

SWALLOWS

PURPLE WILLOW

rib 0[0:0:1], rep from ☆ to last 5[9:13:7] sts, inc in next st, rib to end. 74 sts.
Change to 5mm (US8) needles and P 1 row.
Now cont in patt as given for back and front, inc and work into patt 1 st at each end of 3rd and every foll 5th row until there are 124 sts.
Cont without further shaping until work measures 47[49:51:53]cm, 18½[19¼:20: 21]ins from beg, ending with a WS row. Cast off loosely.

TO MAKE UP/TO FINISH
Join right shoulder seam.

NECKBAND
With RS of work facing, using 4mm (US6) needles and A, K up 26 sts down left side of neck, K across 14[16:18:20] sts at centre front, K up 25 sts up right side of neck, then K across 38[42:50:54] sts on back neck. 103[109:119:125] sts.
Beg with a 2nd row work in K1, P1 rib as given for back and front for 6cm, 2½ins. Cast off loosely in rib.

Join left shoulder and neckband seam. Join side seam Placing centre of cast off edge to shoulder seam, set in sleeves, sewing final rows to cast off sts at underarm. Join sleeve seams.

PURPLE WILLOW
Child's Sweater

Sizes
To fit chest 56[61:66:71]cm, 22[24:26:28]ins
Actual chest 61[66:71:76]cm, 24[26:28:30]ins
Length 34[38:42:46]cm, 13½[15:16½:18¼]ins
Sleeve seam 22[25:28:31]cm, 8¾[9¾:11:12¼]ins

Materials
4[4:5:5] × 25g balls of Sunbeam Sumatra in main colour (A)
1[1:1:1] ball in contrast colour (B)
2[2:3:3] balls in contrast colour (C)
One pair each 4mm (US6) and 5mm (US8) knitting needles
Cable needle

OR

2[2:3:3] × 50g balls of Sunbeam Paris Mohair in main colour (A)
1[1:1:1] ball in contrast colour (B)
1[1:1:1] ball in contrast colour (C)
One pair each 4½mm (US7) and 5½mm (US9) knitting needles
Cable needle

Tension/Gauge
16 sts and 22 rows to 10cm, 4ins over st st using Sumatra and 5mm (US8) needles OR Paris Mohair and 5½mm (US9) needles

PATT PANEL A
(worked over 16 sts with C throughout and bobbles with B)

1st row: (WS) K3, P2, K1, P1, K2, P1, K1, P2, K3.
2nd row: P2, sl next st onto cable needle and hold at back of work, K1 then P1 from cable needle – called Cr2b(P), sl next st onto cable needle and hold at front of work, P1 then K1 from cable needle – called Cr2f(P), P4, Cr2b(P), Cr2f(P), P2.

3rd row: K2, P1, K2, P1, K4, P1, K2, P1, K2.
4th row: P1, Cr2b(P), P2, Cr2f(P), P2, Cr2b(P), P2, Cr2f(P), P1.
5th row: K1, P1, K4, P1, K2, P1, K4, P1, K1.
6th row: Cr2b(P), P4, Cr2f(P), Cr2b(P), P4, Cr2f(P).
7th row: P1, K6, P2, K6, P1.
8th row: K1, P1, make bobble by casting on 2 sts then casting off 2 sts – called MB, P2, MB, P1, sl next st onto cable needle and hold at front of work, K1 then K1 from cable needle – called Cr2f(K), P1, MB, P2, MB, P1, K1.
9th row: P1, K1, P1, K2, P1, K1, P2, K1, P1, K2, P1, K1, P1.
10th row: Cr2f(P), P4, Cr2b(P), Cr2f(P), P4, Cr2b(P).
11th row: As 5th row.
12th row: P1, Cr2f(P), P2, Cr2b(P), P2, Cr2f(P), P2, Cr2b(P), P1.
13th row: As 3rd row.
14th row: P2, Cr2f(P), Cr2b(P), P4, Cr2f(P), Cr2b(P), P2.
15th row: K3, P2, K6, P2, K3.
16th row: P3, Cr2f(K), P1, MB, P2, MB, P1, Cr2f(K), P3.
These 16 rows form patt panel A.

PATT PANEL B
(worked over 22 sts)
1st–7th rows: Beg with a P row work 7 rows st st with A.
8th–9th rows: With B, K.
10th–15th rows: Beg with a K row work 6 rows st st with A.
The 8th–15th rows inclusive form patt panel B.

BACK
☆☆Using smaller needles and A, cast on 49[53:57:61] sts.
Cont in K1, P1 rib as foll:
1st row: K1, ☆P1, K1, rep from ☆ to end.
2nd row: P1, ☆K1, P1, rep from ☆ to end.
Rep these 2 rows for 5[5:6:6]cm, 2[2:2½:2½]ins ending with a 2nd row.
Inc row: Rib 8[10:10:10], ☆inc in next st rib 7[7:8:9], rep from ☆ to last 9[11:11:11] sts, inc in next st, rib to end. 54[58:62:66] sts.
Change to larger needles and commence patt.
1st row: (WS) K0[2:4:6], work 1st row patt panel A, work 1st row patt panel B,

work 1st row patt panel A, K0[2:4:6].
2nd row: P0[2:4:6], work 2nd row patt panel A, work 2nd row patt panel B, work 2nd row patt panel A, P0[2:4:6].
These 2 rows set the position of the patt panels with edge sts in rev st st.
Cont in patt as set until work measures 17.5[20:23:25]cm, 6¾[8:9:9¾]ins from beg, ending with a WS row.
Shape armholes
Cast off 4 sts at beg of next 2 rows. 46[50:54:58] sts. ✫✫
Cont in patt until work measures 34[38:42:46]cm, 13½[15:16½:18¼]ins from beg, ending with a WS row.
Shape shoulders
Cast off 11[13:15:17] sts at beg of next 2 rows. Leave rem 24 sts on a spare needle.

FRONT
Work as given for back from ✫✫ to ✫✫.
Cont in patt until work measures 27[31:35:39]cm, 10¾[12¼:13¾:15½]ins from beg, ending with a WS row.
Shape neck
Next row: Patt 19[21:23:25] and turn, leaving rem sts on a spare needle.
Complete left side of neck first.
Cast off 2 sts at beg of next and 2 foll alt rows, then dec 1 st at beg of next 2 alt rows. 11[13:15:17] sts.
Cont without further shaping until front measures same as back to shoulder shaping, ending at armhole edge.
Shape shoulder
Cast off rem sts.
With RS of work facing return to sts on spare needle, sl centre 8 sts onto a stitch holder, rejoin yarn at neck edge, patt to end.
Patt 1 row. Complete as given for first side of neck.

SLEEVES
Using smaller needles and A, cast on 29[31:33:35] sts.
Work in K1, P1 rib as given for back for 3[3:5:5]cm, 1¼[1¼:2:2]ins ending with a 2nd row.
Inc row: Rib 7[8:8:9], ✫inc in next st, rep from ✫ to last 8[8:9:9] sts, rib to end. 43[46:49:52] sts.
Change to larger needles and beg with 3rd row cont in patt panel B, inc 1 st at each end of 3rd and every foll 6th row until there are 53[58:61:66] sts.
Cont without further shaping until work measures 25[28:31:34]cm, 9¾[11:12¼:

13½]ins from beg, ending with a WS row. Cast off.

TO MAKE UP/TO FINISH
Join right shoulder seam.

NECKBAND
With RS of work facing, using smaller needles and A, K up 17[17:17:19] sts down left side of neck, K across 8 sts at centre front, K up 16[16:16:18] sts up right side of neck, then K across 24 sts on back neck. 65[65:65:69] sts.
Beg with a 2nd row work in K1, P1 rib as given for back for 5cm, 2ins. Cast off in rib.

Join left shoulder and neckband seam. Fold neckband in half to WS and slip stitch in place. Placing centre of cast off edge to shoulder seam, set in sleeves, sewing final rows to cast off sts. Join side and sleeve seams.

SONG THRUSH AND YOUNG
Family Sweaters
See Lambs pattern page 27 for 'Young'

Sizes
To fit chest/bust 76 – 81[86 – 91:97 – 102:107 – 112]cm, 30 – 32[34 – 36:38 – 40:42 – 44]ins
Actual chest/bust 88.5[100:111:123]cm, 34¾[39½:43¾:48½]ins
Length 59[63:66:66]cm, 23¼[24¾:26:26]ins
Sleeve seam 43[45.5:48:50.5]cm, 17[18:19:20]ins

Materials
11[13:16:19] × 50g balls of Sirdar Country Style Chunky
One pair each 5mm (US8) and 6½mm (US10½) knitting needles

Tension/Gauge
14 sts and 20 rows to 10cm, 4ins over patt using 6½mm (US10½) needles

BACK
✫✫Using 5mm (US8) needles, cast on 61[69:77:85] sts.
Cont in K1, P1 rib as foll:
1st row: (RS) K1, ✫P1, K1, rep from ✫ to end.
2nd row: P1, ✫K1, P1, rep from ✫ to end.
Rep these 2 rows for 8cm, 3ins ending with a 2nd row, inc 1 st at end of last row. 62[70:78:86] sts.
Change to 6½mm (US10½) needles and commence patt.
1st row: (RS) K.
2nd row: P.
3rd row: P2, ✫K2, P6, rep from ✫ to last 4 sts, K2, P2.
4th row: K2, ✫P2, K6, rep from ✫ to last 4 sts, P2, K2.
5th–6th rows: Rep 3rd and 4th rows.
7th–8th rows: Rep 1st and 2nd rows.
9th row: ✫P6, K2, rep from ✫ to last 6 sts, P6.
10th row: ✫K6, P2, rep from ✫ to last 6 sts, K6.
11th–12th rows: Rep 9th and 10th rows.
These 12 rows form the patt.
Cont in patt until work measures approximately 47[51:53:53]cm, 18½[20: 21:21]ins from beg, ending with a 2nd, 6th, 8th or 12th patt row.
Next row: K2, ✫P2, K2, rep from ✫ to end.
Next row: P2, ✫K2, P2, rep from ✫ to end. ✫✫
Rep these 2 rows 7[7:8:8] times more.
Shape back neck
Next row: Work 22[25:28:31] sts and turn leaving rem sts on a spare needle.
Complete right side of neck first.
Dec 1 st at neck edge on next 4 rows. 18[21:24:27] sts.
Shape shoulder
Cast off rem sts.
With RS of work facing, return to sts on spare needle, rejoin yarn and cast off centre 18[20:22:24] sts, work to end.
Complete to match first side of neck.

SONG THRUSH AND YOUNG

FRONT

Work as given for back from ✩✩ to ✩✩.
Rep the last 2 rows once more.
Shape neck
Next row: Work 25[28:32:35] sts and turn leaving rem sts on a spare needle.
Dec 1 st at neck edge on every row until 18[21:24:27] sts rem.
Cont without further shaping until work matches back to shoulder shaping.
Shape shoulder
Cast off rem sts.
With RS of work facing, return to sts on spare needle, rejoin yarn and cast off centre 12[14:14:16] sts, work to end.
Complete to match first side of neck.

SLEEVES

Using 5mm (US8) needles, cast on 33[35:39:43] sts. Cont in K1, P1 rib as given for back for 8cm, 3ins ending with a 2nd row.
Inc row: K3[0:0:0], ✩inc in next st, K1, rep from ✩ to last 4[1:1:1] sts, K to end. 46[52:58:64] sts.
Change to 6½mm (US10½) needles and P 1 row.
Commence patt.
1st row: P2[1:0:3], ✩K2, P6, rep from ✩ to last 4[3:2:5] sts, K2, P2[1:0:3].
2nd row: K2[1:0:3], ✩P2, K6, rep from ✩ to last 4[3:2:5] sts, P2, K2[1:0:3].
These 2 rows establish the patt as given on back. Cont in patt inc 1 st at each end of every foll 18th [16th:16th:16th] row until there are 52[60:66:72] sts.
Cont without further shaping until work measures 41.5[44:46.5:49]cm, 16¼[17¼:18¼:19¼]ins from beg, ending with a RS row.
K 4 rows. Cast off fairly loosely.

TO MAKE UP/TO FINISH

Join right shoulder seam

NECKBAND

With RS of work facing, using 5mm (US8) needles, K up 20[20:22:23] sts down left side of neck, 14[16:16:18] sts across centre front, 20[20:22:23] sts up right side of neck and 31[33:35:37] sts around back neck. 85[89:95:101] sts.
Beg with a 2nd row, work 8cm, 3ins in K1, P1 rib as given for back.
Cast off loosely in rib.

Join left shoulder and neckband seam.
Fold neckband in half onto WS and catch down. Placing centre of cast off edge of sleeves to shoulder seams, set in sleeves. Join side and sleeve seams.

Mouse, Hare and Hedgehog

Children's Sweaters

Sizes

To fit chest 56[61:66]cm, 22[24:26]ins
Actual chest 65[69:74]cm, 25½[27¼:29¼]ins
Length 32.5[40:44.5]cm, 12¾[15¾:17½]ins
Sleeve seam 27[29:33]cm, 10¾[11½:13]ins

Materials

4[5:5] × 50g balls of Emu Supermatch Chunky in main colour (A)
1[1:1] ball each in contrast colours (B and C)
Oddment (odds and ends) in contrast colour (D)
One pair each 4mm (US6) and 5mm (US8) knitting needles

Tension/Gauge

17 sts and 24 rows to 10cm, 4ins over st st using 5mm (US8) needles

VERSION 1 MOUSE

FRONT

✩✩Using 4mm (US6) needles and A, cast on 55[59:63] sts.
Cont in K2, P2 rib as foll:
1st row: (RS) ✩K2, P2, rep from ✩ to last 3 sts, K3.
2nd row: K1, P2, ✩K2, P2, rep from ✩ to end.
Rep these 2 rows for 5cm, 2ins ending with a 2nd row.
Change to 5mm (US8) needles.
Beg with a K row work 6 rows in st st
Commence working from chart. Read odd numbered rows (K) from right to left, even numbered rows (P) from left to right. Use separate balls of yarn for each area of colour and twist yarns tog on WS of work when changing from one colour to another to avoid a hole.
1st row: K16[18:20]A, K22 sts from 1st row of chart, K17[19:21]A.
2nd row: P17[19:21]A, P22 sts from 2nd row of chart, P16[18:20]A.
These 2 rows establish the position of the chart. Cont in this way until the chart rows have all been worked, *at the same time*, when work measures 17.5[24:27]cm, 6¾[9½:10¾]ins from beg, ending with a P row.
Shape raglan armholes
Cast off 2 sts at beg of next 2 rows.
Work 2 rows.
Next row: K1, sl 1, K1, psso, K to last 3 sts, K2 tog, K1.
Next row: P. ✩✩
Rep last 2 rows until 27[31:31] sts rem, ending with a K row.
Shape neck
Next row: P9[11:11] and turn, leaving rem sts on a spare needle.
Complete right side of neck first.
Next row: K2 tog, K to last 3 sts, K2 tog, K1.
Next row: P to last 2 sts, P2 tog.
Next row: K2 tog, K to last 3 sts, K2 tog, K1.
Next row: P.
Rep last 2 rows 1[2:2] times more. 2 sts.
K2 tog and fasten off.
With WS of work facing return to sts on spare needle. Sl centre 9[11:11] sts onto a holder, rejoin yarn at neck edge, P to end.

Complete to match first side of neck, reversing shapings and working 'K1, sl 1, K1, psso' at armhole edge instead of 'K2 tog, K1'.

BACK

Work as given for front from ☆☆ to ☆☆.
Rep last 2 rows until 21[23:23] sts rem, ending with a P row.
Next row: K1, sl 1, K2 tog, psso, K to last 4 sts, K3 tog, K1.
Next row: P.
Leave rem 17[19:19] sts on a spare needle.

SLEEVES

Using 4mm (US6) needles and A, cast on 27[31:35] sts.
Cont in K2, P2 rib as given for front for 5cm, 2ins ending with a 2nd row.
Change to 5mm (US8) needles.
Beg with a K row cont in st st inc 1 st at

each end of 5th and every foll 10th[14th:16th] row until there are 37[39:43] sts.
Cont without further shaping until work measures 27[29:33]cm, 10¾[11½:13]ins from beg, ending with a P row.
Shape raglan top
Cast off 2 sts at beg of next 2 rows.
Work 2 rows.
Next row: K1, sl 1, K1, psso, K to last 3 sts, K2 tog, K1.
Next row: P.
Rep last 4 rows 3 times more. 25[27:31] sts.
Now rep last 2 rows until 7 sts rem, ending with a P row.
Leave sts on a spare needle.

TO MAKE UP/TO FINISH

Join raglan seams, leaving right back open.

NECKBAND

Using 4mm (US6) needles and A, with RS of work facing, K across 17[19:19] sts on back neck dec 1 st at centre, K across 7 sts on sleeve top, K up 8[10:10] sts down left front neck, K across 9[11:11] sts

at centre front, K up 8[10:10] sts up right side of neck then K7 sts on sleeve top. 55[63:63] sts.
Beg with a 2nd row, work in K2, P2 rib as given for front for 5cm, 2ins.
Leave sts on a length of yarn.

Join right back raglan seam and neckband. Fold neckband in half onto WS, sew loops to corresponding sts at base of neckband. Join side and sleeve seams.

Using C, embroider eye and form tufts for whiskers. Using three lengths of C make a plait (braid) approximately 18cm, 7ins long and sew in place for tail.

VERSION 2 HARE

Work as given for Version 1, omitting motif on front but working from chart, below, on back as foll on page 25.

Key

A	□	Blue (main)
B	×	Brown
C	•	White
D	▲	Black
	<	Black Whiskers (Embroidery)

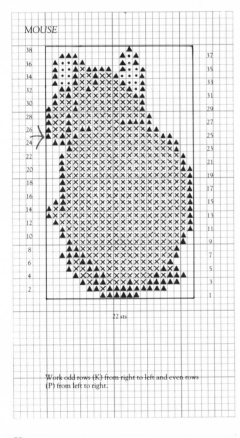

MOUSE

Work odd rows (K) from right to left and even rows (P) from left to right.

22 sts

Key

A	□	Blue (main)
B	×	Grey
C	▲	Black
D	•	Pink
	<	Black Whiskers (Embroidery)

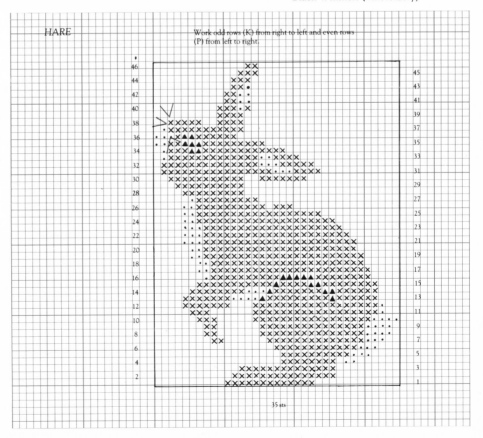

HARE

Work odd rows (K) from right to left and even rows (P) from left to right.

35 sts

MOUSE, HARE and HEDGEHOG

1st row: K10[12:14]A, K35 sts from 1st row of chart, K10[12:14]A.
2nd row: P10[12:14]A, P35 sts from 2nd row of chart, P10[12:14]A.
These 2 rows establish the position of the chart on page 23.

TO MAKE UP/TO FINISH
Work as given for Version 1.
Using D, form tufts for whiskers. Using C make a pom-pon approximately 5cm, 2ins in diameter and sew in place for tail.

VERSION 3 HEDGEHOG

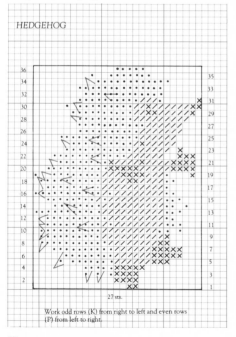

See picture on page 94

HEDGEHOG

27 sts.

Work odd rows (K) from right to left and even rows (P) from left to right.

Key
A	□	Beige (main)
B	/	Grey
C	•	Brown
D	×	Black
	<	Spines (Embroidery)

Work as given for Version 1 working from chart on front as foll:
7th row: K14[16:18]A, K27 sts from 1st row of chart, K14[16:18]A.
8th row: P14[16:18]A, P27 sts from 2nd row of chart, P14[16:18]A.

TO MAKE UP/TO FINISH
Work as given for Version 1.
Using D, embroider 'spines'.

WILLOW CATKINS
His & Her Sweaters

Sizes
To fit bust/chest 71 – 76[81 – 86:91 – 97:102 – 107]cm, 28 – 30[32 – 34:36 – 38: 40 – 42]ins
Actual bust/chest 83[94:105.5:116.5]cm, 32¾[37:41½:45¾]ins
Length 60[63:66:69]cm, 23¾[24¾:26:27¼]ins
Sleeve seam 42.5[44:46:48]cm, 16¾[17¼:18¼:19]ins

Materials
18[19:21:22] × 50g balls of Patons Diploma Aran
One pair each 4mm (US6) and 5mm (US8) knitting needles
Cable needle

Tension/Gauge
28 sts and 26 rows to 11cm, 4¼ins over patt using 5mm (US8) needles

BACK
☆☆Using 4mm (US6) needles, cast on 89[99:109:119] sts.
Cont in K1, P1 rib as foll:
1st row: (RS) K1, ☆P1, K1, rep from ☆ to end.
2nd row: P1, ☆K1, P1, rep from ☆ to end.
Rep these 2 rows for 9cm, 3½ins ending with a 1st row.
Inc row: Rib 12[9:6:17], ☆inc in next st, rib 3[3:3:2], rep from ☆ to last 13[10:7:18] sts, inc in next st, rib to end. 106[120:134:148] sts.
Change to 5mm (US8) needles and commence patt.
1st row: (RS) P3, ☆K into front of 2nd st on left hand needle, K into front of 1st st and sl both off needle tog – called TW2, P4, sl next 2 sts onto cable needle and hold at back of work, K2 then K2 from cable needle – called C4B, P4, rep from ☆ to last 5 sts, TW2, P3.
2nd row: K3, P2, ☆K4, P4, K4, P2, rep from ☆ to last 3 sts, K3.
3rd row: P3, ☆TW2, P3, sl next st onto cable needle and hold at back of work, K2 then K1 from cable needle – called Cr3R, sl next 2 sts onto cable needle and hold at front of work, K1 then K2 from cable needle – called Cr3L, P3, rep from ☆ to last 5 sts, TW2, P3.
4th row: K3, P2, ☆K3, P6, K3, P2, rep from ☆ to last 3 sts, K3.
5th row: P3, ☆TW2, P2, Cr3R, K2, Cr3L, P2, rep from ☆ to last 5 sts, TW2, P3.
6th row: K3, P2, ☆K2, P8, K2, P2, rep from ☆ to last 3 sts, K3.
7th row: P3, ☆TW2, P1, Cr3R, K4, Cr3L, P1, rep from ☆ to last 5 sts, TW2, P3.
8th row: K3, P2, ☆K1, P10, K1, P2, rep from ☆ to last 3 sts, K3.
These 8 rows form the patt. Cont in patt until work measures 34[37:40:43]cm, 13½[14½:15¾:17]ins from beg, ending with a WS row.
Shape armholes
Cast off 14 sts at beg of next 2 rows. 78[92:106:120] sts. ☆☆
Cont in patt without further shaping until work measures 60[63:66:69]cm, 23¾[24¾:26:27¼]ins from beg, ending with a WS row.
Shape shoulders
Cast off 19[25:33:39] sts at beg of next 2 rows. Leave rem 40[42:40:42] sts on a spare needle.

WILLOW CATKINS

FRONT

Work as given for back from ✩✩ to ✩✩. Cont without shaping until work measures 52[55:58:61]cm, 20½[21¾: 22¾:24]ins from beg, ending with a WS row.

Shape neck

Next row: Patt 31[38:45:52] sts and turn leaving rem sts on a spare needle.

Complete left side of neck first.

Cast off 4 sts at beg of next row, 3 sts at beg of foll alt row and 2 sts at beg of next alt row. Dec 1 st at neck edge on every foll alt row until 19[25:33:39] sts rem.

Cont without further shaping until work measures same as back to shoulder shaping, ending at armhole edge.

Shape shoulder

Cast off rem sts.

With RS of work facing return to sts on spare needle. Sl centre 16 sts onto a holder, rejoin yarn at neck edge, patt to end.

Next row: Patt to end.

Complete as given for first side of neck.

SLEEVES

Using 4mm (US6) needles, cast on 41[45:49:53] sts.

Work in K1, P1 rib as given for back for 7cm, 2¾ins ending with a 1st row.

Inc row: Rib 3[6:10:2], ✩inc in next st, rib 0[0:0:1], rep from ✩ to last 2[7:11:3] sts, inc in next st, rib to end. 78 sts.

Change to 5mm (US8) needles and cont in patt as given for back, inc and work into patt 1 st at each end of every 3rd row until there are 132 sts.

Cont without further shaping until work measures 42.5[44:46:48]cm, 16¾[17¼: 18¼:19]ins from beg.

Now work a further 5.5cm, 2¼ins ending with a WS row. Cast off fairly loosely.

TO MAKE UP/TO FINISH

Join right shoulder seam.

NECKBAND

With RS of work facing, using 4mm (US6) needles, K up 26 sts down left side of neck, K across 16 sts at centre front, K up 25 sts up right side of neck then K across 40[42:40:42] sts of back neck. 107[109:107:109] sts.

Beg with a 2nd row, work in K1, P1 rib as given for back for 7cm, 2¾ins.

Cast off loosely in rib.

Fold neckband in half onto WS and slip

stitch down. Placing centre of cast off edge of sleeve to shoulder seam and sewing final rows of sleeve to cast off sts at underarm, set in sleeves. Join side and sleeve seams.

LAMBS

Child's Sweater and Helmet, and Toy Lamb

SWEATER

Sizes

To fit chest 56[61:66:71]cm, 22[24:26:28]ins

Actual chest 60[66:71:77]cm, 23¾[26:28:30¼]ins

Length 35[40:46:49.5]cm, 13¾[15¾:18¼:19½]ins

Sleeve seam 28[31:33:38]cm, 11[12¼:13:15]ins

Materials

6[7:9:11] × 50g balls of Sirdar Country Style Chunky

One pair each 5mm (US8) and 6½mm (US10½) knitting needles

Tension/Gauge

14 sts and 20 rows to 10cm, 4ins over patt using 6½mm (US10½) needles

BACK

✩✩Using 5mm (US8) needles, cast on 41[45:49:53] sts.

Cont in K1, P1 rib as foll:

1st row: (RS) K1, ✩P1, K1, rep from ✩ to end.

2nd row: P1, ✩K1, P1, rep from ✩ to end.

Rep these 2 rows for 5[5:5:6]cm, 2[2:2:2½]ins ending with a 2nd row, inc 1 st at end of last row. 42[46:50:54] sts.

Change to 6½mm (US10½) needles and commence patt.

1st row: (RS) K.

2nd row: P.

3rd row: P0[2:0:2], ✩K2, P6, rep from ✩ to last 2[4:2:4] sts, K2, P to end.

4th row: K0[2:0:2], ✩P2, K6, rep from ✩ to last 2[4:2:4] sts, P2, K to end.

5th–6th rows: Rep 3rd and 4th rows.

7th–8th rows: Rep 1st and 2nd rows.

9th row: P4[6:4:6], ✩K2, P6, rep from ✩ to last 6[8:6:8] sts, K2, P to end.

10th row: K4[6:4:6], ✩P2, K6, rep from ✩ to last 6[8:6:8] sts, P2, K to end.

11th–12th rows: Rep 9th and 10th rows.

These 12 rows form the patt.

Cont in patt until work measures approximately 27[31:37:39]cm, 10¾ [12¼:14½:15½]ins from beg, ending with a 2nd, 6th, 8th or 12th patt row.

Next row: K2, ✩P2, K2, rep from ✩ to end.

Next row: P2, ✩K2, P2, rep from ✩ to end. ✩✩

Rep these 2 rows 5[6:6:7] times more.

Shape back neck

Next row: Work 13[14:15:16] sts and turn, leaving rem sts on a spare needle.

Complete right side of neck first.

Dec 1 st at neck edge on next 2 rows. 11[12:13:14] sts.

Cast off rem sts.

With RS of work facing return to sts on spare needle, rejoin yarn and cast off centre 16[18:20:22] sts, work to end.

Complete to match first side of neck.

FRONT

Work as given for back from ✩✩ to ✩✩.

Shape neck

Next row: Work 18[19:21:22] sts and

turn, leaving rem sts on a spare needle.
Complete left side of neck first.
Dec 1 st at neck edge on every row until 11[12:13:14] sts rem.
Cont without shaping until work matches back to shoulder.
Shape shoulder
Cast off rem sts.
With RS of work facing, return to sts on spare needle, rejoin yarn and cast off centre 6[8:8:10] sts, work to end.
Complete to match first side of neck.

SLEEVES

Using 5mm (US8) needles, cast on 23[25:29:31] sts and work in K1, P1 rib as given for back for 5[5:5:6]cm, 2[2:2:2½] ins ending with a 2nd row.
Inc row: K3[2:4:5], ☆inc in next st, K1, rep from ☆ to last 4[3:5:6] sts, inc in next st, K to end. 32[36:40:42] sts.
Change to 6½mm (US10½) needles and P 1 row.
Commence patt.
1st row: P3[1:3:4], ☆K2, P6, rep from ☆ to last 5[3:5:6] sts, K2, P to end.
2nd row: K3[1:3:4], ☆P2, K6, rep from ☆ to last 5[3:5:6] sts, P2, K to end.
These 2 rows establish the patt as given for back. Cont in patt inc 1 st at each end of every foll 7th[8th:9th:10th] row until there are 42[46:50:52] sts.
Cont without further shaping until work measures 26.5[29.5:31.5:36.5]cm, 10½ [11½:12¼:14¼]ins from beg, ending with a RS row.
K 4 rows. Cast off fairly loosely.

TO MAKE UP/TO FINISH
Join right shoulder seam.

NECKBAND

With RS of work facing, using 5mm (US8) needles, K up 14[14:16:18] sts down left side of neck, 7[9:9:11] sts at centre front, K up 14[14:16:18] sts up right side of neck and 28[30:32:34] sts around back neck. 63[67:73:81] sts.
Beg with a 2nd row, work in K1, P1 rib as given for back for 6[6:6:8]cm, 2½[2½:2½:3]ins. Cast off loosely in rib.

Join left shoulder and neckband seam. Fold neckband in half onto WS and catch down. Placing centre of cast off edge of sleeves to shoulder seams, set in sleeves. Join side and sleeve seams.

HELMET

Size
To fit child 3–6 years

Materials
2 × 50g balls of Sirdar Country Style Chunky
One pair 6½mm (US10½) needles

Tension/Gauge
14 sts and 20 rows to 10cm, 4ins over st st using 6½mm (US10½) needles

MAIN PIECE
Cast on 72 sts.
1st row: (WS) K.
2nd–20th rows: Beg with a K row, work 19 rows st st.
21st row: (WS) K.
22nd–23rd rows: P.
24th–27th rows: ☆K2, P2, rep from ☆ to end.
28th row: ☆K2, P2 tog, rep from ☆ to end. 54 sts.
29th row: ☆K1, P2, rep from ☆ to end.
30th row: ☆K2, P1, rep from ☆ to end.
31st–32nd rows: Rep 29th and 30th rows.
33rd row: As 29th row.
34th row: ☆K2 tog, P1, rep from ☆ to end. 36 sts.
35th row: K.
36th row: ☆P2, tog, rep from ☆ to end. 18 sts.
37th row: ☆K2 tog, rep from ☆ to end. 9 sts.
Cut off yarn, draw through rem sts, draw up and fasten off securely.

EAR MUFFS
(make 2)
Cast on 14 sts.
1st row: (RS) K2, ☆P2, K2, rep from ☆ to end.
2nd row: P2, ☆K2, P2, rep from ☆ to end.
3rd–10th rows: Rep 1st and 2nd rows 4 times more.
11th row: ☆K2, P2 tog, rep from ☆ to last 2 sts, K2.
12th row: P2, ☆K1, P2, rep from ☆ to end.
13th row: K2, ☆P1, K2 tog, rep from ☆ to last 3 sts, P1, K2.
14th row: P2, ☆K1, P1, rep from ☆ to last st, P1.
15th row: K2, P1, K3 tog, P1, K2.
16th row: P2, K1, P1, K1, P2.
17th row: K2, K3 tog, K2.

18th row: P1, P3 tog, P1. Cut off yarn.
Leave rem 3 sts on a safety pin.

EDGING
With RS of work facing, K up 18 sts down first side of muff, K across 3 sts on safety pin, K up 18 sts up second side of muff. 39 sts.
K 1 row. Cast off.

VISOR
Cast on 26 sts and K 1 row.
Beg with a K row, work 6 rows st st.
Next row: K1, K2 tog tbl, K to last 3 sts, K2 tog, K1.
Next row: P1, P2 tog, P to last 3 sts, P2 tog tbl, P1.
Rep the last 2 rows once more. 18 sts.
Cut off yarn and leave sts on a spare needle.

EDGING
With RS of work facing, K up 9 sts down first side of visor, K across 18 sts on spare needle, K up 9 sts up second side of visor. 36 sts.
K 1 row. Cast off.

TO MAKE UP/TO FINISH
Matching centre of visor to centre front of main piece, sew visor flat to helmet along cast on edges, slip stitch side edges. Sew a muff to each side of visor.
Join back seam. Make a loose pom-pon approximately 16cm, 6¼ins in diameter and sew to crown. Make 2 twisted cords 44cm, 17¼ins long and attach to each muff.

TOY LAMB

Size
Length 39cm, 15½ins
Height 39cm, 15½ins

Materials
7 × 50g balls of Sirdar Country Style Chunky
One pair 6½mm (US10½) knitting needles
2 eyes, a nose, a small bell, ribbon for neck and stuffing

Tension/Gauge
12 sts and 12 rows to 10cm, 4ins over loop patt using 6½mm (US10½) needles

LAMBS

MAIN PIECE
(make 2)
Using 6½mm (US10½) needles cast on 47 sts.

K 3 rows.

Commence loop patt.

1st row: (WS) K1, ☆insert right hand needle into next st as if to K, wrap yarn over right hand needle and first and second fingers of left hand twice, then round right hand needle once more, draw 3 loops through and sl onto left hand needle, K3 tog tbl – called loop 1, K1, rep from ☆ to end.

2nd row: K.

3rd row: K1, ☆K1, loop 1, rep from ☆ to last 2 sts, K2.

4th row: K.

These 4 rows form the loop patt.

Cont in loop patt until work measures 31cm, 12¼ins from beg.

Cast off.

LEFT SIDE OF HEAD
Using 6½mm (US10½) needles cast on 23 sts. Beg with a K row, work 4 rows st st.

Shape head
1st row: K to last 2 sts, inc in next st, K1.

2nd row: P.

3rd–6th rows: Rep 1st and 2nd rows twice more.

7th row: Inc in first st, K to last 2 sts, inc in next st, K1.

8th row: P.

9th row: As 1st row.

10th–17th rows: Beg with a P row, work 8 rows st st.

18th row: P2 tog, P to last 2 sts, P2 tog tbl.

19th row: K to last 2 sts, K2 tog.

20th row: Cast off 2 sts, P to last 2 sts, P2 tog tbl.

21st row: K2 tog tbl, K to last 2 sts, K2 tog.

22nd row: P2 tog, P to last 2 sts, P2 tog tbl.

Rep 21st and 22nd rows until 9 sts rem, so ending with a K row. Cast off.

RIGHT SIDE OF HEAD
Work as given for left side of head, reversing all shapings.

EARS (make 4)
Using 6½mm (US10½) needles cast on 12 sts.

Beg with a K row, work 2 rows st st.

Next row: Inc in first st, K to last st, inc in last st.

Beg with a P row, work 5 rows st st.

Next row: K2 tog tbl, K to last 2 sts, K2 tog. 12 sts.

Next row: P.

Rep the last 2 rows until 4 sts rem.

Cast off.

TO MAKE UP/TO FINISH
Join head pieces together, leaving neck open. Stuff firmly.

Join ears, placing a K side and a P side together. Using P side as inner ear, sew in place on head. Sew on eyes and nose.

Join sides of main pieces, leaving a small opening. Stuff firmly. Close opening. Sew head to one top corner of body. Twist 20 strands of yarn together into a skein approximately 23cm, 9in long. Fasten ends in a tuft. Sew to body. Attach bell on ribbon, tie round neck in a bow.

PRIMROSES AND SNOWDROPS

Teddy's 'Fair Maid's of February' Sweater and Scarf *pattern instructions on page 143*

Mother Rabbit's Outfit *pattern instructions on page 150*

GORSE

GORSE *Lady's Cardigan*

Patt instructions for beret, scarf and gloves on pages 141-2

Sizes
To fit bust 81 – 91[91 – 102]cm, 32 – 36 [36 – 40]ins
Actual bust 106[114]cm, 41¾[45]ins
Length 69cm, 27¼ins
Sleeve seam 47[52]cm, 18½[20½]ins

Materials
9[10] × 100g balls of Samband Lopi
One pair each 6mm (US10) and 7mm (US10½) knitting needles
Cable needle
6 'Pikaby' buttons

Tension/Gauge
16 sts and 17 rows to 10cm, 4ins over patt using 7mm (US10½) needles

BACK
Using 7mm (US10½) needles, cast on 90[94] sts.
Cont in K2, P2 rib as foll:
1st row: (RS) K2, ☆P2, K2, rep from ☆ to end.
2nd row: P2, ☆K2, P2, rep from ☆ to end.
Rep these 2 rows for 7cm, 2¾ins ending with a RS row, for *2nd size only* inc 1 st at each end of last row. 90(96) sts.
Commence patt.
1st row: (WS) K0[3], ☆(K1, P1) 3 times, K3, P1, K5, rep from ☆ to last 0[3] sts, K0[3].
2nd row: P0[3], ☆P5, sl next st onto cable needle and hold at front of work, K1, then K1 from cable needle – called Cr2f(K), P2, sl next st onto cable needle and hold at front of work, P1, then K1 from cable needle – called Cr2f(P),

Cr2f(P), P2, rep from ☆ to last 0[3] sts, P0[3].
3rd row: K0[3], ☆K2, P1, K1, P1, K3, P2, K5, rep from ☆ to last 0[3] sts, K0[3].
4th row: P0[3], ☆P4, sl next st onto cable needle and hold at back of work, K1, then P1 from cable needle – called Cr2b(P), Cr2f(K), P2, Cr2f(P), P3, rep from ☆ to last 0[3] sts, P0[3].
5th row: K0[3], ☆K3, P1, K3, P2, K1, P1, K4, rep from ☆ to last 0[3] sts, K0[3].
6th row: P0[3], ☆P3, Cr2b(P) twice, Cr2f(K), P6, rep from ☆ to last 0[3] sts, P0[3].
7th row: K0[3], ☆K6, P2, (K1, P1) twice, K3, rep from ☆ to last 0[3] sts, K0[3].
8th row: P0[3], ☆P2, Cr2b(P) 3 times, Cr2f(P), P5, rep from ☆ to last 0[3] sts, P0[3].
9th row: K0[3], ☆K5, P1, K2, (P1, K1) 3 times, K1, rep from ☆ to last 0[3] sts, K0[3].
10th row: P0[3], ☆P1, Cr2b(P) 3 times, P2, K1, P5, rep from ☆ to last 0[3] sts, P0[3].
11th row: K0[3], ☆K5, P1, K3, (P1, K1) 3 times, rep from ☆ to last 0[3] sts, K0[3].
12th row: P0[3], ☆P2, Cr2b(P) twice, P2, Cr2b(K), P5, rep from ☆ to last 0[3] sts, P0[3].
13th row: K0[3], ☆K5, P2, K3, P1, K1, P1, K2, rep from ☆ to last 0[3] sts, K0[3].
14th row: P0[3], ☆P3, Cr2b(K), P2, Cr2b(P), Cr2f(K), P4, rep from ☆ to last 0[3] sts, P0[3].
15th row: K0[3], ☆K4, P1, K1, P2, K3, P1, K3, rep from ☆ to last 0[3] sts, K0[3].
16th row: P0[3], ☆P6, Cr2b(P), Cr2f(K) twice, P3, rep from ☆ to last 0[3] sts, P0[3].
17th row: K0[3], ☆K3, (P1, K1) twice, P2, K6, rep from ☆ to last 0[3] sts, K0[3].
18th row: P0[3], ☆P5, Cr2b(K), Cr2f(K) 3 times, P2, rep from ☆ to last 0[3] sts, P0[3].
19th row: K0[3], ☆K2, (P1, K1) 3 times, K1, P1, K5, rep from ☆ to last 0[3] sts, K0[3].
20th row: P0[3], ☆P5, K1, P2, Cr2f(K) 3 times, P1, rep from ☆ to last 0[3] sts, P0[3].
These 20 rows form the patt.
Cont in patt until work measures 69cm, 27¼ins from beg, ending with a WS row.
Shape shoulders
Cast off 30[33] sts at beg of next 2 rows.
Leave rem 30 sts on a holder.

LEFT FRONT
Using 7mm (US10½) needles, cast on 36[40] sts.
Cont in K2, P2 rib as foll:
1st row: (RS) ☆K2, P2, rep from ☆ to end.
Rep this row until work measures 7cm, 2¾ins ending with a RS row.
Commence patt.
1st row: (WS) K3, ☆(K1, P1) 3 times, K3, P1, K5, rep from ☆ to last 3[7] sts, K3[7].
This row establishes the patt as given for back. Cont in patt until work measures 61cm, 24ins from beg, ending with a RS row.
Shape neck
Cast off 4 sts at beg of next row, then dec 1 st at beg of every foll alt row until 30[33] sts rem.
Cont without further shaping until work measures same as back to shoulder shaping, ending with a WS row.
Shape shoulder
Cast off rem sts.

RIGHT FRONT
Using 7mm (US10½) needles, cast on 36[40] sts.
Cont in K2, P2 rib as foll:
1st row: (RS) ☆P2, K2, rep from ☆ to end.
Rep this row until work measures 7cm, 2¾ins from beg, ending with a RS row.
Commence patt.
1st row: (WS) K3[7], ☆(K1, P1) 3 times, K3, P1, K5, rep from ☆ to last 3 sts, K3.
This row establishes the patt as given for back.
Complete as given for left front, reversing all shapings.

SLEEVES
Using 6mm (US10) needles, cast on 34 sts.
Work 8cm, 3ins K2, P2 rib as given for back, ending with a WS row.
Inc row: Rib 7, ☆inc in next st, rib 1, rep from ☆ to last 7 sts, inc in next st, rib to end. 45 sts.
Change to 7mm (US10½) needles and cont in patt as given for 1st size of back.
Inc and work into rev st st 1 st at each end of 2nd and every foll 4th row until there are 73[77] sts.
Cont without further shaping until work measures 43[48]cm, 17[19]ins from beg, ending with a WS row.

MEADOWS

Cont in rib as foll:

1st row: P1, ☆K2, P2, rep from ☆ to end.

2nd row: ☆K2, P2, rep from ☆ to last st, K1.

Rep last 2 rows twice more.

Cast off fairly loosely in rib.

POCKET LININGS
(make 2)

Using 7mm (US10½) needles, cast on 26 sts. Work in st st for 15cm, 6ins ending with a P row. Cast off.

BUTTONBAND

Using 7mm (US10½) needles, cast on 10 sts.

Work in K2, P2 rib as given for back until band is long enough, when slightly stretched, to fit up left front to neck edge, ending with a WS row. Cut yarn and leave sts on a safety pin.

TO MAKE UP/TO FINISH

Sew on buttonband. Mark the position of 5 buttons, the first 2cm, ¾in above cast on edge and the last 5cm, 2ins below neck edge with the others evenly spaced between.

BUTTONHOLE BAND

Work as given for buttonband but do not cut yarn and make buttonholes opposite markers as foll:

1st buttonhole row: Rib 3, cast off 3 sts, rib to end.

2nd buttonhole row: Rib to end, casting on 3 sts over those cast off in previous row.

Sew on buttonhole band. Join shoulder seams.

NECKBAND

With RS of work facing, using 6mm (US10) needles, rib across sts of buttonhole band, K up 18 sts up right side of neck, K30 sts across back neck, K up 18 sts down left side of neck, then rib 10 sts of buttonband. 86 sts.

Beg with a WS row, work 3 rows K2, P2 rib as given for back.

Rep 1st and 2nd buttonhole rows again.

Work 2 rows rib. Cast off in rib.

Mark the position of pocket, 9cm, 3½ins and 27cm, 10¾ins above cast on edge of each front at side.

POCKET EDGINGS

With RS of work facing, using 6mm (US10) needles K up 26 sts between pocket markers.

Beg with a WS row, work 5 rows K2, P2 rib as given for back.

Cast off in rib.

Sew pocket linings to correspond with edgings on back at sides.

Placing centre of cast off edge of sleeves to shoulder seams, set in sleeves. Join sleeve and remaining side seams.

Sew on buttons.

MEADOWS
Children's Cardigans

Sizes

To fit chest 51 – 56[61 – 66:71 – 76:81 – 86]cm, 20 – 22[24 – 26:28 – 30:32 – 34]ins

Actual chest 60[72.5:85:98]cm, 23¾[29½:33½:38½]ins

Length 32[39:50:57]cm, 12½[15½:19¾:22½]ins

Sleeve seam 25[29:33:37]cm, 9¾[11½:13:14½]ins

Materials

Striped version

1[1:2:2] × 50g balls of Hayfield Grampian DK in main colour (A)

1[1:2:2] balls each in contrast colours (B, C and D)

Plain version

4[4:5:5] × 50g balls of Hayfield Grampian DK (A)

Both versions

One pair each 3¼mm (US3) and 4mm (US6) knitting needles

5 'Pikaby' buttons

Tension/Gauge

22 sts and 35 rows to 10cm, 4ins over patt using 4mm (US6) needles

STRIPED VERSION

BACK

Using 3¼mm (US3) needles and A, cast on 52[64:76:88] sts.

Cont in K2, P2 rib for 5[5:6:6]cm, 2[2:2½:2½]ins ending with a RS row.

Inc row: Rib 8[4:6:8], ☆inc in next st, rib 2[3:3:3], rep from ☆ to last 8[4:6:8] sts, inc in next st, rib to end. 65[79:93:107] sts.

Change to 4mm (US6) needles and commence patt.

1st row: (RS) With B, K.

2nd row: With B, K8, ☆P7, K7, rep from ☆ to last st, K1.

3rd–6th rows: Rep 1st and 2nd rows twice more.

7th row: With B, K11, ☆(K1, P1, K1) all into next st, turn P3, turn K3, turn P3, turn sl 1, K2 tog, psso – called make bobble MB, K13, rep from ☆ to last 12 sts, MB, K11.

8th row: As 2nd row.

9th–12th rows: Rep 1st and 2nd rows twice more.

13th row: With C, K.

14th row: With C, P8, ☆K7, P7, rep from ☆ to last st, P1.

15th–18th rows: Rep 13th and 14th rows twice more.

19th rows: With C, K4, ☆MB, K13, rep from ☆ to last 5 sts, MB, K4.

20th row: As 14th row.

21st–24th rows: Rep 13th and 14th rows twice more.

25th–36th rows: Rep 1st–12th rows using D instead of B.

37th–48th rows: Rep 13th–24th rows using A instead of C.

These 48 rows form the patt. Cont in patt until work measures approximately 32[39:50:57]cm, 12½[15½:19¾:22½]ins from beg ending with a 12th, 24th, 36th or 48th patt row.

Shape shoulders

Cont in yarn used for previous row, cast off 20[26:32:38] sts at beg of next 2 rows.

Cast off rem 25[27:29:31] sts.

LEFT FRONT

☆☆Using 3¼mm (US3) needles and A, cast on 24[30:36:42] sts.

Cont in K2, P2 rib for 5[5:6:6]cm, 2[2:2½:2½]ins ending with a RS row.

Inc row: Rib 4[6:4:5], ☆inc in next st, rib 2[2:3:3], rep from ☆ to last 5[6:4:5] sts, inc in next st, rib to end. 30[37:44:51] sts. ☆☆

Change to 4mm (US6) needles and commence patt.

1st row: (RS) With B, K.

2nd row: With B, K1[8:1:8], ☆P7, K7, rep from ☆ to last st, K1.

3rd–6th rows: Rep 1st and 2nd rows twice more.

7th row: With B, K11, ☆MB, K13, rep from ☆ to last 5[12:5:12] sts, MB, K4[11:4:11].

8th row: As 2nd row.

9th–12th rows: Rep 1st and 2nd rows twice more.

13th row: With C, K.

14th row: With C, P1[8:1:8], ☆K7, P7, rep from ☆ to last st, P1.

15th–18th rows: Rep 13th and 14th rows twice more.

19th row: With C, K4, ☆MB, K13, rep from ☆ to last 12[5:12:5] sts, MB, K11[4:11:4].

20th row: As 14th row.

21st–24th rows: Rep 13th and 14th rows twice more.

25th–36th rows: Rep 1st–12th rows using D instead of B.

37th–48th rows: Rep 13th–24th rows using A instead of C.

These 48 rows form the patt. Cont in patt until work measures 25[32:43:50]cm, 9¾[12½:17:19¾]ins from beg, ending with a RS row.

Shape neck

Cast off 4[5:6:7] sts at beg of next row, then dec 1 st at neck edge on foll 2 rows. Dec 1 st at neck edge on every foll alt row until 20[26:32:38] sts rem.

Cont without further shaping until work measures same as back to shoulder shaping, ending with a WS row.

Shape shoulder

Cont in yarn used for previous row, cast off rem sts.

RIGHT FRONT

Work as given for left front from ☆☆ to ☆☆.

Change to 4mm (US6) needles and commence patt.

1st row: (RS) With B, K.

2nd row: With B, K1, ☆K7, P7, rep from ☆ to last 1[8:1:8] sts, K1[8:1:8].

3rd–6th rows: Rep 1st and 2nd rows twice more.

7th row: With B, K4[11:4:11], ☆MB, K13, rep from ☆ to last 12 sts, MB, K11.

8th row: As 2nd.

9th–12th rows: Rep 1st and 2nd rows twice more.

13th row: With C, K.

14th row: With C, P1, ☆P7, K7, rep from ☆ to last 1[8:1:8] sts, P1[8:1:8].

15th–18th rows: Rep 13th and 14th rows twice more.

19th row: With C, K11[4:11:4], ☆MB, K13, rep from ☆ to last 5 sts, MB, K4.

20th row: As 14th row.

21st–24th rows: Rep 13th and 14th rows twice more.

25th–36th rows: Rep 1st–12th rows using D instead of B.

37th–48th rows: Rep 13th–24th rows using A instead of C.

These 48 rows form the patt.

Complete as given for left front, reversing all shapings.

SLEEVES

Using 3¼mm (US3) needles and A, cast on 28[36:40:52] sts.

Cont in K2, P2 rib for 5[5:6:6]cm, 2[2:2½:2½]ins ending with a RS row.

Inc row: Rib 6[4:5:10], ☆inc in next st, rib 1[1:2:0], rep from ☆ to last 6[4:5:10] sts, inc in next st, rib to end. 37[51:51:65] sts.

Change to 4mm (US6) needles and cont in patt as given for back, inc and work into patt 1 st at each end of 5th and every foll 4th[5th:6th:7th] row until there are 65[79:79:93] sts.

Cont without further shaping until work measures approximately 25[29:33:37]cm, 9¾[11½:13:14½]ins from beg, ending with a 12th, 24th, 36th or 48th patt row. Cast off loosely.

BUTTONHOLE BAND

With RS of work facing, using 3¼mm (US3) needles and A, K up 70[94:118:142] sts evenly along right front edge for a girl or left front edge for a boy.

1st row: (WS) P2, ☆K2, P2, rep from ☆ to end.

2nd row: K2, ☆P2, K2, rep from ☆ to end.

Work 1 more row in rib.

1st buttonhole row: Rib 4, ☆cast off 2, rib 13[19:25:31] including st used to cast off, rep from ☆ to last 6 sts, cast off 2, rib to end.

2nd buttonhole row: Rib to end, casting on 2 sts over those cast off in previous row.

Work 5 rows in rib. Cast off in rib.

BUTTONBAND

Work to match buttonhole band, omitting buttonholes.

COLLAR

Using 3¼mm (US3) needles and A, cast on 86[98:110:122] sts.

Work in K2, P2, rib as given for buttonhole band for 7cm, 2¾ins. Cast off very loosely in rib.

TO MAKE UP/TO FINISH

Join shoulder seams. Beg and ending at centre of front bands sew cast on edge of collar to neck edge. Placing centre of cast off edge of sleeves to shoulder seam, sew in sleeves. Join side and sleeve seams. Sew on buttons.

PLAIN VERSION

Work as given for striped version but use only A throughout.

DAFFY-DOWN-DILLY *Children's Sweater and Cardigan*

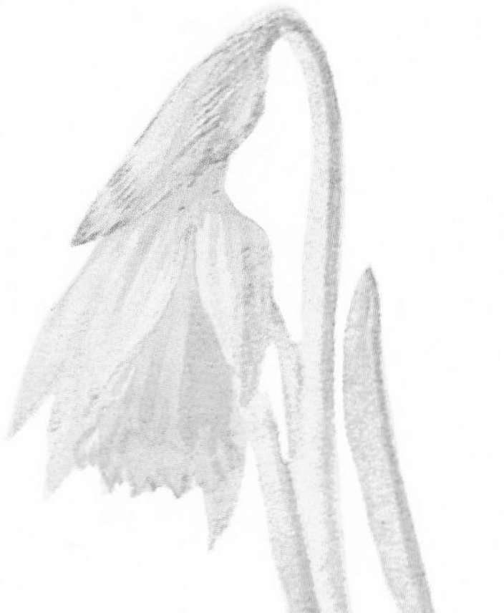

Sizes

To fit chest 51[56:61:66]cm,
20[22:24:26]ins
Actual chest 53[58:62:67]cm,
21[22¾:24½:26½]ins
Length 30[34:38:42]cm,
11¾[13½:15:16½]ins
Sleeve seam 21[26.5:31:35]cm,
8¼[10½:12¼:13¾]ins

Materials

Sweater *OR* cardigan
3[4:4:5] × 50g balls of Phildar Sagittaire
in main colour (A)
1[1:1:1] ball each in contrast colours (B
and C)
One pair each 3mm (US3) and 3¾mm
(US5) knitting needles
6 'Pikaby' buttons for cardigan

Tension/Gauge

22 sts and 32 rows to 10cm, 4ins over st st
using 3¾mm (US5) needles
26 sts and 30 rows to 10cm, 4ins over patt
using 3¾mm (US5) needles

SWEATER

BACK

☆☆Using 3mm (US3) needles and A,
cast on 68[74:80:86] sts.
Cont in K1, P1 rib for 5cm, 2ins ending
with a WS row and inc 1 st at end of last
row. 69[75:81:87] sts.
Change to 3¾mm (US5) needles and
commence patt.
1st row: (RS) K.
2nd–3rd rows: K.
4th row: P.
5th–13th rows: Beg with a K row, work 9
rows st st working colour patt from chart.
Read odd numbered rows (K) from right
to left and even numbered rows (P) from
left to right. Strand yarn loosely on WS

of work and twist yarns when changing
colour to avoid a hole.
14th row: Cont in A only, P.
15th–17th rows: K.
18th row: P.
These 18 rows form the patt. Cont in patt
until work measures 17[20:23:25.5]cm,
6[8:9:10]ins from beg, ending with a WS
row.
Shape armholes
Cast off 5 sts at beg of next 2 rows.
59[65:71:77] sts. ☆☆
Cont without further shaping until work
measures 30[34:38:42]cm, 11¾[13½:15:
16½]ins from beg, ending with a WS
row.
Shape shoulders and neck
Cast off 4[5:6:7] sts at beg of next 2 rows.
Next row: Cast off 4[5:6:7], patt 4[5:6:7]
including st used to cast off, and turn
leaving rem sts on a spare needle.
Complete right side of neck first.
Work 1 row.
Cast off rem 4[5:6:7] sts.
With RS of work facing, return to sts on
spare needle. Rejoin yarn at neck edge,
cast off centre 35 sts, patt to end.
Next row: Cast off 4[5:6:7] sts, patt to
end.
Work 1 row.
Cast off rem 4[5:6:7] sts.

FRONT

Work as given for back from ☆☆ to ☆☆.
Cont without further shaping until work
measures 26[29.5:33.5:37]cm, 10¼[11¾:
13¼:14½]ins from beg, ending with a
WS row.
Shape neck
Next row: Patt 21[24:27:30] sts and turn,
leaving rem sts on a spare needle.
Complete left side of neck first.
Cast off 2 sts at beg of next and 2 foll alt
rows. Dec 1 st at neck edge on next 3
rows. 12[15:18:21] sts. Cont without
further shaping until work measures same
as back to shoulder shaping, ending at
armhole edge.
Shape shoulder
Cast off 4[5:6:7] sts at beg of next and foll
alt row. Work 1 row. Cast off rem
4[5:6:7] sts.
With RS of work facing, return to sts on
spare needle. Rejoin yarn at neck edge
and cast off centre 17 sts, patt to end.
Work 1 row.
Complete as given for first side of neck.

SLEEVES

Using 3mm (US3) needles and A, cast
on 36[38:40:42] sts.
Cont in K1, P1 rib for 6cm, 2½ins.
Change to 3¾mm (US5) needles and
commence patt, *at the same time*, inc 1 st
at each end of 3rd and every foll 4th row
until there are 58[62:68:72] sts.
1st row: (RS) K.
2nd–3rd rows: K.
4th–14th rows: Beg with a P row, work
11 rows st st.
15th–17th rows: K.
18th row: P.
These 18 rows form the patt.
Cont without further shaping until work
measures 23[28.5:33:37]cm, 9[11¼:13:
14½]ins from beg, ending with a WS
row.
Cast off loosely.

TO MAKE UP/TO FINISH

Join right shoulder seam.

NECKBAND

With RS of work facing, using 3mm
(US3) needles and A, K up 92[94:94:96]
sts evenly around neck edge.
Cont in K1, P1 rib for 3cm, 1¼ins. Cast
off loosely in rib.

Join left shoulder and neckband seam.
Placing centre of cast off edge of sleeve to
shoulder seam, set in sleeves, sewing final
rows to cast off sts at underarm. Join side
and sleeve seams.

CARDIGAN

BACK

Work as given for back of sweater.

LEFT FRONT

Using 3mm (US3) needles and A, cast
on 32[36:38:42] sts.
Cont in K1, P1 rib for 5cm, 2ins.
Change to 3¾mm (US5) needles and
cont in patt as given for sweater back
until work measures same as back to
armhole shaping, ending with a WS row.
Shape armhole
Cast off 5 sts at beg of next row.
27[31:33:37] sts.
Cont without further shaping until work
measures 25[28·5:32·5:36]cm, 9¾[11¼:
12¾:14¼]ins from beg, ending with a RS
row.
Shape neck
Cast off 6[7:6:7] sts at beg of next row and

* on page 38

DAFFY-DOWN-DILLY

2 sts at beg of foll 3 alt rows.
Dec 1 st at neck edge on next 3 rows.
12[15:18:21] sts.
Cont without further shaping until work measures same as back to shoulder shaping, ending with a WS row.
Shape shoulder
Cast off 4[5:6:7] sts at beg of next and foll alt row. Work 1 row. Cast off rem 4[5:6:7] sts.

RIGHT FRONT
Work as given for left front, reversing all shapings.

SLEEVES
Work as given for sleeves of sweater.

BUTTONBAND
Using 3mm (US3) needles and A, cast on 6 sts.

Cont in K1, P1 rib until band is long enough, when slightly stretched, to fit up left front edge, ending at inner neck edge. Cut yarn and leave sts on a safety pin.

TO MAKE UP/TO FINISH
Sew on buttonband. Mark the position of 5 buttons, the first in the 5th row from cast on edge and the rem 4 evenly spaced between it and the 6th buttonhole to be made in 5th row of neckband.

BUTTONHOLE BAND
Work as given for buttonband but end at outer edge and do not cut yarn, making buttonholes opposite markers as foll:
1st buttonhole row: (RS) Rib 2, cast off 2, rib to end.
2nd buttonhole row: Rib to end, casting on over cast off sts in previous row.

Sew on buttonhole band. Join shoulder seams.

NECKBAND
Using 3mm (US3) needles and A, rib 6 sts of buttonhole band, K up 92[94:94:96] sts evenly around neck edge, then rib 6 sts from buttonband. 104[106:106:108] sts.
Work 3 rows K1, P1 rib then work 1st and 2nd buttonhole rows again.
Work 3 rows rib, cast off loosely in rib.

Placing centre of cast off edge of sleeve to shoulder seam, set in sleeves, sewing final rows to cast off sts at underarm. Join side and sleeve seams. Sew on buttons.

Key
A   □
B   ●
C   ×

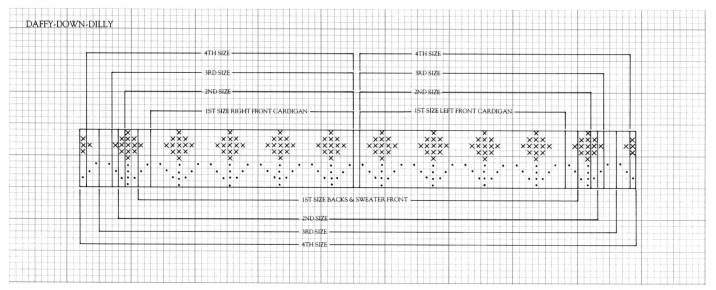

DAFFY·DOWN·DILLY

4TH SIZE   4TH SIZE
3RD SIZE   3RD SIZE
2ND SIZE   2ND SIZE
1ST SIZE RIGHT FRONT CARDIGAN   1ST SIZE LEFT FRONT CARDIGAN

1ST SIZE BACKS & SWEATER FRONT
2ND SIZE
3RD SIZE
4TH SIZE

BUTTERCUPS AND DAISIES

Children's Waistcoats

Sizes
To fit chest 56 – 61[61 – 66]cm, 22 – 24[24 – 26]ins
Actual chest 61[66]cm, 24[26]ins
Length 24[30]cm, 9½[11¾]ins

Materials
2[3] × 50g balls of Patons Beehive Double Knitting
One pair each 2¾mm (US2) and 3¼mm (US3) knitting needles
Ribbon, lace and oddments (odds and ends) of yarn for trimming (optional)

Tension/Gauge
27 sts and 40 rows to 10cm, 4ins over st st using 3¼mm (US3) needles

BACK
Using 2¾mm (US2) needles, cast on 83[89] sts.
Cont in K1, P1 rib as foll:
1st row: (RS) K1, ☆P1, K1, rep from ☆ to end.
2nd row: P1, ☆K1, P1, rep from ☆ to end.

Rep these 2 rows twice more.
Change to 3¼mm (US3) needles. Beg with a K row cont in st st until work measures 9[12]cm, 3½[4¾]ins from beg, ending with a P row.
Shape armholes
Cast off 6 sts at beg of next 2 rows. Dec 1 st at each end of next and every foll alt row until 61[65] sts rem.
Cont without further shaping until work measures 24[30]cm, 9½[11¾]ins from beg, ending with a P row.
Shape shoulders
Cast off 15[16] sts at beg of next 2 rows.
Leave rem 31[33] sts on a spare needle.

BUTTERCUPS AND DAISIES

LEFT FRONT

☆☆Using 2¾mm (US2) needles, cast on 41[45] sts.

Work 6 rows K1, P1 rib as given for back. Change to 3¼mm (US3) needles. Beg with a K row cont in st st until work measures same as back to armhole shaping, ending at side edge.

Shape armhole

Cast off 6 sts at beg of next row. Dec 1 st at armhole edge on every foll alt row until 30[33] sts rem. ☆☆

Cont without further shaping until work measures 17[21] rows less than back to shoulder shaping, ending at front edge.

Shape neck

Cast off 5 sts at beg of next row. Dec 1 st at neck edge on every row until 15[16] sts rem.

Cont without further shaping until work measures same as back to shoulder shaping, ending at armhole edge.

Shape shoulder

Cast off rem sts.

RIGHT FRONT

Work as given for left front from ☆☆ to ☆☆.

Cont without further shaping until work measures 16[20] rows less than back to shoulder shaping, ending at front edge.

Complete as given for left front.

TO MAKE UP/TO FINISH

Join shoulder seams.

ARMBANDS

With RS of work facing, using 2¾mm (US2) needles, K up 99[105] sts evenly around armhole edge.

Beg with 2nd row, work 5 rows K1, P1 rib as given for back. Cast off in rib.

FRONTBANDS

With RS of work facing, using 2¾mm (US2) needles, K up 55[63] sts evenly from front edge.

Complete as given for armbands.

NECKBAND

With RS of work facing, using 2¾mm (US2) needles, beg at outer edge of right frontband, K up 25[29] sts up right side of neck, K across 31[33] sts at back neck, K up 25[29] sts down left side of neck and top of left frontband. 81[91] sts.

Complete as given for armbands.

Join side seams. Trim garment as desired – make a ribbon tie at neck, sew on lace around neckline. Embroider flowers in oddments of yarn.

WILD PEAR

Lady's Sweater and Scarf

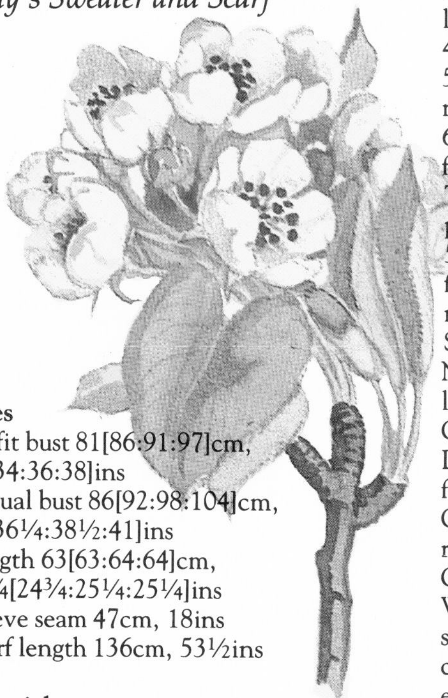

Sizes

To fit bust 81[86:91:97]cm, 32[34:36:38]ins
Actual bust 86[92:98:104]cm, 34[36¼:38½:41]ins
Length 63[63:64:64]cm, 24¾[24¾:25¼:25¼]ins
Sleeve seam 47cm, 18ins
Scarf length 136cm, 53½ins

Materials

5[6:6:7] × 50g balls of Argyll Chameleon for sweater
2 balls for scarf
One pair each 3¾mm (US5) and 5mm (US8) knitting needles

Tension/Gauge

18 sts (3 patt reps) to 9cm, 3½ins and 24 rows (4 patt reps) to 15cm, 6ins on 5mm (US8) needles

SWEATER

FRONT

☆☆Using 3¾mm (US5) needles, cast on 73[79:85:91] sts.

Cont in K1, P1 rib as foll:

1st row: K1, ☆P1, K1, rep from ☆ to end.

2nd row: P1, ☆K1, P1, rep from ☆ to end.

Rep these 2 rows for 8cm, 3ins, ending with a 2nd row.

Inc row: Rib 6[3:6:3], inc in next st, ☆rib 4[5:5:6], inc in next st, rep from ☆ to last 6[3:6:3] sts, rib to end. 86[92:98:104] sts.

Change to 5mm (US8) needles and cont in patt.

1st row: (WS) K1, ☆P5 tog, work (K1, P1, K1, P1, K1) all into next st, rep from ☆ to last st, K1.

2nd row: P.

3rd row: K1, ☆work (K1, P1, K1, P1, K1) all into next st, P5 tog, rep from ☆ to last st, K1.

4th row: P.

5th row: K to end winding yarn twice round needle for each st.

6th row: P to end allowing extra loops to fall from needle.

These 6 rows form the patt. ☆☆Cont in patt until work measures approximately 54[54:55:55]cm, 21¼[21¼:21¾:21¾]ins from beg, ending with a 2nd or 4th patt row.

Shape neck

Next row: Patt 35[37:39:41] sts and turn leaving rem sts on a spare needle.

Complete left side of neck first.

Dec 1 st at neck edge on next and every foll alt row until 30[32:34:36] sts rem.

Cont without further shaping. Work 4 rows, ending with a 4th or 6th patt row.

Cast off.

With RS of work facing, return to sts on spare needle. Rejoin yarn at neck edge, cast off centre 16[18:20:22] sts, patt to end.

Complete as given for first side of neck.

BACK

Work as given for front from ☆☆ to ☆☆.

Cont in patt until work measures same as front, ending with same patt row.

Cast off marking 30th [32nd:34th:36th] st from each side edge for shoulders.

SLEEVES

Using 3¾mm (US5) needles, cast on 47[47:51:51] sts.

Work in K1, P1 rib as given for front for 8cm, 3ins, ending with a 2nd row.

Inc row: K1[1:2:2], ☆inc in next st, rep from ☆ to last 1[1:2:2] sts, K1[1:2:2]. 92[92:98:98] sts.

Change to 5mm (US8) needles and cont in patt as given for front until work measures approximately 47cm, 18½ins from beg, ending with a 2nd or 4th patt row. Cast off loosely.

COLLAR

Using 3¾mm (US5) needles, cast on 133[137:141:145] sts.

WILD PEAR

Work in K1, P1 rib as given for front for 10cm, 4ins.
Cast off loosely in rib.

TO MAKE UP/TO FINISH

Join shoulder seams. Placing centre of cast off edge to shoulder seams, set in sleeves. Join side and sleeve seams. Sew collar to neck edge. Brush fabric with a teazle to enhance appearance.

SCARF

Using 5mm (US8) needles, cast on 56 sts.
K 1 row.
Cont in patt as given for front of sweater until work measures approximately 136cm, 53½ins from beg, ending with a 2nd or 4th patt row. Cast off. Brush fabric with a teazle to enhance appearance.

LADY'S SMOCK

Child's Cardigan

Sizes

To fit chest 56[61:66]cm, 22[24:26]ins
Actual chest 62[68:73]cm, 24½[26¾:28¾]ins
Length 33[35:37]cm, 13[13¾:14½]ins
Sleeve seam 11cm, 4¼ins

Materials

7[8:9] × 20g balls of Jarol Imps and Angels Baby DK
One pair each 3¼mm (US3) and 4mm (US6) knitting needles
Cable needle
43cm, 17ins ribbon
1 'Pikaby' button

Tension/Gauge

23 sts and 30 rows to 10cm, 4ins over patt using 4mm (US6) needles

LACE PATT PANEL

(worked over 9 sts)
1st row: (RS) P1, K1, K2 tog, yfwd, K1, yfwd, K2 tog tbl, K1, P1.
2nd row: K1, P7, K1.
3rd row: P1, K2 tog, yfwd, K3, yfwd, K2 tog tbl, P1.
4th row: As 2nd row.
These 4 rows form the lace patt panel.

FLOWER PATT PANEL

(worked over 9 sts but sts are made and lost within patt)
1st row: (RS) P1, K3, (K1, yfwd, K1, yfwd, K1) all into next st, K3, P1.
2nd row: K1, P3, P5 winding yarn twice round needle for each st, P3, K1.
3rd row: P1, K3, keeping yarn at back of work sl 5 purlwise allowing extra loops to fall, K3, P1.
4th row: K1, P3, keeping yarn at front of work, sl 5 purlwise, P3, K1.
5th row: P1, K1, sl next st onto cable needle and hold at back of work, K3 tog, K1 from cable needle, K1, sl next 3 sts onto cable needle and hold at front of work, K1, K3 tog tbl from cable needle, K1, P1.
6th row: K1, P7, K1.
7th–8th rows: Rep 1st–2nd rows.
9th row: P1, K3, keeping yarn at back of work sl 3 purlwise, K2 tog allowing extra loops to fall, p3sso, K3, P1.
10th row: As 6th row.
11th row: P1, K7, P1.
12th row: As 6th row.
These 12 rows form the flower patt panel.

BACK

Using 3¼mm (US3) needles, cast on 60[66:74] sts.
Work 7 rows K1, P1 rib.
Inc row: Rib 6[9:7], ☆inc in next st, rib 3[3:4], rep from ☆ to last 6[9:7] sts, inc in next st, rib to end. 73[79:87] sts.

Change to 4mm (US6) needles and commence patt.
1st row: (RS) K2[2:3], ☆work 1st row of lace panel, K1[2:3], work 1st row of flower panel, K1[2:3], rep from ☆ to last 11[11:12] sts, work 1st row of lace panel, K2[2:3].
2nd row: P2[2:3], ☆work 2nd row of lace panel, P1[2:3], work 2nd row of flower panel, P1[2:3], rep from ☆ to last 11[11:12] sts, work 2nd row of lace panel, P2[2:3].
These 2 rows establish the position of lace and flower patt panels with st st between. Keeping panels correct, cont as set until work measures 17.5[18:18]cm, 6¾[7:7]ins from beg, ending with a WS row.
Shape armholes
Cast off 6 sts at beg of next 2 rows. 61[67:75] sts.
Next row: K5[5:6], patt to last 5[5:6] sts, K to end.
Cont as set, keeping patt correct and edge sts in g st until work measures 33[35:37]cm, 13[13¾:14½]ins from beg, ending with a WS row.
Shape shoulders
Cast off 9[10:12] sts at beg of next 2 rows and 9[11:13] sts at beg of foll 2 rows.
Leave rem 25 sts on a spare needle.

LEFT FRONT

☆☆Using 3¼mm (US3) needles, cast on 32[34:36] sts.
Work 7 rows K1, P1 rib.
Inc row: Rib 6[7:6], ☆inc in next st, rib 3, rep from ☆ to last 6[7:6] sts, inc in next st, rib 5[6:5]. 38[40:43] sts. ☆☆
Change to 4mm (US6) needles and commence patt.
1st row: (RS) K2[2:3], work 1st row of lace panel, K1[2:3], work 1st row of flower panel, K1[2:3], work 1st row of lace panel, K1, P1, K5.
2nd row: K6, P1, work 2nd row of lace panel, P1[2:3], work 2nd row of flower panel, P1[2:3], work 2nd row of lace panel, P2[2:3].
These 2 rows establish the position of the lace and flower patt panels with st st between and g st at front edge. Keeping panels correct, cont in patt as set until work measures same as back to armhole shaping, ending with a WS row.
Shape armhole
Cast off 6 sts at beg of next row. 32[34:37] sts.

LADY'S SMOCK

Next row: Patt to last 6 sts, K6.

Cont as set, keeping patt correct and sts at armhole edge in g st until work measures 27[29:31]cm, 10¾[11½: 12¼]ins from beg, ending with a WS row.

Shape neck

Next row: Patt to last 6 sts and turn leaving rem sts on a safety pin.

Dec 1 st at neck edge on every row until 18[21:25] sts rem.

Cont without further shaping until work measures same as back to shoulder shaping, ending with a WS row.

Shape shoulder

Cast off 9[10:12] sts at beg of next row. Work 1 row. Cast off rem 9[11:13] sts.

RIGHT FRONT

Work as given for left front from ☆☆ to ☆☆.

Change to 4mm (US6) needles and commence patt.

1st row: (RS) K5, P1, K1, work 1st row of lace panel, K1[2:3], work 1st row of flower panel, K1[2:3], work 1st row of lace panel, K2[2:3].

2nd row: P2[2:3], work 2nd row of lace panel, P1[2:3] work 1st row of flower panel, P1[2:3], work 2nd row of lace panel, P1, K6.

These 2 rows establish the position of the lace and flower patt panels with st st between and g st at front edge.

Complete as given for left front, reversing all shapings.

SLEEVES

Using 3¼mm (US3) needles, cast on 42[48:54] sts.

Work 7 rows K1, P1 rib.

Inc row: Rib 5[8:10], ☆inc in next st, rep from ☆ to last 6[9:11] sts, rib to end. 73[79:87] sts.

Change to 4mm (US6) needles and cont in patt as given for back.

Keeping panels correct, work 34 rows ending with a WS row.

Cast off loosely.

TO MAKE UP/TO FINISH

Join shoulder seams.

NECKBAND

With RS of work facing, using 3¼mm (US3) needles, K across 6 sts on right front safety pin, K up 20 sts up right side of neck, K across 25 sts on back neck, K up 20 sts down left side of neck, then K across 6 sts on left front safety pin. 77 sts.

1st row: K6, ☆P1, K1, rep from ☆ to last 7 sts, P1, K6.

2nd row: K5, ☆P1, K1, rep from ☆ to last 6 sts, P1, K5.

3rd row: As 1st row.

4th row: (make buttonhole) K2, K2 tog, yfwd, work to end.

5th–6th rows: Rep 1st and 2nd rows.

7th row: As 1st row.

Cast off, in rib over ribbed section.

Placing centre of cast off edge of sleeve to shoulder seam, set in sleeves, sewing final rows to cast off sts at underarm. Join side and sleeve seams. Sew on button. Catch centre of length of ribbon to right front neckband and tie in a bow. Oversew 'flower buds' on WS of work to emphasise them.

SUMMER

WILD GUELDER ROSE *Lady's Cardigan*

Tension/Gauge

16 sts and 22 rows to 10cm, 4ins over st st using 4mm (US6) needles

BACK

Using 4½mm (US7) needles and A, cast on 80 sts.

Cont in K1, P1 rib for 7cm, 2¾ins ending with a WS row.

Change to 5½mm (US9) needles. Beg with a K row, cont in st st working colour patt from chart. Use small separate balls of yarn for each area of colour, twisting them tog on WS of work when changing colour to avoid a hole. Read odd numbered rows (K) from right to left and even numbered rows (P) from left to right.

Work 106 rows from chart.

Shape back neck

Next row: Patt 28, cast off 24 sts, patt to end.

Cont on last set of sts, completing right side of back neck first.

Dec 1 st at neck edge on next row.

Work 1 row.

Shape shoulder

Cast off rem 27 sts.

With WS of work facing, return to sts for left side of neck, rejoin yarn and patt to end.

Dec 1 st at neck edge on next row.

Shape shoulder

Cast off rem 27 sts.

LEFT FRONT

☆☆Using 4½mm (US7) needles and A, cast on 40 sts.

Cont in K1, P1 rib for 7cm, 2¾ins ending with a WS row.

Change to 5½mm (US9) needles. Beg with a K row cont in st st working colour patt from chart.☆☆

Work 97 rows.

Shape neck

Cast off 5 sts at beg of next row, 4 sts at beg of next alt row and 2 sts at beg of foll 2 alt rows. 27 sts.

Cont without further shaping until work measures same as back to shoulder shaping, ending with a K row.

Shape shoulder

Cast off rem sts.

RIGHT FRONT

Work as given for left front from ☆☆ to ☆☆.

Work 98 rows.

Shape neck

Work as given for left front.

SLEEVES

First half (make 2)

Using 4½mm (US7) needles and A, cast on 22 sts.

Cont in K1, P1 rib for 5cm, 2ins ending with a RS row.

Inc row: Rib 4, ☆rib 1, inc in next st, rep from ☆ to end. 31 sts.

Change to 5½mm (US9) needles. Beg with a K row cont in st st, inc 1 st at end of every alt row until there are 77 sts.

Cont without further shaping until work measures 52cm, 20½ins from beg, ending with a P row.

Cast off loosely.

Second half (make 2)

Using 4½mm (US7) needles and A, cast on 22 sts.

Cont in K1, P1 rib for 5cm, 2ins ending with a RS row.

Inc row: ☆Inc in next st, rib 1, rep from

Size

To fit bust 81 – 97cm, 32 – 38ins
Actual bust 100cm, 39½ins
Length 56.5cm, 22¼ins
Sleeve seam 52cm, 20½ins

Materials

10 × 50g balls of Sunbeam Paris Mohair in main colour (A)
1 ball in contrast colour (B)
2 × 50g balls of Sunbeam Sapphire DK (C)
One pair each 4½mm (US7), 5½mm (US9), 3¾mm (US5) and 4mm (US6) knitting needles
4.00mm (USF/5) crochet hook
7 large pearl beads for buttons
Small pearl beads for decoration

• on opposite page

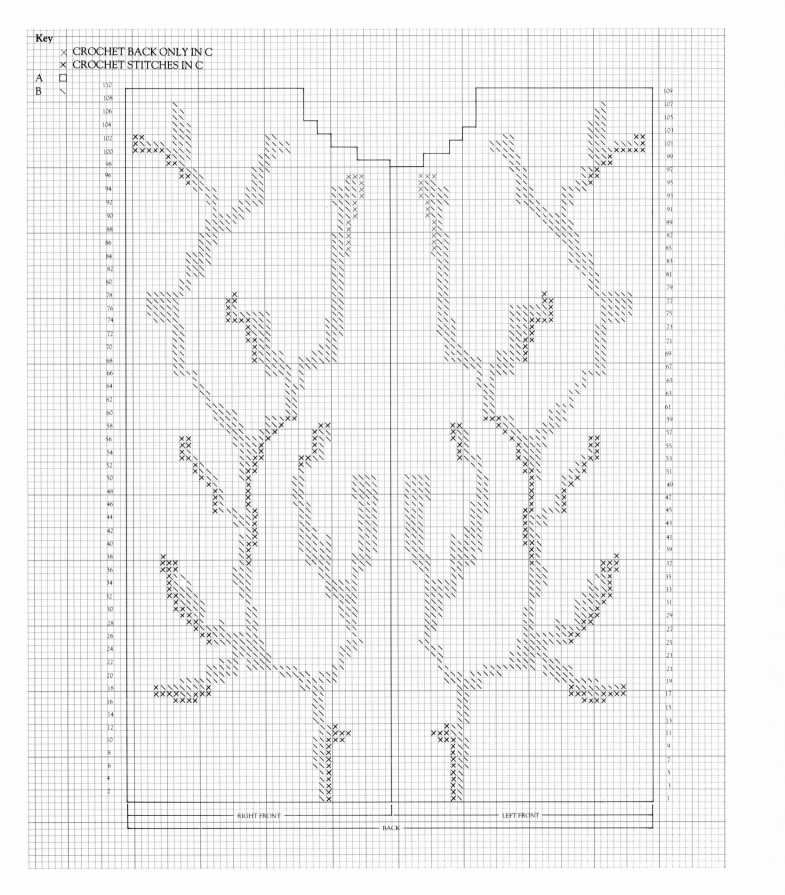

Key

✕	CROCHET BACK ONLY IN C
✕	CROCHET STITCHES IN C
A	☐
B	╲

RIGHT FRONT

LEFT FRONT

BACK

WILD GUELDER ROSE

MAY *Lady's Sweater*

☆ to last 4 sts, rib 4. 31 sts.
Complete as given for first half, reversing shaping.

BUTTONHOLE BAND
With RS of work facing, using 3¾mm (US5) needles and C, K up 110 sts evenly up right front edge.
K 3 rows.
Buttonhole row: K3, ☆K2 tog, yfwd, K15, rep from ☆ to last 5 sts, K2 tog, yfwd, K3.
K 2 rows. Cast off.

BUTTONBAND
With RS of work facing, using 3¾mm (US5) needles and C, K up 110 sts evenly down left front edge.
K 6 rows. Cast off.

TO MAKE UP/TO FINISH
Join shoulder seams.

COLLAR
With RS of work facing, using 3¾mm (US5) needles and C, K up 87 sts evenly from across buttonhole band, round neck edge and across buttonband.
Work 4cm, 1½ins in g st.
Change to 4mm (US6) needles and cont in g st until collar measures 6cm, 2½ins. Cast off.

Using 4.00mm (USF/5) crochet hook join in short lengths of C to positions indicated on chart. Work 3 ch into each st marked. Fasten off securely.

Join sleeve halves. Set in sleeves, placing centre seam to shoulder seam. Join side and underarm seams. Sew on buttons. Decorate with small pearl beads sewn close to crochet chains.

Sizes
To fit bust 76 – 81[86 – 91:91 – 97:102 – 107]cm, 30 – 32[34 – 36:36 – 38:40 – 42]ins
Actual bust 89[97:104:112]cm, 35[38:41:44]ins
Length 53[56:56:60]cm, 21[22:22:23¾]ins
Sleeve seam 43[43:46:46]cm, 17[17:18¼:18¼]ins

Materials
8[9:10:11] × 50g balls of Sunbeam St-Ives 4 ply
One pair each 2¾mm (US2) and 3¼mm (US3) knitting needles

Tension/Gauge
27 sts and 29 rows to 10cm, 4ins over patt using 3¼mm (US3) needles

BACK
Using 2¾mm (US2) needles, cast on 122[130:142:150] sts.
Cont in K2, P2 rib as foll:
1st row: (RS) K2, ☆P2, K2, rep from ☆ to end.
2nd row: P2, ☆K2, P2, rep from ☆ to end.
Rep these 2 rows for 8cm, 3ins ending with a WS row, dec [inc:dec:inc] 1 st in centre of last row. 121[131:141:151] sts.
Change to 3¼mm (US3) needles and commence patt.
1st row: (RS) K1, ☆yfwd, K3, sl 1, K2 tog, psso, K3, yfwd, K1, rep from ☆ to end.
2nd row: P.
3rd–7th rows: Rep 1st and 2nd rows twice more, then work 1st row again.
8th row: K.
9th row: K1, ☆K1 winding yarn 3 times round needle, rep from ☆ to last st, K1.
10th row: K to end dropping extra loops of previous row.
These 10 rows form the patt. Cont in patt until work measures approximately 49[53:53:56]cm, 19¼[21:21:22]ins from beg, ending with a 10th patt row.
Shape neck
Next row: Patt 41[46:51:56] and turn, leaving rem sts on a spare needle.
Complete this side of neck first. Note, extra loops on 10th row count as 1 st when shaping.
Dec 1 st at neck edge on next 8 rows. 33[38:43:48] sts.
Cont without further shaping until work measures 53[56:56:60]cm, 21[22:22:23¾]ins from beg, ending with a WS row.
Shape shoulder
Cast off 17[19:22:24] sts at beg of next row.
Work 1 row.
Cast off rem 16[19:21:24] sts.
With RS of work facing, return to sts on spare needle. Sl centre 39 sts onto a holder, rejoin yarn at neck edge, patt to end.
Complete to match first side of neck reversing all shapings.

FRONT
Work as given for back.

MAY

CRAB APPLE

SLEEVES

Using 2¾mm (US2) needles, cast on 58[58:62:62] sts.

Cont in K2, P2 rib as given on back for 8cm, 3ins, ending with a RS row.

Inc row: Rib 3[3:2:2], ☆inc in next st, rep from ☆ to last 3[3:2:2] sts, inc in next st, rib to end. 111[111:121:121] sts.

Change to 3¼mm (US3) needles. Cont in patt as given on back until work measures approximately 43[43:46:46]cm, 17[17:18¼:18¼]ins from beg, ending with a 10th patt row.

Cast off loosely.

TO MAKE UP/TO FINISH

Join right shoulder seam.

NECKBAND

With RS of work facing, using 2¾mm (US2) needles, K up 12 sts down left side of neck, K across 39 sts at centre front, K up 12 sts up right side of neck, 12 sts down right back neck, K across 39 sts at centre back neck then K up 12 sts up left back neck. 126 sts.

Beg with a 2nd row, cont in K2, P2 rib as given for back for 5cm, 2ins.

Cast off loosely in rib.

Join left shoulder and neckband seam. Fold neckband in half onto WS and catch down. Placing centre of cast off edge of sleeve to shoulder seam, set in sleeves. Join side and sleeve seams.

CRAB APPLE

Lady's Twinset

Sizes

To fit bust 81[86:91:97]cm,
32[34:36:38]ins
Actual sweater bust 89[101:114:126]cm,
35[39¾:45:49¾]ins
Actual cardigan bust 104[129]cm,
41[50¾]ins
Length 64cm, 25¼ins
Sleeve seam 48cm, 19ins

Materials

Sweater
8[8:9:9] × 50g balls of Sirdar Romance

Cardigan
8[9] × 50g balls of Sirdar Romance
5 'Pikaby' buttons

Both versions
One pair each 4mm (US6) and 5mm (US8) knitting needles

Tension/Gauge

16 sts and 23 rows to 10cm, 4ins over patt using 5mm (US8) needles

SWEATER

BACK

☆☆Using 4mm (US6) needles, cast on 70[80:90:100] sts.

Cont in K1, P1 rib for 6cm, 2½ins ending with a RS row, inc 1 st at end of last row. 71[81:91:101] sts.

Change to 5mm (US8) needles. Cont in patt as foll:

1st row: (WS) P.

2nd row: K3, ☆K2 tog, yfwd, K1, yfwd, sl 1, K1, psso, K5, rep from ☆ to last 8 sts, K2 tog, yfwd, K1, yfwd, sl 1, K1, psso, K3.

3rd and every foll alt row: P.

4th row: K2, ☆K2 tog, (K1, yfwd) twice, K1, sl 1, K1, psso, K3, rep from ☆ to last 9 sts, K2 tog, (K1, yfwd) twice, K1, sl 1, K1, psso, K2.

6th row: K1 ☆K2 tog, K2, yfwd, K1, yfwd, K2, sl 1, K1, psso, K1, rep from ☆ to end.

8th row: K2 tog, ☆K3, yfwd, K1, yfwd, K3, sl 1, K2 tog, psso, rep from ☆ to last 9 sts, K3, yfwd, K1, yfwd, K3, sl 1, K1, psso.

10th row: K1, ☆yfwd, sl 1, K1, psso, K5, K2 tog, yfwd, K1, rep from ☆ to end.

12th row: K1, ☆yfwd, K1, sl 1, K1, psso, K3, K2 tog, K1, yfwd, K1, rep from ☆ to end.

14th row: K1, ☆yfwd, K2, sl 1, K1, psso, K1, K2 tog, K2, yfwd, K1, rep from ☆ to end.

16th row: K1, ☆yfwd, K3, sl 1, K2 tog, psso, K3, yfwd, K1, rep from ☆ to end.

These 16 rows form the patt.☆☆ Rep these 16 rows 7 times more, then work 1st–5th rows again.

Shape shoulders

2nd, 3rd and 4th sizes only

Cast off [5:10:15] sts at beg of next 2 rows.

All sizes

Cast off 5 sts at beg of next 2 rows.

Shape back neck

Next row: Cast off 7, patt 9 including st used to cast off and turn, leaving rem sts on a spare needle.

Complete right side of neck first.

Dec 1 st at neck edge on next row. Cast off rem 8 sts.

With RS of work facing, return to sts on spare needle. Rejoin yarn at neck edge cast off centre 29 sts, patt to end.

Next row: Cast off 7 sts, patt to last 2 sts, work 2 tog.

Work 1 row. Cast off rem 8 sts.

FRONT

Work as given for back from ☆☆ to ☆☆. Rep these 16 rows 6 times more, then work 1st–9th rows again.

Shape neck

Next row: Patt 29[34:39:44] sts and turn, leaving rem sts on a spare needle.

Complete left side of neck first.

Cast off 2 sts at beg of next and 3 foll alt rows, then dec 1 st at neck edge on foll alt row. 20[25:30:35] sts.

Work 2 rows.

Shape shoulder

1st size only

Cast off 5 sts at beg of next row and 7 sts at beg of foll alt row. Work 1 row.

Cast off rem 8 sts.

2nd, 3rd and 4th sizes only

Cast off [5:10:15] sts at beg of next row and 5 sts at beg of foll alt row.
Cast off 7 sts at beg of next alt row.
Work 1 row. Cast off rem 8 sts.
With RS of work facing, return to sts on spare needle. Rejoin yarn at neck edge, cast off centre 13 sts, patt to end.
Work 1 row, then complete as given for first side of neck.

SLEEVES
Using 4mm (US6) needles, cast on 40 sts. Cont in K1, P1 rib for 6cm, 2½ins ending with a RS row, inc 1 st at end of last row. 41 sts.
Change to 5mm (US8) needles. Cont in patt as given for back, inc and work into patt 1 st at each end of 3rd and every foll 5th row until there are 71 sts.
Cont without further shaping until the 16 patt rows have been worked 6 times. Cast off loosely.

TO MAKE UP/TO FINISH
Join right shoulder seam.

NECKBAND
With RS of work facing, using 4mm (US6) needles, K up 94 sts evenly around neck edge.
Beg with a P row, work 3 rows st st.
Form picot edge
Next row: K1, ☆yfwd, K2 tog, rep from ☆ to last st, K1.
Beg with a P row, work 3 rows st st.
Cast off very loosely.

Join left shoulder and neckband seam. Fold neckband onto WS at picot edge and catch down. Placing centre of cast off edge of sleeve to shoulder seam, set in sleeves. Join side and sleeve seams.

CARDIGAN

BACK
Work as given for 2nd[4th] sizes of sweater back.

LEFT FRONT
Using 4mm (US6) needles, cast on 40[50] sts.
Cont in K1, P1 rib for 6cm, 2½ins ending with a RS row, inc 1 st at end of last row. 41[51] sts.
Change to 5mm (US8) needles. Cont in patt as given for back of sweater. Rep 16 patt rows 3 times.

Shape neck
Keeping patt correct, dec 1 st at neck edge on next and every foll 4th row until 25[35] sts rem.
Cont without further shaping until work measures same as back to shoulder shaping, ending at armhole edge.
Shape shoulder
Cast off 5[15] sts at beg of next row, 5 sts at beg of foll alt row, 7 sts at beg of next alt row. Work 1 row. Cast off rem 8 sts.

RIGHT FRONT
Work as given for left front, reversing shapings.

SLEEVES
Work as given for sleeves of sweater.

FRONTBAND
Using 4mm (US6) needles, cast on 6 sts.
Cont in K1, P1 rib. Work 2 rows.
1st buttonhole row: Rib 2, cast off 2, rib to end.
2nd buttonhole row: Rib to end, casting on 2 sts over those cast off in previous row.
Rib 12 rows.
Rep last 14 rows 4 times more.
Now cont in rib until band, when slightly stretched, fits up right front, across back neck and down left front.
Cast off in rib.

TO MAKE UP/TO FINISH
Join shoulder seams.
Placing centre of cast off edge of sleeve to shoulder seam, set in sleeves. Join side and sleeve seams. Sew on front band. Sew on buttons.

HONEYSUCKLE
Children's Sweater and Cardigan

Sizes
To fit chest 56 – 61[66 – 71]cm, 22 – 24[26 – 28]ins
Cardigan actual chest 65[74]cm, 25½[29¼]ins
Sweater actual chest 61[73]cm, 24[28¾]ins
Length 30[35]cm, 11¾[13¾]ins
Sleeve seam 26[30]cm, 10¼[11¾]ins

Materials
Cardigan *OR* sweater
4[5] × 40g balls of Hayfield Pretty Whites
One pair each 3¼mm (US3) and 4mm (US6) knitting needles
6 'Pikaby' buttons for cardigan
Narrow ribbon for trimming

Tension/Gauge
20 sts and 28 rows to 10cm, 4ins over patt using 4mm (US6) needles

CARDIGAN

BACK
Using 3¼mm (US3) needles, cast on 61[73] sts.
Cont in K1, P1 rib as foll:
1st row: (RS) K1, ☆P1, K1, rep from ☆ to end.
2nd row: P1, ☆K1, P1, rep from ☆ to end.
Rep these 2 rows for 5cm, 2ins ending with a RS row.
Change to 4mm (US6) needles and commence patt.
1st row: (WS) P.
2nd row: K6, ☆yfwd, sl 1, K1, psso, K10,

HONEYSUCKLE

rep from ☆ to last 7 sts, yfwd, sl 1, K1, psso, K5.

3rd and every foll alt row: P.

4th row: K4, ☆K2 tog, yfwd, K1, yfwd, sl 1, K1, psso, K7, rep from ☆ to last 9 sts, K2 tog, yfwd, K1, yfwd, sl 1, K1, psso, K4.

6th row: K3, ☆K2 tog, yfwd, K3, yfwd, sl 1, K1, psso, K5, rep from ☆ to last 10 sts, K2 tog, yfwd, K3, yfwd, sl 1, K1, psso, K3.

8th row: K2, ☆K2 tog, yfwd, K5, yfwd, sl 1, K1, psso, K3, rep from ☆ to last 11 sts, K2 tog, yfwd, K5, yfwd, sl 1, K1, psso, K2.

10th row: K1, ☆K2 tog, yfwd, K7, yfwd, sl 1, K1, psso, K1, rep from ☆ to end.

12th row: K2 tog, ☆yfwd, K9, yfwd, sl 1, K2 tog, psso, rep from ☆ to last 11 sts, yfwd, K9, yfwd, sl 1, K1, psso.

These 12 rows form the patt. Cont in patt until work measures approximately 30[35]cm, 11¾[13¾]ins from beg, ending with a 12th patt row.

Next row: P.

Shape shoulders

Cont in st st, cast off 20[23] sts at beg of next 2 rows. Leave rem 21[27] sts on a spare needle.

LEFT FRONT

Using 3¼mm (US3) needles, cast on 41[45] sts.

Cont in rib as given for back for 6cm, 2½ins ending with a WS row.

Next row: Rib to last 9[10] sts and turn, leaving rem sts on a safety pin. 32[35] sts.

Change to 4mm (US6) needles and commence patt.

1st row: (WS) P.

2nd row: K6, ☆yfwd, sl 1, K1, psso, K10, rep from ☆ to last 2[5] sts, yfwd, sl 1, K1, psso, K0[3].

3rd and every foll alt row: P.

4th row: K4, ☆K2 tog, yfwd, K1, yfwd, sl 1, K1, psso, K7, rep from ☆ to last 4[7] sts, K2 tog, yfwd, K2[5].

6th row: K3, ☆K2 tog, yfwd, K3, yfwd, sl 1, K1, psso, K5, rep from ☆ to last 5[8] sts, K2 tog, yfwd, K3[6].

8th row: K2, ☆K2 tog, yfwd, K5, yfwd, sl 1, K1, psso, K3, rep from ☆ to last 6[9] sts, K2 tog, yfwd, K4[7].

10th row: K1, ☆K2 tog, yfwd, K7, yfwd, sl 1, K1, psso, K1, rep from ☆ to last 7[10] sts, K2 tog, yfwd, K5[8].

12th row: K2 tog, yfwd, K9, ☆yfwd, sl 1, K2 tog, psso, yfwd, K9, rep from ☆ to last

10 sts, yfwd, sl 1, K2 tog, psso, yfwd, K6[9].

These 12 rows form the patt. Cont in patt until work measures 11[15] rows less than back to shoulder shaping, ending with a RS row.

Shape neck

Cast off 4 sts at beg of next row. Dec 1 st at neck edge on every row until 20[23] sts rem.

Cont without further shaping until work measures same as back to shoulder shaping, ending with a 12th patt row.

Next row: P.

Shape shoulder

Cast off rem sts.

RIGHT FRONT

Using 3¼mm (US3) needles, cast on 41[45] sts.

Cont in rib as given for back. Work 4 rows.

1st buttonhole row: Rib 4, yon, K2 tog, rib to end.

Cont in rib until work measures 5cm, 2ins ending with a WS row.

Next row: Rib 9[10] and sl sts onto a safety pin, rib to end. 32[35] sts.

Change to 4mm (US6) needles and commence patt.

1st row: (WS) P.

2nd row: K1[4], ☆yfwd, sl 1, K1, psso, K10, rep from ☆ to last 7 sts, yfwd, sl 1, K1, psso, K5.

3rd and every foll alt row: P.

4th row: K2[5], yfwd, sl 1, K1, psso, ☆K7, K2 tog, yfwd, K1, yfwd, sl 1, K1, psso, rep from ☆ to last 4 sts, K4.

6th row: K3[6], yfwd, sl 1, K1, psso, ☆K5, K2 tog, yfwd, K3, yfwd, sl 1, K1, psso, rep from ☆ to last 3 sts, K3.

8th row: K4[7], yfwd, sl 1, K1, psso, ☆K3, K2 tog, yfwd, K5, yfwd, sl 1, K1, psso, rep from ☆ to last 2 sts, K2.

10th row: K5[8], yfwd, sl 1, K1, psso, ☆K1, K2 tog, yfwd, K7, yfwd, sl 1, K1, psso, rep from ☆ to last st, K1.

12th row: K6[9], ☆yfwd, sl 1, K2 tog, psso, yfwd, K9, rep from ☆ to last 2 sts, yfwd, K2 tog.

These 12 rows form the patt. Cont in patt until work measures 12[16] rows less than back to shoulder shaping, ending with a WS row.

Shape neck

Complete to match left front, reversing shapings.

SLEEVES

Using 3¼mm (US3) needles, cast on 27[35] sts.

Cont in K1, P1 rib as given for back for 5cm, 2ins ending with a WS row.

Inc row: Rib 4, inc in next st, ☆rib 1, inc in next st, rep from ☆ to last 4 sts, rib 4. 37[49] sts.

Change to 4mm (US6) needles and cont in patt as given for back. Inc 1 st at each end of 3rd and every foll 4th row until there are 61[73] sts. Cont without further shaping until work measures approximately 26[30]cm, 10¼[11¾]ins from beg, ending with a 12th patt row.

Next row: P.

Cast off loosely.

BUTTONBAND

With WS of work facing, return to sts on left front safety pin.

Using 3¼mm (US3) needles, rejoin yarn and cont in rib until band, when slightly stretched, fits up left front to neck, ending at inner edge. Cut yarn and leave sts on a safety pin.

Mark the positions of 4 buttons, the first at top of ribbing and the last 5cm, 2ins from neck edge, with the others evenly spaced between.

TO MAKE UP/TO FINISH

Join shoulder seams. Sew on button band.

BUTTONHOLE BAND

Work as given for buttonband, but end at outer edge; do not cut yarn and make buttonholes opposite markers as foll:

1st buttonhole row: (RS) Rib 4, yon, K2 tog, rib to end.

NECKBAND

With RS of work facing, using 3¼mm (US3) needles, work buttonhole row across sts of buttonhole band, K up 19[23] sts up right side of neck, K21[27] sts at back neck, K up 19[23] sts down left side of neck, then rib across sts of button-band. 77[93] sts.

Beg with a 2nd row, work 7 rows K1, P1 rib as given for back.

Cast off in rib.

Sew on buttonhole band. Placing centre of cast off edge of sleeve to shoulder seam, set in sleeves. Join side and sleeve seams. Sew on buttons. Thread ribbon

Dog Roses *Lady's Jacket*

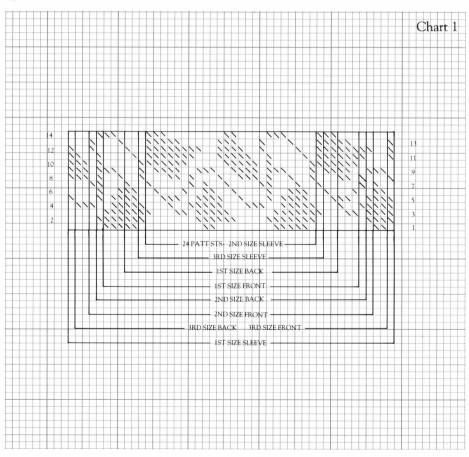

through alternate bands of pattern and tie in small bows as shown.

SWEATER

BACK

Work as given for back of cardigan.

FRONT

Work as given for back of cardigan until work measures 12[16] rows less than back to shoulder shaping, ending with a WS row.
Shape neck
Next row: Patt 26[31] and turn, leaving rem sts on a spare needle.
Complete left side of neck first.
Dec 1 st at neck edge on every row until 20[23] sts rem.
Cont without further shaping until work measures same as back to shoulder shaping, ending with a 12th patt row.
Next row: P.
Shape shoulder
Cast off rem sts.
With RS of work facing, return to sts on spare needle. Sl centre 9[11] sts onto a holder, rejoin yarn at neck edge, patt to end.
Complete to match first side of neck, reversing shapings.

SLEEVES

Work as given for sleeves of cardigan.

TO MAKE UP/TO FINISH

Join right shoulder seam.

NECKBAND

With RS of work facing, using 3¼mm (US3) needles, K up 18[22] sts down left side of neck, K across 9[11] sts at centre front, K up 19[23] sts up right side of neck, then K across 21[27] back neck sts. 67[83] sts.
Beg with a 2nd row, work 7 rows K1, P1 rib as given for back. Cast off in rib.

Join left shoulder and neckband seam. Placing centre of cast off edge of sleeve to shoulder seam, set in sleeves. Join side and sleeve seams. Join side and sleeve seams. Thread ribbon through alternate bands of pattern and tie in small bows as shown.

Sizes

To fit bust 81 – 86[91 – 97:102 – 107]cm,
32 – 34[36 – 38:40 – 42]ins
Actual bust 111[122:132]cm,
43¾[48:52]ins
Length 69[71:73]cm, 27¼[28:28¾]ins
Sleeve seam 46[46:48]cm,
18¼[18¼:19]ins

Materials

18[19:19] × 50g balls of Wendy Family Choice Chunky in main colour (A)
2 balls in contrast colour (B)

Key
A   □
B   \

1[2:2] balls each in 3 contrast colours (C, D and E)
1 ball each in 2 contrast colours (F and G)
One pair each 5½mm (US5) and 6½mm (US10½) knitting needles
4 'Pikaby' buttons

Tension/Gauge

14 sts and 20 rows to 10cm, 4ins over st st using 6½mm (US10½) needles

BACK

Using 5½mm (US5) needles and C, cast on 63[73:77] sts.
☆☆Cont in K1, P1 rib as foll:
1st row: (RS) K1, ☆P1, K1, rep from ☆ to end.
2nd row: P1, ☆K1, P1, rep from ☆ to end.
Change to D and rep these 2 rows, change to E and rep these 2 rows again then change to A and cont in rib until work measures 6cm, 2½ins from beg, ending with a RS row. ☆☆
Inc row: Rib 3[6:3], ☆inc in next st, rib 3[4:4], rep from ☆ to last 4[7:4] sts, inc in next st, rib to end. 78[86:92] sts.

Chart 1

24 PATT STS - 2ND SIZE SLEEVE
3RD SIZE SLEEVE
1ST SIZE BACK
1ST SIZE FRONT
2ND SIZE BACK
2ND SIZE FRONT
3RD SIZE BACK   3RD SIZE FRONT
1ST SIZE SLEEVE

DOG ROSES

Chart 2

Change to 6½mm (US10½) needles. ☆☆☆Beg with a K row cont in st st. Work 4 rows.

Now commence colour patt from chart 1.* Read odd numbered rows (K) from right to left and even numbered rows (P) from left to right. Strand yarn not in use loosely across back of work and twist yarn when changing colour to avoid a hole.

Work 14 rows from chart 1, then cont in A only. ☆☆☆ Work 12 rows.

Now commence colour patt from chart 2.† Use small separate balls of yarn for each area of colour.

Work 76 rows from chart 2, then cont in A only until work measures 69[71:73]cm, 27¼[28:28¾]ins from beg, ending with a P row.

Cast off.

LEFT FRONT

Using 5½mm (US5) needles and C, cast on 29[33:37] sts.

Work as given for back from ☆☆ to ☆☆.

Inc row: Rib 2[4:3], ☆inc in next st, rib 3[3:4], rep from ☆ to last 3[5:4] sts, inc in next st, rib to end. 36[40:44] sts.

Change to 6½mm (US10½) needles.

Work as given for back from ☆☆☆ to ☆☆☆.

Cont until work measures 28cm, 11ins from beg, ending with a P row.

Shape front edge

Dec 1 st at end of next and every foll 9th[9th:7th] row until 27[30:32] sts rem.

Cont without further shaping until work measures same as back to shoulder, ending with a P row.

Shape shoulder

Cast off rem sts.

RIGHT FRONT

Work as given for left front, reversing shapings.

SLEEVES

Using 5½mm (US5) needles and C, cast on 31[33:35] sts.

Work as given for back from ☆☆ to ☆☆.

Inc row: Rib 1[2:3], ☆inc in next st, rib 1, rep from ☆ to last 2[3:4] sts, inc in next st, rib to end. 46[48:50] sts.

Change to 6½mm (US10½) needles.

Work as given for back from ☆☆☆ to ☆☆☆, *at the same time*, inc 1 st at each end of 3rd and every foll 4th row until there are 84[86:90] sts.

Cont without further shaping until work measures 46[46:48]cm, 18¼[18¼:19]ins from beg, ending with a P row. Cast off loosely.

LEFT FRONT BORDER

Using 5½mm (US5) needles and C, cast on 124[126:128] sts.

Cont in rib as foll:

1st row: (RS) K2, ☆P1, K1, rep from ☆ to end.

2nd row: ☆P1, K1, rep from ☆ to end.

Change to D and rep these 2 rows, change to E and rep these 2 rows again.

Next row: Using E, cast off 42, cut off E, join in A and rib to end. 82[84:86] sts

Cast off 2 sts at beg of foll 6[3:2] alt rows then cast off 3 sts at beg of every foll alt row until 13[15:16] sts rem.

Work 1 row. Cast off loosely in rib.

RIGHT FRONT BORDER

Using 5½mm (US5) needles and C, cast on 124[126:128] sts.

Cont in rib as foll:

1st row: (RS) K1, ☆P1, K1, rep from ☆ to last st, K1.

2nd row: ☆K1, P1, rep from ☆ to end.

Change to D and rep the 1st row again.

1st buttonhole row: Rib 2, cast off 2, (rib 10, including st used to cast off, cast off 2) 3 times, rib to end.

Change to E.

2nd buttonhole row: Rib to end, casting on 2 sts over those cast off in previous row.

Rib 1 row.

Change to A.

Next row: Rib 82[84:86] sts, rejoin E, rib to end.

Next row: Using E, cast off 42 sts, using A, rib to end.

Complete to match left front border, reversing shaping.

POCKET LININGS
(make 2)

Using 6½mm (US10½) needles and A, cast on 30 sts.

Work in st st for 12cm, 4¾ins, ending with a P row.

Cast off.

TO MAKE UP/TO FINISH

Join shoulder seams. Sew on front bands, placing cast off edges to front and joining centre back seam.

Placing centre of cast off edge of sleeve to shoulder seam, set in sleeves.

Fold pocket linings in half, catching together cast on and cast off edges. Sew row ends to side seams of back and fronts above border pattern. Join side seams above and below pocket. Join sleeve seams. Sew on buttons.

TRAILING ROSE AND FOXGLOVE
Lady's Sweater

Sizes

To fit bust 76 – 81[86 – 91:97 – 102]cm, 30 – 32[34 – 36:38 – 40]ins

Actual bust 87[102:116.5]cm, 34¼[40:45¾]ins

Length 57[58:59]cm, 22½[22¾:23¼]ins

Sleeve seam 41cm, 16ins

Materials

6[7:8] × 50g balls of Rowan Designer Collection DK in main colour (A)

3[3:3] balls in contrast colour (B)

1 ball in each of 4 contrast colours (C, D, E and F)

One pair each 3¼mm (US3) and 4mm (US6) knitting needles

Tension/Gauge

22 sts and 25 rows to 10cm, 4ins over st st using 4mm (US6) needles

BACK

☆☆Using 3¼mm (US3) needles and A, cast on 96[112:128] sts.

* on page 56   † on facing page

TRAILING ROSE AND FOXGLOVE

Cont in K2, P2 rib for 8cm, 3ins ending with a WS row, inc 1 st at end of last row. 97[113:129] sts.

Change to 4mm (US6) needles. Beg with a K row, cont in st st working colour patt from chart. Read odd numbered rows (K) from right to left and even numbered rows (P) from left to right. Use small separate balls of yarn for each area of colour, twisting yarns on WS of work when changing colour to avoid a hole.☆☆

Cont until work measures 57[58:59]cm, 22½[22¾:23¼]ins from beg, ending with a WS row.

Shape shoulders

Cast off 31[38:45] sts at beg of next 2 rows. Leave rem 35[37:39] sts on a spare needle.

FRONT

Work as given for back from ☆☆ to ☆☆.

Cont until work measures 49[50:51]cm, 19¼[19¾:20]ins from beg, ending with WS row.

Shape neck

Next row: Patt 41[48:55] and turn, leaving rem sts on a spare needle.

Complete left side of neck first.

Dec 1 st at neck edge on every row until 31[38:45] sts rem.

Cont without further shaping until work measures same as back to shoulder shaping, ending at armhole edge.

Shape shoulder

Cast off rem sts.

With RS of work facing, return to sts on spare needle. Sl centre 15[17:19] sts onto a holder, rejoin yarn at neck edge, patt to end.

Complete as given for first side of neck.

SLEEVES

Using 3¼mm (US3) needles and A, cast on 56 sts.

Work in K2, P2 rib for 8cm, 3ins ending with a RS row.

Inc row: Rib 4, ☆inc in next st, rib 5, rep from ☆ to last 4 sts, inc in next st, rib 3. 65 sts.

Change to 4mm (US6) needles and beg with a K row cont in st st working colour patt from chart. *At the same time*, inc 1 st at each end of every 3rd then 2nd row alternately until there are 121 sts.

Cont without further shaping until work measures 41cm, 16ins from beg, ending with a WS row. Cast off loosely.

TO MAKE UP/TO FINISH

Join left shoulder seam.

NECKBAND

With RS of work facing, using 3¼mm (US3) needles and A, K6[4:5], inc in next st, (K2[3:3], inc in next st) 7 times, K7[4:5] across 35[37:39] sts from back neck, K up 25 sts down left side of neck, K across 15[17:19] sts at centre front, then K up 25 sts up right side of neck. 108[112:116] sts.

Work 7 rows in K2, P2 rib. Cast off in rib.

Join right shoulder and neckband seam. Placing centre of cast off edge of sleeve to shoulder seam, set in sleeves. Join side and sleeve seams.

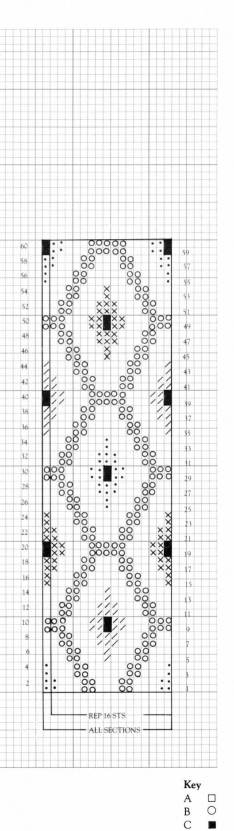

REP 16 STS

ALL SECTIONS

Key

A	□
B	○
C	■
D	/
E	×
F	•

WILLOW HERB *Child's Sweater*

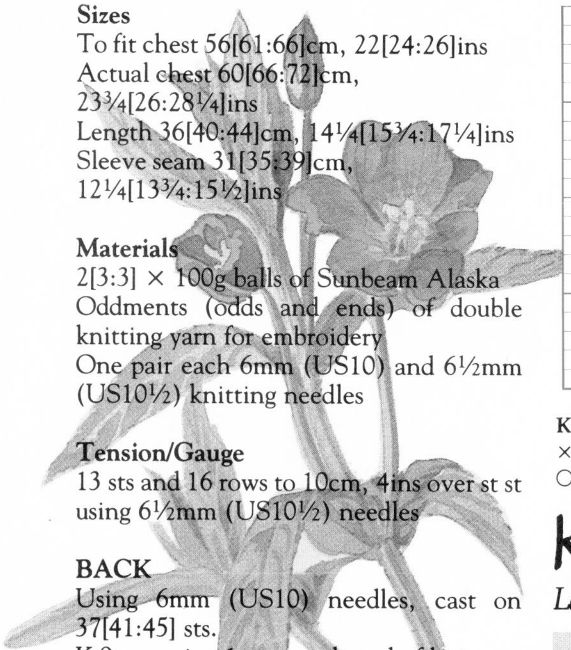

Sizes
To fit chest 56[61:66]cm, 22[24:26]ins
Actual chest 60[66:72]cm,
23¾[26:28¼]ins
Length 36[40:44]cm, 14¼[15¾:17¼]ins
Sleeve seam 31[35:39]cm,
12¼[13¾:15½]ins

Materials
2[3:3] × 100g balls of Sunbeam Alaska
Oddments (odds and ends) of double
knitting yarn for embroidery
One pair each 6mm (US10) and 6½mm
(US10½) knitting needles

Tension/Gauge
13 sts and 16 rows to 10cm, 4ins over st st
using 6½mm (US10½) needles

BACK
Using 6mm (US10) needles, cast on
37[41:45] sts.
K 9 rows, inc 1 st at each end of last row.
39[43:47] sts.
Change to 6½mm (US10½) needles.
Beg with a K row cont in st st until work
measures 34[38:42]cm, 13½[15:16½]ins
from beg, ending with a P row.
K 4 rows.
Cast off loosely.

FRONT
Work as given for back.

SLEEVES
Using 6mm (US10) needles, cast on
20[22:24] sts.
K 11 rows.
Change to 6½mm (US10½) needles.
Beg with a K row cont in st st, inc 1 st at
each end of 3rd and every foll 3rd
[4th:4th] row until there are 42[44:46]
sts.
Cont without further shaping until work
measures 31[35:39]cm, 12¼[13¾:15½]ins
from beg, ending with a P row. Cast off
loosely.

TO MAKE UP/TO FINISH
Using double knitting yarns, working in
cross stitch from chart, embroider flowers
on back, front and sleeves randomly as
shown.
Join shoulder seams for 7[8:8.5]cm,
2¾[3:3¼]ins leaving centre open for
neck. Placing centre of cast off edge of
sleeve to shoulder seams, set in sleeves.
Join side seams above g st hem and sleeve
seams.

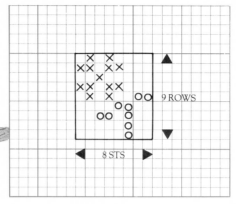

Key
×   red
○   green

KINGFISHER
Lady's Jacket

Sizes
To fit bust 81[86:91:97]cm,
32[34:36:38]ins
Actual width cuff to cuff
146.5[148.5:150.5:152.5]cm,
57½[58½:59¼:60]ins
Length 68[68:70:70]cm,
26¾[26¾:27½:27½]ins

Materials
8[8:9:9] × 50g balls of Pingouin
Mohair 50
One pair each 3¾mm (US5), 4½mm
(US7) knitting needles
3¾mm (US5) circular needle
Medium size crochet hook

Tension/Gauge
18 sts and 26 rows to 10cm, 4in over rev
st st using 4½mm (US7) needles

BACK
☆☆Using 4½mm (US7) needles, cast on
35[35:39:39] sts for cuff edge.
Beg with a P row, cont in rev st st until
work measures 14cm, 5½ins ending with
a K row.
Shape sleeve
Inc 1 st at end of next and every foll alt
row until there are 61[61:65:65] sts, then
at same edge on every row until there are
77[77:81:81] sts, ending with a P row.
Shape side edge
Cast on 24 sts at beg of next row.
101[101:105:105] sts.☆☆
Cont in rev st st without further shaping
until work measures 18.5[19.5:20.5:
21.5]cm, 7¼[7¾:8¼:8½]ins from side
edge, ending with a K row.

WILLOW HERB

Mark end of last row to denote shoulder. Now cont in rev st st for 16cm, 6¼ins from shoulder, ending with a K row.
Mark end of last row with a coloured thread to denote shoulder.
Cont in rev st st until work measures 53[55:57:59]cm, 21[21¾:22½:23¼]ins from side edge, ending with a P row.
Shape side edge
Cast off 24 sts at beg of next row. 77[77:81:81] sts.
Shape sleeve
Dec 1 st at end of next and at same edge on every row until 61[61:65:65] sts rem, then at end of every foll alt row until 35[35:39:39] sts rem.
Cont without further shaping until work measures same as first sleeve from side edge to cuff, ending with a K row.
Cast off.

LEFT FRONT

Work as given for back from ☆☆ to ☆☆.
Cont in rev st st without further shaping until work measures 18.5[19.5:20.5: 21.5]cm, 7¼[7¾:8¼:8½]ins from side edge, ending with a P row.
Shape front edge
Next row: K to last 5 sts, turn.
Next and foll alt rows: Sl 1, P to end.
Next row: K to last 10 sts, turn.
Next row: K to last 15 sts, turn.
Cont in this way working 5 sts less on every alt row until 50[50:55:55] sts are unworked, ending with a P row.
Next row: K to end across all sts.
Cut yarn and leave sts on a spare needle.

RIGHT FRONT

Work as given for left front, reversing shapings by reading K for P and P for K.

TO MAKE UP/TO FINISH

Join upper sleeve and shoulder seams to markers.

CUFFS

With RS of work facing, using 3¾mm (US5) needles, K up 35 sts from sleeve edge.
Cont in K1, P1 rib as foll:
1st row: (WS) P1, ☆K1, P1, rep from ☆ to end.
2nd row: K1, ☆P1, K1, rep from ☆ to end.
Rep these 2 rows for 7cm, 2¾ins ending with a WS row. Cast off loosely in rib.

Join underarm and side seams.

LOWER RIBBING

With RS of work facing, using 3¾mm (US5) circular needle, K up 36[38:42:44] sts from lower edge of left front, 73[79:85:91] sts from back and 36[38:42:44] sts from right front. 145[155:169:179] sts.
Cont to work in rows.
Inc row: K9[4:11:5], inc in next st, ☆ K5[6:6:7], inc in next st, rep from ☆ to last 9[3:10:5] sts, K to end. 167[177:191: 201] sts.
Beg with a RS row, cont in rib as given for cuffs for 12cm, 4¾ins ending with a WS row. Cast off loosely in rib.

FRONT EDGE

With RS of work facing, using 3¾mm (US5) circular needle, K up 29 sts from row ends of lower ribbing, K across 101[101:105:105] sts of right front, K up 30[30:32:32] sts across back neck, K across 101[101:105:105] sts of left front, then K up 29 sts from row ends of lower ribbing. 290[290:300:300] sts.
Work in rows.
Beg with a P row, work 10 rows st st.
Cast off.

Allow front edge to roll onto RS and slip stitch down.

CROCHET BUTTON

Wrap yarn twice round index finger to form a ring, then using crochet hook work 6 dc (sc) into ring, sl st into first dc (sc).
Pull up end to close ring.
Next round: Work 2 dc (sc) into each dc (sc), sl st into first dc (sc).
Next round: Work 1 dc (sc) into each dc (sc), sl st into first dc (sc) and fasten off leaving a long end.
Close top of button, sew in position to top of ribbing.

BUTTON LOOP

Using yarn double and crochet hook, make 8 ch. Fasten off.
Sew ends of loop on right front to correspond with button.

HAWTHORN BLOSSOM *Lady's Sleeveless Top and Matching Cardigan*

Sizes

To fit bust 81[86:91]cm, 32[34:36]ins
Sweater actual bust 93[97.5:102]cm, 36¾[38¼:40]ins
Length 45[46:47]cm, 17¾[18¼:18½]ins
Cardigan actual bust 96[102:108.5]cm, 37¾[40:42¾]ins
Length 61[62:63]cm, 24[24½:24¾]ins
Sleeve seam 46cm, 18¼ins

Materials

17[18:20] × 50g balls of Twilleys Perlespun
One pair each 2¾mm (US2) and 3¼mm (US3) knitting needles
7 'Pikaby' buttons for cardigan

Tension/Gauge

26 sts and 32 rows to 10cm, 4ins over st st using 3¼mm (US3) needles

PATT PANEL

(worked over 27 sts)
1st row: (WS) K2, P23, K2.
2nd row: P2, sl 1, K1, psso, K6, (yfwd, K1) twice, sl 1, K2 tog, psso, (K1, yfwd) twice, K6, K2 tog, P2.
3rd and every foll alt row: As 1st row.
4th row: P2, sl 1, K1, psso, K5, yfwd, K1, yfwd, K2, sl 1, K2 tog, psso, K2, yfwd, K1, yfwd, K5, K2 tog, P2.
6th row: P2, sl 1, K1, psso, K4, yfwd, K1, yfwd, (K1, P1, K1, P1, K1) all into next st, then pass 4th, 3rd, 2nd and 1st sts in turn over 5th st – called MB, K2, sl 1, K2 tog, psso, K2, MB, yfwd, K1, yfwd, K4, K2 tog, P2.

KINGFISHER

8th row: P2, sl 1, K1, psso, K3, yfwd, K1, yfwd, MB, K3, sl 1, K2 tog, psso, K3, MB, yfwd, K1, yfwd, K3, K2 tog, P2.

10th row: P2, sl 1, K1, psso, K2, yfwd, K1, yfwd, MB, K4, sl 1, K2 tog, psso, K4, MB, yfwd, K1, yfwd, K2, K2 tog, P2.

These 10 rows form the patt panel.

SWEATER

FRONT

☆☆Using 2¾mm (US2) needles, cast on 97[103:109] sts.

Cont in K1, P1 rib as foll:

1st row: (RS) K1, ☆P1, K1, rep from ☆ to end.

2nd row: P1, ☆K1, P1, rep from ☆ to end.

Rep these 2 rows for 6cm, 2½ins ending with a WS row.

Inc row: Rib 2[5:8], ☆inc in next st, rib 3, rep from ☆ to last 3[6:9] sts, inc in next st, rib to end. 121[127:133] sts.☆☆

Change to 3¼mm (US3) needles and commence patt.

1st row: (WS) P47[50:53], work 1st row of patt panel, P47[50:53].

2nd row: K47[50:53], work 2nd row of patt panel, K47[50:53].

These 2 rows establish the position of the patt panel with edge sts in st st.

Keeping patt panel correct, cont as set until work measures 28cm, 11ins from beg, ending with a WS row.

Shape armholes

Cast off 13 sts at beg of next 2 rows. 95[101:107] sts.

Cont without further shaping until work measures 13[14:15]cm, 5¼[5½:6]ins from beg of armhole shaping, ending with a WS row.

Shape neck

Next row: K35[37:39] turn, leaving rem sts on a spare needle.

Complete left side of neck first.

Dec 1 st at neck edge on next and every foll alt row until 28[30:32] sts rem, ending with a WS row.

Shape shoulder

Cast off rem sts.

With RS of work facing, return to sts on spare needle. Sl centre 25[27:29] sts onto a holder, rejoin yarn at neck edge, K to end.

Complete as given for first side of neck reversing shapings.

BACK

Work as given for front from ☆☆ to ☆☆.

Change to 3¼mm (US3) needles. Beg with a P row cont in st st until work measures same as front to armhole shaping, ending with a P row.

Shape armholes

Cast off 13 sts at beg of next 2 rows. 95[101:107] sts.

Cont without further shaping until work measures same as front to shoulder shaping, ending with a P row.

Shape shoulders

Cast off 28[30:32] sts at beg of next 2 rows. Leave rem 39[41:43] sts on a spare needle.

TO MAKE UP/TO FINISH

Join right shoulder seam.

NECKBAND

With RS of work facing, using 2¾mm (US2) needles, K up 18 sts down left side of neck, K across 25[27:29] sts at centre front, K up 17 sts up right side of neck, then K across 39[41:43] sts on back neck. 99[103:107] sts.

Beg with a WS row work in K1, P1 rib as given for front for 3cm, 1¼ins, ending with a WS row. Cast off in rib.

Join left shoulder and neckband seam.

ARMBANDS

With RS of work facing, using 2¾mm (US2) needles, K up 107[115:123] sts evenly around armhole, beg and end at inner edge of cast off sts at underarm.

Beg with a WS row, work in K1, P1 rib as given for front for 5cm, 2ins ending with a WS row. Cast off in rib.

Sew ends of armbands to cast off sts at underarms. Join side seams.

CARDIGAN

LEFT FRONT

Using 2¾mm (US2) needles, cast on 49[53:57] sts.

Work in K1, P1 rib as given for sweater front for 6cm, 2½ins, ending with a WS row.

Inc row: Rib 2[4:1], ☆inc in next st, rib 3[3:4], rep from ☆ to last 3[5:1] sts, inc in next st, rib 2[4:0]. 61[65:69] sts.

Change to 3¼mm (US3) needles and cont in patt.

1st row: (WS) P17[19:21], work 1st row of patt panel, P17[19:21].

2nd row: K17[19:21], work 2nd row of patt panel, K17[19:21].

These 2 rows establish the position of the patt panel with edge sts in st st.

Keeping patt correct, cont as set until work measures 38cm, 15ins from beg, ending at side edge.

Shape armhole

Cast off 13 sts at beg of next row. 48[52:56] sts.

Work 1 row.

Shape front edge

Dec 1 st at neck edge on next and every foll 4th row until 32[35:38] sts rem. Cont without further shaping until work measures 61[62:63]cm, 24[24½:24¾]ins from beg, ending with a WS row.

Shape shoulder

Cast off rem sts.

RIGHT FRONT

Work as given for left front, reversing shapings.

BACK

Using 2¾mm (US2) needles, cast on 99[107:115] sts.

Cont in K1, P1 rib as given for front of sweater for 6cm, 2½ins ending with a WS row.

Inc row: Rib 3[7:11], ☆inc in next st, rib 3, rep from ☆ to last 4[8:12] sts, inc in next st, rib to end. 123[131:139] sts.

Change to 3¼mm (US3) needles. Beg with a P row, cont in st st until work measures same as front to armhole shaping, ending with a P row.

Shape armholes

Cast off 13 sts at beg of next 2 rows. 97[105:113] sts.

Cont without further shaping until work measures same as fronts to shoulder shaping, ending with a P row.

Shape shoulders

Cast off 32[35:38] sts at beg of next 2 rows. Cast off rem 33[35:37] sts.

SLEEVES

Using 2¾mm (US2) needles, cast on 59[61:61] sts.

Cont in K1, P1 rib as given for sweater front for 6cm, 2½ins, ending with a WS row.

Inc row: Rib 1, ☆inc in next st, rib 1, rep from ☆ to end. 88[91:91] sts.

Change to 3¼mm (US3) needles. Beg with a P row, cont in st st inc 1 st at each end of 5th and every foll 6th row until there are 120[125:131] sts.

SPEEDWELL *Lady's V-neck Slipover*

Cont without further shaping until work measures 46cm, 18¼ins from beg, ending with a P row.

Mark each end of last row. Work a further 16 rows. Cast off loosely.

FRONT BAND

Using 2¾mm (US2) needles, cast on 11 sts. Cont in K1, P1 rib as foll:

1st row: P1, ☆K1, P1, rep from ☆ to end.
2nd row: K1, ☆P1, K1, rep from ☆ to end. Rep these 2 rows once more.
Buttonhole row: Rib 4, K2 tog, yrn, rib to end.
Rib 17 rows.

Rep the last 18 rows 5 times more, then work the buttonhole row again. Cont in rib until band, when slightly stretched, fits up right front, across back neck and down left front. Cast off in rib.

TO MAKE UP/TO FINISH

Join shoulder seams. Placing centre of cast off edge of sleeve to shoulder seam, set in sleeves, sewing final 16 rows to cast off sts at underarm. Join side and sleeve seams. Sew on front band. Sew on buttons.

Sizes

To fit bust 76 – 81[86 – 91:97 – 102]cm, 30 – 32[34 – 36:38 – 40]ins
Actual bust 87[96:106]cm, 34¼[37¾:41¾]ins
Length 56cm, 22ins

Materials

4[5:6] × 50g balls of DK cotton type yarn in main colour (A)
2[3:4] balls in contrast colour (B)
One pair each 3¼mm (US3) and 4mm (US6) knitting needles

Tension/Gauge

23 sts and 25 rows to 10cm, 4ins over patt using 4mm (US6) needles

BACK

☆☆Using 3¼mm (US3) needles and B, cast on 70[80:90] sts.
Work 2 rows K1, P1 rib. Change to A, work 12 rows. Change to B, work 2 rows. Change to A and cont in rib until work measures 10cm, 4ins from beg, ending with a RS row.
Inc row: Rib 6[11:14], ☆inc in next st, rib 1, rep from ☆ to last 6[11:14] sts, inc in next st, rib to end. 100[110:122] sts.
Change to 4mm (US6) needles. Beg with a K row cont in st st working colour patt from chart.* Read odd numbered rows (K) from right to left and even numbered rows (P) from left to right. Strand yarn not in use loosely across WS of work. ☆☆
Cont working from chart until work measures 56cm, 22ins from beg, ending with a P row.

Shape shoulders
Cast off 10[11:13] sts at beg of next 4 rows and 10[13:15] sts at beg of foll 2 rows. Leave rem 40 sts on a spare needle.

FRONT

Work as given for back from ☆☆ to ☆☆.
Cont working from chart until work measures 34cm, 13½ins from beg, ending with a P row.
Divide for neck
Next row: Patt 50[55:61] and turn, leaving rem sts on a spare needle.
Complete left side of neck first.
Dec 1 st at neck edge on next and every foll 3rd then 2nd row alternately until 30[35:41] sts rem.
Cont without further shaping until work measures same as back to shoulder shaping, ending with a P row.
Shape shoulder
Cast off 10[11:13] sts at beg of next and foll alt row. Work 1 row. Cast off rem 10[13:15] sts.
With RS of work facing, return to sts on spare needle. Rejoin yarn and patt to end.
Complete as given for first side of neck, reversing shapings.

TO MAKE UP/TO FINISH

Join right shoulder seam.

NECKBAND

With RS of work facing, using 3¼mm (US3) needles and A, K up 60 sts down left side of neck, K up 1 st at centre front and mark this st, K up 60 sts up right side of neck, then K across 40 sts on back neck. 161 sts.
Work 5 rows K1, P1 rib dec 1 st at each side of marked centre st on every row.
Change to B and rib 2 rows, dec as before. Cast off in rib, dec again.

Join left shoulder and neckband seam.

ARMBANDS

Mark a point 20.5cm, 8¼ins down from shoulder seam on back and front.
With RS of work facing, using 3¼mm (US3) needles and A, K up 108 sts evenly between markers.
Work 7 rows K1, P1 rib.
Change to B and rib 2 rows.
Cast off in rib.

Join side seams.

* Chart page 70.

HAWTHORN BLOSSOM

SPEEDWELL

FORGET~ME~NOT

WILD HYACINTHS

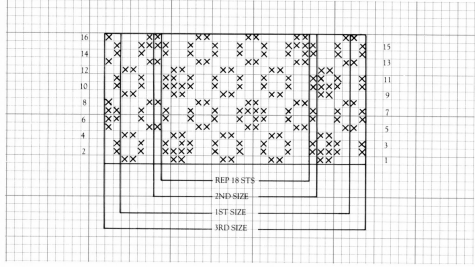

Key

A ☐

B ✕

Forget-Me-Not

Child's Sweater

Sizes

To fit chest/bust 46 – 51[56 – 61:66 – 71:76 – 81]cm, 18¼ – 20[22 – 24:26 – 28:30 – 32]ins
Actual chest/bust 56[66:76:86]cm, 22[26:30:34]ins
Length 35.5[37.5:39:41.5]cm, 14[14¾:15½:16¼]ins
Sleeve seam 24[26:34:38]cm, 9½[10¼:13½:15]ins

Materials

4[4:5:5] × 50g balls of Sunbeam Pure Wool DK in main colour (A)
1 ball in contrast colour (B)
One pair each 3¼mm (US3) and 4mm (US6) knitting needles
8 'Pikaby' buttons

Tension/Gauge

24 sts and 30 rows to 10cm, 4ins over st st using 4mm (US6) needles

BACK

☆☆Using 3¼mm (US3) needles and A, cast on 61[69:77:85] sts.
Cont in K1, P1 rib as foll:
☆☆☆1st row: (RS) K1, ☆P1, K1, rep from ☆ to end.
2nd row: P1, ☆K1, P1, rep from ☆ to end.
Change to B, rep these 2 rows once more.
Change to A, rep last 2 rows twice more.
Now rep last 6 rows once more, then the first 3 rows again. ☆☆☆
Inc row: Using A, rib 3[3:6:8], ☆inc in next st, rib 10[6:4:3], rep from ☆ to last 3[3:6:9] sts, inc in next st, rib to end. 67[79:91:103] sts.

Change to 4mm (US6) needles. Beg with a K row work 11 rows in st st.
Change to B, work 2 rows.
Change to A and cont until work measures 20.5cm, 8¼ins from beg, ending with a P row.
Shape raglan armholes
Cast off 2[3:4:6] sts at beg of next 2 rows.
1st, 2nd and 3rd sizes only
K 1 row.
Dec 1 st at each end of next and every foll 3rd row until 43[61:79] sts rem, ending with a P row. ☆☆
All sizes
Dec 1 st at each end of every foll alt row until 31 sts rem, ending with a P row.
Leave rem sts on a spare needle.

FRONT

Work as given for back from ☆☆ to ☆☆.
2nd, 3rd and 4th sizes only
Dec 1 st at each end of next and every foll alt row until 45 sts rem, ending with a P row.
All sizes
Shape neck
Next row: K2 tog, K13[15:15:15] and turn, leaving rem sts on a spare needle.
Complete left side of neck first.
Still dec at armhole edge as before on every foll alt row, cast off 2 sts at neck edge on next and 2 foll alt rows, then dec 1 st at neck edge on 2 foll alt rows.
Keeping neck edge straight, cont to dec at armhole edge only until 2 sts rem, ending with a P row.
Next row: K2 tog and fasten off.
With RS of work facing, return to sts on spare needle. Sl centre 11 sts on a holder, rejoin yarn at neck edge, K to last 2 sts, K2 tog.
Complete to match first side of neck, reversing shapings.

SLEEVES

Using 3¼mm (US3) needles and A, cast on 31[35:39:43] sts.
Cont in K1, P1 rib as given for back from ☆☆☆ to ☆☆☆.
Inc row: Using A, rib 5[7:7:7], ☆inc in next st, rib 4[4:5:6], rep from ☆ to last 6[8:8:8] sts, inc in next st, rib to end. 36[40:44:48] sts.
Change to 4mm (US6) needles. Beg with a K row, work 11 rows st st inc 1 st at each end of every 3rd[3rd:4th:4th] row.
Change to B and work 2 rows then change to A still inc as before until there

are 64[70:76:84] sts.

Cont without further shaping until work measures 24[26:34:38]cm, 9½[10¼:13½: 15]ins from beg, ending with a P row.

Shape raglan top

Cast off 2[3:4:6] sts at beg of next 2 rows. Dec 1 st at each end of next and every foll alt row until 30[26:22:18] sts rem, ending with a P row.

Next row: K2 tog, K11[9:7:5], K2 tog, K2 tog tbl, K to last 2 sts, K2 tog.

Next row: P.

Next row: K2 tog, K9[7:5:3], K2 tog, K2 tog tbl, K to last 2 sts, K2 tog.

Next row: P.

Cont in this way, dec 4 sts on next and every foll alt row until 6 sts rem, ending with a P row. Leave sts on a spare needle.

FRONT RAGLAN EDGINGS

Mark a point 14cm, 5½ins down from neck on raglan edge.

With RS of work facing, using 3¼mm (US3) needles and A, K up 35 sts from raglan edge, between neck and marker.

Beg with a WS row, work 1 row K1, P1 rib as given for back.

Cont in A only.

Buttonhole row: Rib 3, ☆yfwd, K2 tog, rib 7, rep from ☆ to last 5 sts, yfwd, K2 tog, rib 3.

Rib 1 row. Cast off in rib.

FRONT SLEEVE RAGLAN EDGES

Mark a point 14cm, 5½ins down from top of sleeve on front raglan edge.

With RS of work facing, using 3¼mm (US3) needles and A, K up 35 sts from sleeve raglan edge between top and marker. Cast off knit-wise.

TO MAKE UP/TO FINISH

Join back raglan seams and rem front raglan seams.

BACK NECKBAND

With RS of work facing, using 3¼mm (US3) needles and A, K across 6 sts on right sleeve top, K across 31 sts on back neck inc 1 st in first and last st, K across 6 sts on left sleeve top. 45 sts.

Beg with a WS row, cont in A only working in K1, P1 rib as given for back for 4cm, 1½ins. Cast off loosely in rib.

FRONT NECKBAND

With RS of work facing, using 3¼mm (US3) needles and A, K up 21 sts down left side of neck, K across 11 sts at centre front, K up 21 sts up right side of neck. 53 sts.

Complete as given for back neckband.

Using chart and B, Swiss darn motif from chart. Place one motif on each sleeve, two at lower edge of front and one at neck.

Fold neckbands in half onto WS and catch down. Join side and sleeve seams. Sew on buttons.

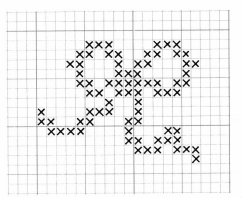

Key
A ☐
B ✗

WILD HYACINTHS
Child's Sweater

Sizes
To fit chest 56 – 61[66 – 71]cm, 22 – 24[26 – 28]ins
Actual chest 66.5[76.5]cm, 26¼[30¼]ins

Length 30[35]cm, 11¾[13¾]ins
Sleeve seam 25[29]cm, 9¾[11½]ins

Materials
4[5] × 50g balls of DK cotton type yarn in main colour (A)
2 balls in contrast colour (B)
One pair each 3¼mm (US3) and 4mm (US6) knitting needles

Tension/Gauge
22 sts and 28 rows to 10cm, 4ins over st st using 4mm (US6) needles
24 sts and 21 rows to 10cm, 4ins over patt using 4mm (US6) needles

BACK
Using 3¼mm (US3) needles and A, cast on 61[71] sts.

Cont in K1, P1 rib as foll:

1st row: (RS) K1, ☆P1, K1, rep from ☆ to end.

2nd row: P1, ☆K1, P1, rep from ☆ to end.

Rep these 2 rows for 6cm, 2½ins ending with a WS row.

Inc row: Rib 3[5], ☆inc in next st, rib 2, rep from ☆ to last 4[6] sts, inc in next st, rib to end. 80[92] sts.

Change to 4mm (US6) needles. Commence patt.

1st row: (WS) Using B, P1, ☆P5 tog, (K1, P1, K1, P1, K1) all into next st, rep from ☆ to last st, P1.

2nd row: Using B, P.

3rd row: Using A, P1, ☆(K1, P1, K1, P1, K1) all into next st, P5 tog, rep from ☆ to last st, P1.

4th row: Using A, P.

5th row: Using A, K to end winding yarn 3 times round needle for each st.

6th row: Using A, P to end dropping extra loops of previous row.

These 6 rows form the patt.

Cont in patt until work measures approximately 30[35]cm, 11¾[13¾]ins from beg, ending with a 4th patt row. Cast off using A.

FRONT
Work as given for back.

SLEEVES
Using 3¼mm (US3) needles and A, cast on 31[35] sts.

Cont in K1, P1 rib as given for back for 4cm, 1½ins ending with a WS row.

Inc row: Rib 0[1], ☆inc in next st, rep

from ☆ to last 0[1] sts, rib 0[1]. 62[68] sts. Change to 4mm (US6) needles. Cont in patt as given for back inc 1 st at each end of 4th and every foll 6th row until there are 74[80] sts.

Cont without further shaping until work measures approximately 25[29]cm, 9¾ [11½]ins from beg, ending with a 4th patt row. Cast off loosely.

TO MAKE UP/TO FINISH

Join shoulder seams for 9[10]cm, 3½[4]ins leaving opening for neck. Placing centre of cast off edge of sleeve to shoulder seams, set in sleeves. Join side and sleeve seams.

BUTTERFLY

Lady's Jacket

Sizes

To fit bust 86 – 91[97 – 102]cm, 34 – 36[38 – 40]ins
Actual bust 104[114]cm, 41[45]ins
Length 66cm, 26ins
Sleeve seam 48cm, 19ins

Materials

10[11] × 50g balls of Sirdar Nocturne in main colour (A)
3 balls each in 2 contrast colours (B and C)
2 balls in contrast colour (D)
One pair each 4½mm (US7) and 5½mm (US9) knitting needles
9 'Pikaby' buttons

Tension/Gauge

17 sts and 18 rows to 10cm, 4ins over patt using 5½mm (US9) needles

BACK

Using 4½mm (US7) needles and A, cast on 76[86] sts.
Cont in K1, P1 rib for 5cm, 2ins ending with a RS row.
Inc row: Rib 2, ☆inc in next st, rib 7[8],

rep from ☆ to last 2[3] sts, inc in next st, rib to end. 86[96] sts.
Change to 5½mm (US9) needles. Beg with a K row, cont in st st working colour patt from chart.* Read odd numbered rows (K) from right to left and even numbered rows (P) from left to right. Strand yarn loosely across back of work, twisting yarns when changing colour to avoid a hole.
Cont until work measures 66cm, 26ins from beg, ending with a P row.
Shape shoulders
Cont in A only. Cast off 14[16] sts at beg of next 2 rows and 15[16] sts at beg of foll 2 rows. Leave rem 28[32] sts on a spare needle.

LEFT FRONT

Using 4½mm (US7) needles and A, cast on 37[41] sts.
Cont in K1, P1 rib as foll:
1st row: (RS) K1, ☆P1, K1, rep from ☆ to end.
2nd row: P1, ☆K1, P1, rep from ☆ to end.
Rep these 2 rows for 5cm, 2ins ending with a 1st row.
Inc row: Rib 2, ☆inc in next st, rib 7[8], rep from ☆ to last 3 sts, inc in next st, rib to end. 42[46] sts.
Change to 5½mm (US9) needles and beg with a K row, cont in st st working colour patt from chart.
Cont until work measures 58.5cm, 23ins from beg, ending with a P row.
Shape neck
Next row: Patt to last 6 sts, turn and leave these sts on a safety pin.
Dec 1 st at neck edge on every row until 29[32] sts rem.
Cont without further shaping until work measures same as back to shoulder shaping, ending with a P row.
Shape shoulder
Cont in A only. Cast off 14[16] sts at beg of next row. Work 1 row.
Cast off rem 15[16] sts.

RIGHT FRONT

Work as given for left front, reversing all shapings.

SLEEVES

Using 4½mm (US7) needles and A, cast on 36 sts. Cont in K1, P1 rib for 8cm, 3ins ending with a RS row.
Inc row: Rib 5, ☆inc in next st, rib 1, rep

from ☆ to last 5 sts, inc in next st, rib to end. 50 sts.
Change to 5½mm (US9) needles. Beg with a K row, cont in st st working colour patt from chart, *at the same time*, inc and work into patt 1 st at each end of every 3rd row until there are 78 sts, then at each end of every alt row until there are 98 sts.
Cont without further shaping until work measures 48cm, 19ins from beg, ending with a P row. Cast off loosely.

BUTTONBAND

Using 4½mm (US7) needles and A, cast on 10 sts.
Cont in K1, P1 rib until band is long enough to fit, when slightly stretched, up left front to neck edge, ending with a WS row. Cut yarn and leave sts on a safety pin.

TO MAKE UP/TO FINISH

Sew on button band. Mark the positions of 8 buttons, the first in the 5th row from cast on edge and the last 5cm, 2ins from neck edge with the others evenly spaced between.

BUTTONHOLE BAND

Work as given for buttonband but do not cut yarn and make buttonholes opposite markers as foll:
Buttonhole row: (RS) Rib 4, yon, K2 tog, rib to end.

Join shoulder seams. Sew on buttonhole band.

NECKBAND

With RS of work facing, using 4½mm (US7) needles and A, rib across 10 sts of buttonhole band, K across 6 sts at front neck, K up 15 sts up right side of neck, K across 32 sts on back neck, K up 15 sts down left side of neck, K6 sts from front neck then rib across 10 sts of button band. 94 sts.
Work 5 rows K1, P1 rib.
Work the buttonhole row again. Work 3 rows rib, then work buttonhole row once more.
Work 5 rows in rib. Cast off loosely in rib.

Fold neckband in half onto WS and catch down. Oversew around double buttonhole.

(cont'd page 75)

* on page 75

BUTTERFLY

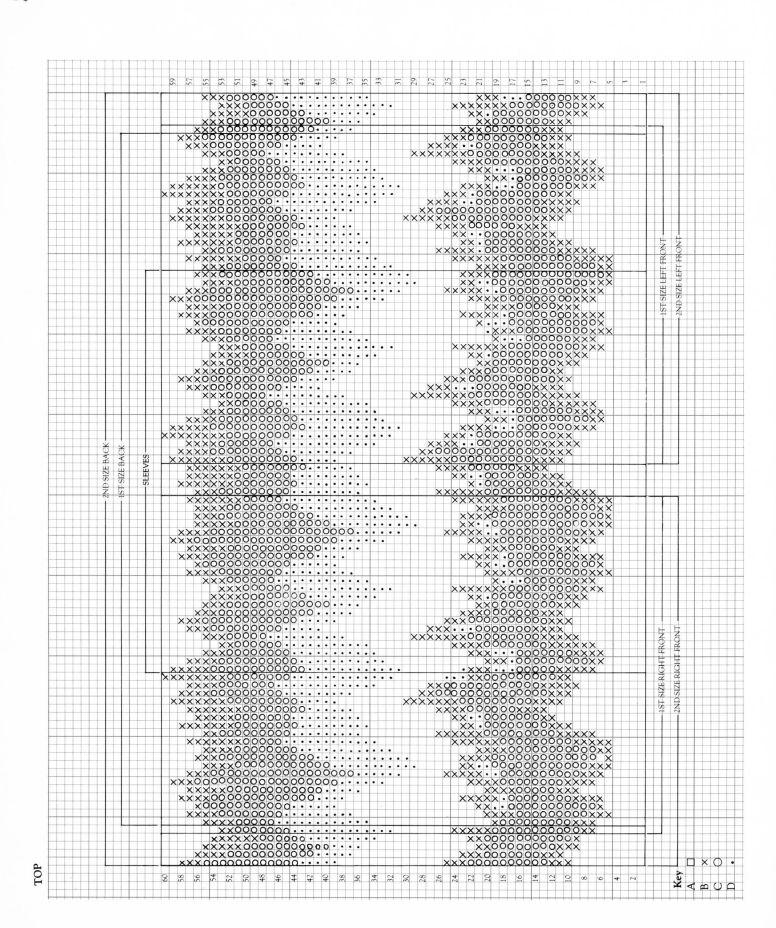

74

Placing centre of cast off edge of sleeve to shoulder seam, set in sleeves.
Join side and sleeve seams. Sew on buttons.

LADYBIRDS

Children's Sweater and Cardigan

Sizes

To fit chest 56-61[66-71]cm,
22-24[26-28]ins
Sweater actual chest 68[76.5]cm,
26¾[30¼]ins
Cardigan actual chest 67[76]cm,
26½[30]ins
Length 34[41]cm, 13½[16]ins
Sleeve seam 25[29]cm, 9¾[11½]ins

Materials

Sweater OR cardigan
1[2] × 100g balls of Jarol Supersaver Double Knitting in main colour (A)
1[2] balls in contrast colour (B)
One pair each 3mm (US3) and 4mm (US6) knitting needles
8 Ladybird buttons

Tension/Gauge

21 sts and 42 rows to 10cm, 4ins over patt using 4mm (US6) needles

SWEATER

BACK

☆☆Using 3mm (US3) needles and A, cast on 71[81] sts.
Cont in K1, Pl rib as foll:
1st row: (RS) K1, ☆P1, K1, rep from ☆ to end.
2nd row: P1, ☆K1, P1, rep from ☆ to end.
Rep these 2 rows for 6cm, 2½ins ending with a 2nd row.
Change to 4mm (US6) needles and commence patt.
1st row: (RS) K.
2nd row: P1, ☆K through centre of st in row below next st on left hand needle and allow both sts to sl off needle tog, P1, rep from ☆ to end.
These 2 rows form the patt.
Cont in patt until work measures 22[26]cm, 8¾[10¼]ins from beg, ending with a WS row.
Shape raglan armholes
☆☆☆Cast off 4 sts at beg of next 2 rows.
Next row: S1 1, K2 tog, psso, patt to last 3 sts, K3 tog.
Patt 5 rows. ☆☆
Rep the last 6 rows until 27[29] sts rem, ending with the dec row.
Patt 1 row.
Leave rem sts on spare needle.

FRONT

Work as given for back from ☆☆ to ☆☆.
Rep the last 6 rows until 43[49] sts rem, ending with the dec row.
Patt 5 rows.
Shape neck
Next row: S1 1, K2 tog, psso, patt 10[13], K2 tog and turn, leaving rem sts on a spare needle.
Complete left side of neck first.
Patt 5 rows.
Next row: S1 1, K2 tog, psso, patt to last

2 sts, K2 tog.
Rep the last 6 rows until 3 sts rem, ending with the dec row.
Patt 1 row.
Next row: S1 1, K2 tog, psso and fasten off.
With RS of work facing, return to sts on spare needle. S1 centre 13 sts onto a holder, rejoin yarn to next st, K2 tog, patt to last 3 sts, K3 tog.
Patt 5 rows.
Next row: K2 tog, patt to last 3 sts, K3 tog.
Rep the last 6 rows until 3 sts rem, ending with the dec row.
Patt 1 row.
Next row: K3 tog and fasten off.

SLEEVES

Using 3mm (US3) needles and B, cast on 39[47] sts.
Work in K1, P1 rib as given for back for 6cm, 2½ins ending with a 2nd row.
Change to 4mm (US6) needles and cont in patt as given for back. Inc and work into patt 1 st at each end of 7th and every foll 8th row until there are 53[61] sts.
Cont without further shaping until work measures 25[29]cm, 9¾[11½]ins from beg, ending with a WS row.
Shape raglan top
Work as given for raglan armhole of back from ☆☆☆ to ☆☆.
Rep the last 6 rows until 9 sts rem, ending with the dec row.
Patt 1 row.
Leave rem sts on a holder.

TO MAKE UP/TO FINISH

Join raglan seams, leaving left back raglan open.

NECKBAND

With RS of work facing, using 3mm (US3) needles and A, K9 sts of sleeve, K up 12[14] sts down left side of neck, K across 13 sts at centre front, K up 11[13] sts up right side of neck, K9 sts from sleeve and K across 27[29] sts on back neck. 81[87] sts.
Beg with 2nd row, work in K1, P1 rib as given for back for 5cm, 2ins.
Cast off loosely in rib.
Join left back raglan and neckband seam.
Fold neckband in half to WS and slip stitch in place. Join side and sleeve seams.

LADYBIRDS

BOW TIE

Using 3mm (US3) needles and B, cast on 10 sts.
Cont in g st for 16cm, 6¼ins.
Cast off.
Using 3mm (US3) needles and B, cast on 4 sts.
Work in g st for 4cm, 1½ins.
Cast off.
Join short ends of larger piece together. Using the seam as centre back, fold the piece in half, gather at the centre and secure to form bow shape.
Wrap the smaller piece around the centre of the bow and join ends at the back.
Embroider spots with A as shown.
Sew bow tie to centre front neck of sweater.

CARDIGAN

Work as given for back of sweater.

LEFT FRONT

☆☆☆☆Using 3mm (US3) needles and A, cast on 33[37] sts.
Cont in K1, P1 rib as given for back of sweater for 6cm, 2½ins ending with a 2nd row.
Change to 4mm (US6) needles and cont in patt as given for back of sweater until work measures 22[24]cm, 8¾[9½]ins from beg, ending at side edge.
Shape raglan armhole
Cast off 4 sts at beg of next row.☆☆☆☆
Patt 1 row.
Next row: S1 1, K2 tog, psso, patt to end.
Patt 5 rows.

Rep the last 6 rows until 19[21] sts rem, ending with the dec row.
Patt 4 rows.
Shape neck
Next row: Cast off 4[3] sts, patt to end.
Next row: S1 1, K2 tog, psso, patt to last 2 sts, K2 tog.
Patt 5 rows.
Rep the last 6 rows until 3 sts rem, ending with the dec row.
Patt 1 row.
Next row: S1 1, K2 tog, psso and fasten off.

RIGHT FRONT

Work as given for left front from ☆☆☆☆ to ☆☆☆☆.
Next row: Patt to last 3 sts, K3 tog.
Patt 5 rows.
Rep the last 6 rows until 19[21] sts rem, ending with the dec row.
Patt 5 rows.
Shape neck
Next row: Cast off 5[4] sts, patt to last 3 sts, K3 tog.
Patt 5 rows.
Next row: K2 tog, patt to last 3 sts, K3 tog.
Rep the last 6 rows until 3 sts rem, ending with the dec row.
Patt 1 row.
Next row: K3 tog and fasten off.

SLEEVES

Work as given for sleeves of sweater.

TO MAKE UP/TO FINISH

Join raglan seams.

BUTTONBAND

Using 3mm (US3) needles and B, cast on 9 sts.
Cont in K1, P1 rib as given for back of sweater until band, when slightly stretched, fits up left front edge to neck, ending with a 2nd row. Cut yarn and leave sts on a holder.

Sew buttonband in place. Mark the positions of 7 buttons, the first 1cm, ½in above cast on edge and the last 2cm, ¾in below neck with the others evenly spaced between.

BUTTONHOLE BAND

Work as given for buttonband but do not cut yarn and make buttonholes opposite markers as foll:
Buttonhole row: (RS) Rib 4, yrn, P2 tog, rib to end.

NECKBAND

Using 3mm (US3) needles and B, rib across 9 sts of buttonhole band, K up 16[18] sts up right side of neck, K across 9 sts on sleeve, 27[29] sts on back neck and 9 sts on left sleeve, then K up 16[18] sts down left side of neck, and rib across 9 sts on buttonband. 95[101] sts.
Rib 1 row then work buttonhole row again.
Rib 5 rows. Cast off in rib.
Sew on buttonhole band. Join side and sleeve seams. Sew on buttons.

AUTUMN

RED POPPY

POPPIES

RED POPPY *Lady's Sweater*

Sizes
To fit bust 86[91:97]cm, 34[36:38]ins
Actual bust 109[114:120]cm, 43[45:47¼]ins
Length 64cm, 25¼ins
Sleeve seam 48cm, 19ins

Materials
10[11:12] × 50g balls of Rowan Designer DK in main colour (A)
2[2:3] balls in contrast colour (B)
2[2:2] balls in contrast colour (C)
1 ball each in contrast colours (D and E)
One pair each 3¼mm (US3) and 4mm (US6) knitting needles

Tension/Gauge
22 sts and 30 rows to 10cm, 4ins over st st using 4mm (US6) needles

BACK
☆☆Using 3¼mm (US3) needles and A, cast on 90[96:102] sts.
Cont in K1, P1 rib for 7cm, 2¾ins ending with a RS row.
Inc row: Rib 16[4:7], ☆inc in next st, rib 1[2:2], rep from ☆ to last 16[5:8] sts, inc in next st, rib to end. 120[126:132] sts.
Change to 4mm (US6) needles. Beg with a K row work 4 rows st st. Now commence working in st st from chart. Use small separate balls of yarn for each area of colour, twisting yarns on WS of work when changing colour to avoid a hole.
1st row (RS) K0[3:6]A, reading from right to left, K 1st row of chart, K0[3:6]A.
2nd row: P0[3:6]A, reading from left to right, P 2nd row of chart, P0[3:6]. ☆☆
Keeping chart correct, cont in this way until 152 rows have been worked from chart.
Cont in A only until work measures 64cm, 25¼ins from beg, ending with a P row.
Shape shoulders
Cast off 13[14:15] sts at beg of next 6 rows. Leave rem 42 sts on a spare needle.

FRONT
Work as given for back from ☆☆ to ☆☆.
Keeping chart correct, cont in this way until 132 rows have been worked from chart.
Divide for neck
Next row: Patt 51[54:57] sts and turn, leaving rem sts on a spare needle.
Complete left side of neck first.
Dec 1 st at neck edge on every row until 39[42:45] sts rem.
Cont without further shaping until work measures same as back to shoulder shaping, ending with a P row.
Shape shoulder
Cast off 13[14:15] sts at beg of next and foll alt row. Work 1 row. Cast off rem 13[14:15] sts.
With RS of work facing, return to sts on spare needle. Sl centre 18 sts onto a holder, rejoin yarn at neck edge and patt to end.
Complete to match first side of neck, reversing all shapings.

SLEEVES
Using 3¼mm (US3) needles and A, cast on 46 sts.
Cont in K1, P1 rib for 7cm, 2¾ins ending with a RS row.
Inc row: Rib 3, ☆inc in next st, rib 2, rep from ☆ to last 4 sts, inc in next st, rib to end. 60 sts.
Change to 4mm (US6) needles. Beg with a K row work 4 rows st st.
Now commence working in st st from chart, inc 1 st at each end of 2nd and every foll 3rd row until there are 126 sts, working extra sts into patt.
Cont without further shaping until work measures 48cm, 19ins from beg, ending with a P row. Cast off loosely.

TO MAKE UP/TO FINISH
Join right shoulder seam.

NECKBAND
With RS of work facing, using 3¼mm (US3) needles and A, K up 22 sts down left side of neck, K across 18 sts at centre front neck, K up 22 sts up right side of neck, then K across 42 sts on back neck. 104 sts.
Cont in K1, P1 rib for 5cm, 2ins. Cast off loosely in rib.

Join left shoulder and neckband seam. Fold neckband in half onto WS and catch down. Placing centre of cast off edge of sleeve to shoulder seam, set in sleeves. Join side and sleeve seams.

POPPIES
Children's Sweater and Cardigan

Sizes
To fit chest 51 – 56[61 – 66]cm, 20 – 22[24 – 26]ins
Jacket actual chest 67[77.5]cm, 26½[30½]ins
Sweater actual chest 65.5[77]cm, 25¾[30½]ins
Length 38[46]cm, 15[18¼]ins
Sleeve seam 26[32]cm, 10¼[12½]ins

Materials
Jacket
6[7] × 50g balls of Sunbeam Aran Knit in main colour (A)
1[1] ball in contrast colour (B)
1[1] ball in contrast colour (C)
5 'Pikaby' buttons

Sweater
5[6] × 50g balls of Sunbeam Aran Knit in main colour (A)
1[1] ball in contrast colour (B)
1[1] ball in contrast colour (C)

Both versions
One pair each 3¾mm (US5), 4½mm (US7) and 5mm (US8) knitting needles

• on page 82

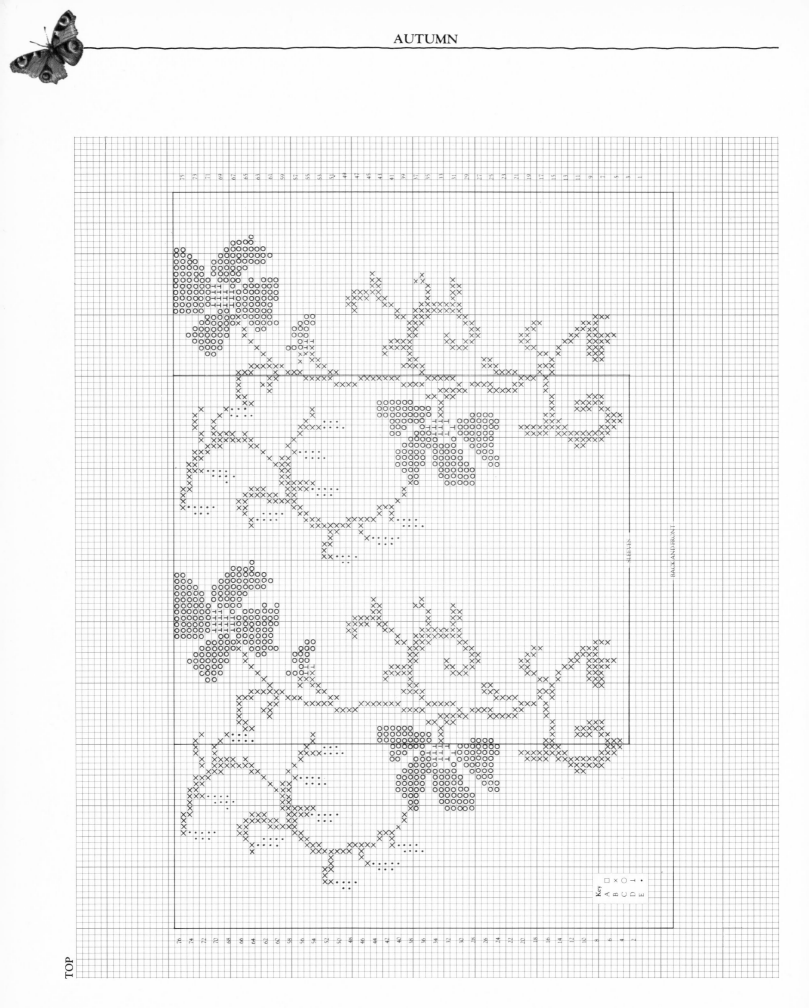

Tension/Gauge

18 sts and 24 rows to 10cm, 4ins over st st using 4½mm (US7) needles
18 sts and 20 rows to 10cm, 4ins over patt using 5mm (US8) needles

JACKET

BACK

Using 3¾mm (US5) needles and A, cast on 49[59] sts.
Cont in K1, P1 rib as foll:
1st row: (RS) K1, ☆P1, K1, rep from ☆ to end.
2nd row: P1, ☆K1, P1, rep from ☆ to end.
Rep these 2 rows for 6[7]cm, 2½[2¾]ins ending with a RS row.
Inc row: Rib 6[7], ☆inc in next st, rib 3[4], rep from ☆ to last 7 sts, inc in next st, rib to end. 59[69] sts.
Change to 4½mm (US7) needles. Beg with a K row cont in st st until work measures 24[29]cm, 9½[11½]ins from beg, ending with a P row.
Change to C and work 2 rows.
Change to 5mm (US8) needles and commence yoke patt.
1st row: (RS) K1A, ☆1B, 1A, rep from ☆ to end.
2nd row: P1B, ☆1A, 1B, rep from ☆ to end.
These 2 rows form the yoke patt. Keeping yoke patt correct, place poppy motifs working from chart.* Read odd numbered rows (K) from right to left and even numbered rows (P) from left to right. Use small separate balls of yarn for each area of colour, twisting yarns when changing colour to avoid a hole.
Next row: Patt 2, (work 1st row of chart, patt 3[5]) twice, work 1st row of chart, patt 1[3], (work 1st row of chart, patt 3[5]) twice, work 1st row of chart, patt 2.
This row establishes the position of 6 poppy motifs with yoke patt between. Keeping patt and chart correct cont until 6 rows of chart have been completed.
Cont in yoke patt only. Work 2[4] rows.
Now place poppy motif.
Next row: Patt 2, work 1st row of chart, patt to last 9 sts, work 1st row of chart, patt to end.
This row establishes the position of 2 poppy motifs with yoke patt between. Keeping patt and chart correct, cont until 6 rows of chart have been completed.
Rep the last 8[10] rows again, then cont in yoke patt only. Work 2[4] rows.
Shape shoulders
Cast off 18[22] sts at beg of next 2 rows.
Leave rem 23[25] sts on a spare needle.

LEFT FRONT

☆☆Using 3¾mm (US5) needles and A, cast on 23[27] sts
Cont in K1, P1 rib as given for back for 6[7]cm, 2½[2¾]ins ending with a RS row.
Inc row: Rib 4[6], ☆inc in next st, rib 2, rep from ☆ to last 4[6] sts, inc in next st, rib to end. 29[33] sts.
Change to 4½mm (US7) needles. Beg with a K row cont in st st until work measures 24[29]cm, 9½[11½]ins from beg, ending with a P row.
Change to C and work 2 rows.☆☆
Change to 5mm (US8) needles and commence yoke patt.
1st row: (RS) ☆K1B, 1A, rep from ☆ to last st, K1B.
2nd row: P1A, ☆1B, 1A, rep from ☆ to end.
These 2 rows form the yoke patt. Keeping yoke patt correct, place poppy motifs, working from chart.
Next row: Patt 2, (work 1st row of chart, patt 3[5]) twice, work 1st row of chart.
This row establishes the position of 3 poppy motifs with yoke patt between. Keeping patt and chart correct cont until 6 rows of chart have been worked.
Cont in yoke patt only. Work 2[4] rows.
Place poppy motif
Next row: Patt 2, work 1st row of chart, patt to end.
This row establishes the position of poppy motif and edge sts in yoke patt. Keeping patt and chart correct, cont until 6 rows of chart have been worked.
Rep the last 8[10] rows again, then cont in yoke patt only, *at the same time*, when 13[19] rows have been worked from beg of yoke, ending with a RS row.
Shape neck
Cast off 5 sts at beg of next row. Dec 1 st at neck edge on next 3 rows, then on every foll alt row until 18[22] sts rem.
Cont without further shaping until work measures same as back to shoulder shaping, ending at armhole edge.
Shape shoulder
Cast off rem sts.

RIGHT FRONT

Work as given for left front from ☆☆ to ☆☆.

Change to 5mm (US8) needles and commence yoke patt.
1st row: (RS) K1B, ☆1A, 1B, rep from ☆ to end.
2nd row: ☆P1A, 1B, rep from ☆ to last st, P1A.
These 2 rows form the yoke patt. Keeping yoke patt correct, place poppy motifs, working from chart.
Next row: Work 1st row of chart, (patt 3[5], work 1st row of chart) twice, patt 2.
This row establishes the position of 3 poppy motifs with yoke patt between. Keeping patt and chart correct cont until 6 rows of chart have been worked.
Cont in yoke patt only. Work 2[4] rows.
Place poppy motif
Next row: Patt to last 9 sts, work 1st row of chart, patt to end.
This row establishes the position of poppy motif with edge sts in yoke patt. Keeping patt and chart correct, cont until 6 rows of chart have been worked.
Rep the last 8[10] rows again, then cont in yoke patt only, *at the same time*, when 14[20] rows have been worked from beg of yoke, ending with a WS row,
Shape neck
Complete as given for left front.

SLEEVES

Using 3¾mm (US5) needles and A, cast on 23[31] sts.
Cont in K1, P1 rib as given for back for 6[7]cm, 2½[2¾]ins ending with a RS row.
Inc row: Rib 4[5], ☆inc in next st, rib 1[2], rep from ☆ to last 5 sts, inc in next st, rib to end. 31[39] sts.
Change to 4½mm (US7) needles. Beg with a K row cont in st st inc 1 st at each end of 3rd and every foll 3rd[4th] row until there are 51[61] sts.
Cont without further shaping until work measures 25[31]cm, 9¾[12¼]ins from beg, ending with a K row.
Change to C, work 3 rows, ending with a P row.
Cast off loosely.

TO MAKE UP/TO FINISH

Join shoulder seams.

NECKBAND

With RS of work facing, using 3¾mm (US5) needles and A, K up 18[20] sts up right front neck, K across 23[25] back neck sts, K up 18[20] sts down left front neck. 59[65] sts.

* on page 84 (above)

Beg with a WS row, cont in K1, P1 rib as given for back for 2[2.5]cm, ¾[1]in. Cast off in rib.

BUTTONHOLE BAND

With RS of work facing, using 3¾mm (US5) needles and A, K up 67[87] sts evenly up right front edge.
Beg with a WS row, work 1[3] rows K1, P1 rib as given for back.
1st buttonhole row: Rib 3, ☆cast off 2, rib 13[18] including st used to cast off, rep from ☆ to last 4 sts, cast off 2, rib to end.
2nd buttonhole row: Rib to end, casting on 2 sts over those cast off in previous row.
Cont in K1, P1 rib until work measures 2[2.5]cm, ¾[1]in ending with a WS row. Cast off in rib.

BUTTONBAND

Work to match buttonhole band, omitting buttonholes.

POCKET LININGS
(make 2)

Using 4½mm (US7) needles and A, cast on 14[15] sts and beg with a K row cont in st st for 8[9]cm, 3[3½]ins. Cast off.
Position linings above welt on WS of fronts at side edges. Catch down inner side edges.

POCKET EDGINGS
(make 2)

With RS of work facing, using 3¾mm (US5) needles and A, K up 19[21] sts along front pocket opening edge.
Beg with a WS row, work 2 rows K1, P1 rib as given for back. Cast off in rib.
Follow Swiss Darning chart, embroider extra sts in C.
Placing centre of cast off edge of sleeves to shoulder seams, set in sleeves. Join sleeve seams and side seams, sewing pocket linings to back. Sew on buttons.

SWEATER

BACK

Work as given for back of jacket.

FRONT

Work as given for back until work measures 7cm, 2¾ins less than back to shoulder shaping, ending with a WS row.
Divide for neck
Next row: Patt 24[28] and turn, leaving rem sts on a spare needle.

Complete left side of neck first.
Dec 1 st at neck edge on next 3 rows then on every foll alt row until 18[22] sts rem. Cont without further shaping until work measures same as back to shoulder shaping, ending at armhole edge.
Shape shoulder
Cast off rem sts.
With RS of work facing, return to sts on spare needle. Sl centre 11[13] sts onto a holder, rejoin yarn at neck edge, patt to end.
Complete as given for first side of neck.

SLEEVES

Work as given for sleeves of jacket.

TO MAKE UP/TO FINISH

Join right shoulder seam.

NECKBAND

With RS of work facing, using 3¾mm (US5) needles and A, K up 14[15] sts down left side of neck, K across 11[13] sts at centre front, K up 14[15] sts up right side of neck, then K across 23[25] sts on back neck. 62[68] sts.
Cont in K1, P1 rib for 2[2.5]cm, ¾[1]in. Cast off in rib.
Follow Swiss Darning chart, embroider extra sts in C.
Join left shoulder and neckband seam. Placing centre of cast off edge of sleeve to shoulder seam, set in sleeves. Join side and sleeve seams.

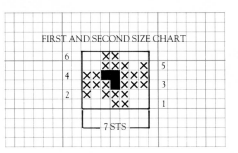

FIRST AND SECOND SIZE CHART

7 STS

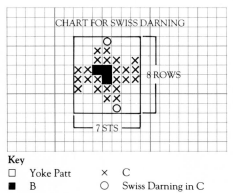

CHART FOR SWISS DARNING

8 ROWS

7 STS

Key

□ Yoke Patt	× C	
■ B	○ Swiss Darning in C	

SPARROW
Lady's V-neck Slipover

Sizes

To fit bust 76 – 81[86 – 91:97 – 102:107 – 112]cm, 30 – 32[34 – 36:38 – 40:42 – 44]ins
Actual bust 94[104:114:124]cm, 37[41:45:48¾]ins
Length 58[60:66:68]cm, 22¾[23¾:26:26¾]ins

Materials

5[5:6:7] × 50g balls of Rowan DK in main colour (A)
2[2:2:3] balls in contrast colour (B)
1[1:2:2] balls in contrast colour (C)
1[1:1:1] ball each in contrast colours (D and E)
One pair each 3¼mm (US3) and 4mm (US6) knitting needles
3¼mm (US3) circular needle

Tension/Gauge

24 sts and 24 rows to 10cm, 4ins over patt using 4mm (US6) needles

FRONT

☆☆Using 3¼mm (US3) needles and A, cast on 112[124:136:148] sts.
Cont in K1, P1 rib for 8cm, 3ins ending with a WS row, inc 1 st at end of last row. 113[125:137:149] sts.
Change to 4mm (US6) needles. Beg with a K row cont in st st working colour patt from chart. Read odd numbered rows (K) from right to left and even numbered rows (P) from left to right. Strand yarn not in use loosely on WS of work and twist yarns when changing colour to avoid a hole.
Cont from chart until work measures 30[32:37.5:37.5]cm, 11¾[12½:14¾:14¾]ins, ending with a P row.☆☆

SPARROW

Shape armholes
Cast off 5 sts at beg of next 2 rows. Dec 1 st at each end of 4 foll alt rows ending with a P row. 95[107:119:131] sts.
Divide for neck
Next row: Patt 47[53:59:65] sts, cast off 1, patt to end.
Complete right side of neck first.
Cont to dec at armhole edge as before on next and 4 foll alt rows, *at the same time*, dec 1 st at neck edge on next 14 rows then on every foll alt row until 23[29:35:41] sts rem.
Cont without further shaping until work measures 58[60:66:68]cm, 22¾[23¾:26:26¾]ins from beg, ending at armhole edge.
Shape shoulder
Cast off 6[7:9:10] sts at beg of next and 2 foll alt rows.
Work 1 row. Cast off rem 5[8:8:11] sts.
With WS of work facing, return to sts for left side of neck.
Rejoin yarn at neck edge and complete as given for first side of neck.

BACK
Work as given for front from ☆☆ to ☆☆.
Shape armholes
Cast off 5 sts at beg of next 2 rows. Dec 1 st at each end of every alt row until 85[97:109:121] sts rem.
Cont without further shaping until work measures same as front to shoulder shaping, ending with a P row.
Shape shoulders
Cast off 6[7:9:10] sts at beg of next 4 rows.
Shape back neck
Next row: Cast off 6[7:9:10], patt 6[9:9:12] including st used to cast off, turn leaving rem sts on a spare needle.
Complete right side of neck first.
Next row: Work 2 tog, patt to end.
Cast off rem 5[8:8:11] sts.
With RS of work facing return to sts on spare needle, rejoin yarn and cast off centre 37 sts, patt to end.
Next row: Cast off 6[7:9:10] sts patt to end.
Next row: Work 2 tog, patt to end.
Cast off rem 5[8:8:11] sts.

TO MAKE UP/TO FINISH
Join shoulder seams.

NECKBAND
With RS of work facing, using 3¼mm

(US3) circular needle and A, beg at centre front neck, K up 190[190:190:202] sts evenly all round neck edge.
Work in rows.
Cont in K1, P1 rib for 3cm, 1¼ins.
Cast off loosely in rib.

ARMBANDS
With RS of work facing, using 3¼mm (US3) needles and A, K up 156[156:156:166] sts evenly around armhole edge.
Cont in K1, P1 rib for 3cm, 1¼ins. Cast off loosely in rib.

Overlap neckband left front over right front and catch down row ends. Join side seams.

Key
A □
B •
C /
D ×
E ○

BACK & FRONT
REP 12 STS

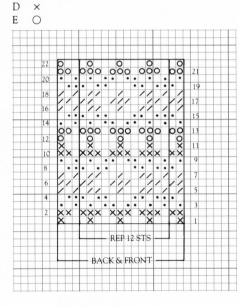

CORNFIELD
Lady's Longline Slipover with Matching Skirt

Sizes
To fit bust 76 – 81[86 – 91:97 – 102]cm, 30 – 32[34 – 36:38 – 40]ins
Actual bust 96[101:107]cm, 37¾[39¾:42]ins
Length 70cm, 27½ins

Materials
11[12:13] × 50g balls of Wendy Ascot DK
One pair each 3¼mm (US3) and 4mm (US6) knitting needles
3¼mm (US3) circular needle
Cable needle

Tension/Gauge
28 sts and 30 rows to 10cm, 4ins over patt using 4mm (US6) needles

CABLE PANEL A
(worked over 17 sts)
1st row: (RS) P5, sl next 2 sts onto cable needle and hold at front of work, P1 then K2 from cable needle – called Cr3L, P1, sl next st onto cable needle and hold at back of work, K2 then P1 from cable needle – called Cr3R, P5.
2nd row: K3, K into front and back of next st twice, then K into front again – called inc 5, K2, P2, K1, P2, K2, inc 5, K3.
3rd row: P3, K5 tog tbl, P2, sl next 3 sts onto cable needle and hold at front of work, K2, sl P st from cable needle onto left needle and P it, K2 from cable needle – called C5, P2, K5 tog tbl, P3.
P2, K5 tog tbl, P3.
4th row: K6, P2, K1, P2, K6.
5th row: P5, Cr3R, P1, Cr3L, P5.
6th row: K5, P2, K3, P2, K5.
7th row: P4, Cr3R, P3, Cr3L, P4.
8th row: K4, P2, K2, inc 5, K2, P2, K4.
9th row: P3, Cr3R, P2, K5 tog tbl, P2, Cr3L, P3.
10th row: K3, P2, K7, P2, K3.
11th row: P2, Cr3R, P7, Cr3L, P2.
12th row: K2, P2, K2, inc 5, K3, inc 5, K2, P2, K2.
13th row: P1, Cr3R, P2, K5 tog tbl, P3, K5 tog tbl, P2, Cr3L, P1.
14th row: K1, P2, K11, P2, K1.
15th row: P1, K2, P11, K2, P1.
16th row: K1, P2, K3, inc 5, K3, inc 5, K3, P2, K1.
17th row: P1, Cr3L, P2, K5 tog tbl, P3, K5 tog tbl, P2, Cr3R, P1.
18th row: K2, P2, K9, P2, K2.

CORNFIELD

19th row: P2, Cr3L, P7, Cr3R, P2.
20th row: K3, P2, K3, inc 5, K3, P2, K3.
21st row: P3, Cr3L, P2, K5 tog tbl, P2, Cr3R, P3.
22nd row: K4, P2, K5, P2, K4.
23rd row: P4, Cr3L, P3, Cr3R, P4.
24th row: K5, P2, K3, P2, K5.
These 24 rows form cable panel A.

CABLE PANEL B
(worked over 9 sts)
1st row: (RS) P3, K3 tbl, P3.
2nd row: K3, P3 tbl, K3.
3rd row: P2, sl next st onto cable needle and hold at back of work, K1 tbl then P1 from cable needle – called Tw2b, K1 tbl, sl next st onto cable needle and hold at front of work, P1 then K1 tbl from cable needle – called Tw2f, P2.
4th row: K2, (P1 tbl, K1) twice, P1 tbl, K2.
5th row: P1, Tw2b, P1, K1 tbl, P1, Tw2f, P1.
6th row: K1, (P1 tbl, K2) twice, P1 tbl, K1.
7th row: Tw2b, P1, K3 tbl, P1, Tw2f.
8th row: P1 tbl, K2, P3 tbl, K2, P1 tbl.
These 8 rows form cable panel B.

CABLE PANEL C
(worked over 30[34:38] sts)
1st row: (RS) P6[8:10], sl next 2 sts onto cable needle and hold at front of work, K2 tbl then K2 tbl from cable needle – called C4Fb, P10, C4Fb, P6[8:10].
2nd and every foll alt row: K the P sts and P the K sts of previous row.
3rd row: P5[7:9], sl next st onto cable needle and hold at back of work, K2 tbl then P1 from cable needle – called Cr3Rb, sl next 2 sts onto cable needle and hold at front of work, P1 then K2 tbl from cable needle – called Cr3Lb, P8, Cr3Rb, Cr3Lb, P5[7:9].
5th row: P4[6:8], Cr3Rb, K1, P1, Cr3Lb, P6, Cr3Rb, K1, P1, Cr3Lb, P4[6:8].
7th row: P3[5:7], Cr3Rb, (K1, P1) twice, Cr3Lb, P4, Cr3Rb, (K1, P1) twice, Cr3Lb, P3[5:7].
9th row: P2[4:6], Cr3Rb, (K1, P1) 3 times, Cr3Lb, P2, Cr3Rb, (K1, P1) 3 times, Cr3Lb, P2[4:6].
11th row: P1[3:5], ☆Cr3Rb, (K1, P1) 4 times, Cr3Lb, rep from ☆ once more, P1[3:5].
13th row: P1[3:5], K2 tbl, (K1, P1) 5 times, C4Fb, (K1, P1) 5 times, K2 tbl, P1[3:5].

15th row: P1[3:5], ☆Cr3Lb, (K1, P1) 4 times, Cr3Rb, rep from ☆ once more, P1[3:5].
17th row: P2[4:6], Cr3Lb, (K1, P1) 3 times, Cr3Rb, P2, Cr3Lb, (K1, P1) 3 times, Cr3Rb, P2[4:6].
19th row: P3[5:7], Cr3Lb, (K1, P1) twice, Cr3Rb, P4, Cr3Lb, (K1, P1) twice, Cr3R, P3[5:7].
21st row: P4[6:8], Cr3Lb, K1, P1, Cr3Rb, P6, Cr3Lb, K1, P1, Cr3Rb, P4[6:8].
23rd row: P5[7:9], Cr3Lb, Cr3Rb, P8, Cr3Lb, Cr3Rb, P5[7:9].
24th row: As 2nd row.
These 24 rows form cable panel C.

BACK
Using 3¼mm (US3) needles, cast on 120[128:136] sts.
Work in K2, P2 rib for 12cm, 4¾ins ending with a RS row.
Inc row: Rib 1[5:9], ☆inc in next st, rib 8, rep from ☆ to last 2[6:10] sts, inc in next st, rib to end. 134[142:150] sts.
Change to 4mm (US8) needles and commence patt.
1st row: (RS) K1, P0[2:4], ☆K2, work 1st row cable panel A, K2, work 1st row cable panel B, K2, work 1st row cable panel A, K2,☆ work 1st row cable panel C, rep from ☆ to ☆ again, P0[2:4], K1.
2nd row: K1[3:5], ☆P2, work 2nd row cable panel A, P2, work 2nd row cable panel B, P2, work 2nd row cable panel A, P2,☆ work 2nd row cable panel C, rep from ☆ to ☆ again, K1[3:5].
These 2 rows establish the position of cable panels with st st between. ☆☆Cont in this way, keeping panels correct until work measures 70cm, 27½ins from beg, ending with a WS row.
Shape shoulders
Cast off 45[49:53] sts at beg of next 2 rows. Leave rem 44 sts on a spare needle.

POCKET LININGS
(make 2)
Using 4mm (US6) needles, cast on 28 sts.
Work in st st for 12.5cm, 5ins ending with a P row.
Leave sts on a spare needle.

FRONT
Work as given for back from ☆☆ to ☆☆.
Cont in this way, keeping panels correct until work measures 25cm, 9¾ins from

beg, ending with a WS row.
Place pockets
Next row: Patt 3[5:7], sl next 28 sts on a holder, patt across 28 sts of first pocket lining, patt 72[76:80] sts, sl next 28 sts on a holder, patt across 28 sts of second pocket lining, patt to end.
Cont in patt until work measures 41cm, 16ins from beg, ending with a WS row.
Shape neck
Next row: Patt 67[71:75] sts and turn leaving rem sts on a spare needle.
Complete left side of neck first.
Dec 1 st at neck edge on every foll 3rd row until 45[49:53] sts rem.
Cont without further shaping until work matches back to shoulder shaping, ending at side edge.
Shape shoulder
Cast off rem sts.
With RS of work facing, return to sts on spare needle, rejoin yarn and patt to end.
Complete as given for first side of neck.

TO MAKE UP/TO FINISH
Join left shoulder seam.

NECKBAND
With RS of work facing, using 3¼mm (US3) circular needle, K44 sts across back neck, K up 100 sts down left side of neck, 2 sts from centre front and 100 sts up right side of neck. 246 sts.
Work in rows.
1st row: (WS) (P2, K2) 24 times, P2, K2 tog, P2 centre sts, K2 tog, ☆P2, K2, rep from ☆ to last 2 sts, P2.
2nd row: Work in K2, P2 rib to within 2 sts of centre 2 sts, P2 tog, K2, P2 tog, rib to end.
Cont in this way, dec 1 st at each side of centre 2 sts. Work a further 10 rows. Cast off in rib, dec on this row as before.

ARMBANDS
Join right shoulder and neckband seam.
Mark position of armholes 23cm, 9ins down from shoulder seams on back and front.
With RS of work facing, using 3¼mm (US3) needles, K up 128 sts between markers.
Work 12 rows K2, P2 rib. Cast off in rib.
Join side seams.

SKIRT
The pattern for this is exactly the same as that for 'Thistle' skirt on pages 96-7.

RED BERRIES *Children's Sweater and Cardigan*

Sizes

To fit chest 56 – 61[61 – 66]cm, 22 – 24[24 – 26]ins
Actual sweater chest 62[68]cm, 24½[26¾]ins
Length 24[33]cm, 9½[13]ins
Actual cardigan chest 64[70]cm, 25¼[27½]ins
Length 29[38]cm, 11½[15]ins
Sleeve seam 29[30]cm, 11½[11¾]ins

Materials

Sweater OR cardigan
4[5] × 50g balls of Poppletons
Emmerdale DK in main colour (A)
1 ball in each of contrast colours (B, C and D)
One pair each 3¼mm (US3) and 4mm (US6) knitting needles
Cable needle
Medium size crochet hook
7 buttons for cardigan

Tension/Gauge

27 sts and 30 rows to 10cm, 4ins over patt using 4mm (US6) needles

SWEATER

BACK

☆☆Using 3¼mm (US3) needles and A, cast on 83[91] sts.
Cont in K1, P1 rib as foll:
1st row: (RS) K1, ☆P1, K1, rep from ☆ to end.
2nd row: P1, ☆K1, P1, rep from ☆ to end.
Rep these 2 rows for 5[6]cm, 2[2½]ins

ending with a RS row, inc 1 st at end of last row. 84[92] sts.
Change to 4mm (US6) needles and commence patt.
1st row: (WS) K4[5], P1, ☆K8[9], P8, K8[9], P1, rep from ☆ to last 4[5] sts, K4[5].
2nd row: P4[5], K1 tbl, ☆P8[9], K8, P8[9], K1 tbl, rep from ☆ to last 4[5] sts, P4[5].
3rd row: As 1st row.
4th row: P4[5], (K1, yfwd, K1) all into next st, ☆P8[9], sl next 4 sts onto cable needle and hold at front of work, K4 then K4 from cable needle – called C8F, P8[9], (K1, yfwd, K1) all into next st, rep from ☆ to last 4[5] sts, P4[5].
5th row: K4[5], P3, ☆K8[9], P8, K8[9], P3, rep from ☆ to last 4[5] sts, K4[5].
6th row: P4[5], K1, (yfwd, K1) twice, ☆P8[9], K8, P8[9], K1, (yfwd, K1) twice, rep from ☆ to last 4[5] sts, P4[5].
7th row: K4[5], P5, ☆K8[9], P8, K8[9], P5, rep from ☆ to last 4[5] sts, K4[5].
8th row: P4[5], K2, yfwd, K1, yfwd, K2, ☆P8[9], K8, P8[9], K2, yfwd, K1, yfwd, K2, rep from ☆ to last 4[5] sts, P4[5].
9th row: K4[5], P7, ☆K8[9], P8, K8[9], P7, rep from ☆ to last 4[5] sts, K4[5].
10th row: P4[5], K3, yfwd, K1, yfwd, K3, ☆P8[9], K8, P8[9], K3, yfwd, K1, yfwd, K3, rep from ☆ to last 4[5] sts, P4[5].
11th row: K4[5], P9, ☆K8[9], P8, K8[9], P9, rep from ☆ to last 4[5] sts, K4[5].
12th row: P4[5], K4, yfwd, K1, yfwd, K4, ☆P8[9], C8F, P8[9], K4, yfwd, K1, yfwd, K4, rep from ☆ to last 4[5] sts, P4[5].
13th row: K4[5], P11, ☆K8[9], P8, K8[9], P11, rep from ☆ to last 4[5] sts, K4[5].
14th row: P4[5], K3, sl 1, K1, psso, yfwd, K1, yfwd, K2 tog, K3, ☆P8[9], K8, P8[9], K3, sl 1, K1, psso, yfwd, K1, yfwd, K2 tog, K3, rep from ☆ to last 4[5] sts, P4[5].
15th row: As 13th row.
16th row: P4[5], sl 1, K1, psso, K1, sl 1, K1, psso, yfwd, K1, yfwd, K2 tog, K1, K2 tog, ☆P8[9], K8, P8[9], sl 1, K1, psso, K1, sl 1, K1, psso, yfwd, K1, yfwd, K2 tog, K1, K2 tog, rep from ☆ to last 4[5] sts, P4[5].
17th row: As 11th row.
18th row: P4[5], sl 1, K1, psso, K5, K2 tog, ☆P8[9], K8, P8[9], sl 1, K1, psso, K5, K2 tog, rep from ☆ to last 4[5] sts, P4[5].
19th row: As 9th row.
20th row: P4[5], sl 1, K1, psso, K3, K2 tog, ☆P8[9], C8F, P8[9], sl 1, K1, psso,

K3, K2 tog, rep from ☆ to last 4[5] sts, P4[5].
21st row: As 7th row.
22nd row: P4[5], sl 1, K1, psso, K1, K2 tog, ☆P8[9], K8, P8[9], sl 1, K1, psso, K1, K2 tog, rep from ☆ to last 4[5] sts, P4[5].
23rd row: As 5th row.
24th row: P4[5], sl 1, K2 tog, psso, ☆P8[9], K8, P8[9], sl 1, K2 tog, psso, rep from ☆ to last 4[5] sts, P4[5].
These 24 rows form the patt. ☆☆
Cont patt, work a further 25[49] rows.
Change to 3¼mm (US3) needles.
Dec 1 st at centre of 1st row, cont in K1, P1 rib as given for welt for 3cm, 1¼ins ending with a 2nd row. Cast off in rib.

FRONT

Work as given for back.

SLEEVES

Using 3¼mm (US3) needles and A, cast on 37[41] sts.
Cont in K1, P1 rib as given for back for 5[6]cm, 2[2½]ins ending with a WS row.
Inc row: Rib 8, ☆inc in next st, rib 6[7], rep from ☆ to last 8[9] sts, inc in next st, rib to end. 41[45] sts.
Change to 4mm (US6) needles. Commence patt.
1st row: (WS) K4[5], P8, K8[9], P1, K8[9], P8, K4[5].
2nd row: P4[5], K8, P8[9], K1 tbl, P8[9], K8, P4[5].
3rd row: As 1st row.
4th row: P4[5], C8F, P8[9], (K1, yfwd, K1) all into next st, P8[9], C8F, P4[5].
These 4 rows establish the patt as given for back. Cont in patt as set, inc and work into rev st st 1 st at each end of next and 12[13] foll 4th rows.
Cont without further shaping until 73 rows have been worked in patt.
Cast off loosely.

TO MAKE UP/TO FINISH

Join shoulder seams for 7[8]cm, 2¾[3]ins, leaving centre open for neck.
Placing centre of cast off edge of sleeves to shoulder seams, set in sleeves. Join side and sleeve seams.
Using B, oversew the K sts between 'leaves' to form berries.
Using C and D double, make crochet chains long enough to weave through the cables as shown. Secure ends on WS.

RED BERRIES

CARDIGAN

Note, sts are made and lost within the patt; allow for this when shaping garment.

BACK

Work as given for back of sweater from ☆☆ to ☆☆.

Cont in patt, work a further 49[73] rows.
Shape shoulders
Cast off 29[31] sts at beg of next 2 rows.
Leave rem 26[30] sts on a spare needle.

LEFT FRONT

☆☆☆Using 3¼mm (US3) needles and A, cast on 41[45] sts.

Cont in K1, P1 rib as given for back of sweater for 5[6]cm, 2[2½]ins ending with a RS row.

Change to 4mm (US6) needles.
Commence patt.

1st row: (WS) K4[5], P8, K8[9], P1, K8[9], P8, K4[5].
2nd row: P4[5], K8, P8[9], K1 tbl, P8[9], K8, P4[5].
3rd row: As 1st row.
4th row: P4[5], C8F, P8[9], (K1, yfwd, K1) all into next st, P8[9], C8F, P4[5].

These 4 rows establish the patt as given for back of sweater. Cont in patt until 60[82] rows have been worked in patt. ☆☆☆

Shape neck
Cast off 7[8] sts at beg of next row.
Dec 1 st at neck edge on next 5[6] rows. 29[31] sts.

Cont without further shaping until work measures same as back to shoulder shaping, ending at armhole edge.
Shape shoulder
Cast off rem sts.

RIGHT FRONT

Work as given for left front from ☆☆☆ to ☆☆☆. Work 1 row. Complete to match left front reversing all shapings.

SLEEVES

Work as given for sleeves of sweater.

BUTTONBAND

Using 3¼mm (US3) needles and A, cast on 9 sts.

Work in K1, P1 rib as given for sweater back until band is long enough, when slightly stretched, to fit up left front edge to neck, ending at inner neck edge. Cut yarn and leave sts on a safety pin.

TO MAKE UP/TO FINISH

Sew on buttonband. Mark the position of 6 buttons, the first 1cm, ½in from cast on edge the last 2cm, ¾in from neck edge with the others evenly spaced between.

BUTTONHOLE BAND

Work as given for buttonband but do not cut yarn and make buttonholes opposite markers as foll:
Buttonhole row: (RS) Rib 4, yon, K2 tog, rib to end.

Sew on buttonhole band. Join shoulder seams.

NECKBAND

With RS of work facing, using 3¼mm (US3) needles and A, rib sts of buttonhole band, K up 16[18] sts up right front neck, K across 26[30] sts on back neck, K up 15[17] sts down left front neck, then rib sts of buttonband. 75[83] sts.
Rib 3 rows then work the buttonhole row again.
Rib 3 rows. Cast off in rib.

Placing centre of cast off edge of sleeve to shoulder seams, set in sleeves. Join side and sleeve seams. Sew on buttons.
Complete cardigan as given for sweater.

JUNIPER BERRIES

Lady's Sweater

Sizes

To fit bust 76 – 81[86 – 91:97 – 102]cm, 30 – 32[34 – 36:38 – 40]ins
Actual bust 94[103:112]cm, 37[40½: 44]ins
Length 60[62:64]cm, 23¾[24½:25¼]ins
Sleeve seam 45cm, 17¾ins

Materials

6[6:7] × 50g balls of Sunbeam Pure New Wool DK in main colour (A)
3[3:4] balls in contrast colour (B)
3[3:4] balls in contrast colour (C)
2[2:3] balls in contrast colour (D)
One pair each 3¼mm (US3) and 4mm (US6) knitting needle

Tension/Gauge

27 sts and 28 rows to 10cm, 4ins over patt using 4mm (US6) needles

BACK

Using 3¼mm (US3) needles and A, cast on 111[123:133] sts.
Cont in K1, P1 rib as foll:
1st row: (RS) K1, ☆P1, K1, rep from ☆ to end.
2nd row: P1, ☆K1, P1, rep from ☆ to end.
Rep these 2 rows for 7cm, 2¾ins ending with a RS row.
Inc row: Rib 2[1:6], ☆inc in next st, rib 6[7:6], rep from ☆ to last 4[2:8] sts, inc in next st, rib to end. 127[139:151] sts.
Change to 4mm (US6) needles. Commence working colour patt from chart, read odd numbered rows (RS) from right to left and even numbered rows (WS) from left to right. Work g st ridges as indicated and fairisle bands in st st. Strand yarn not in use loosely across WS of work and twist yarns when changing colour to avoid a hole.
Work 96 rows.
Shape armholes
Keeping patt correct, cast off 12 sts at beg of next 2 rows. 103[115:127] sts.
Cont without further shaping until work measures 60[62:64]cm, 23¾[24½:25¼] ins from beg, ending with a WS row.
Shape shoulders
Cast off 10[12:13] sts at beg of next 4 rows and 12[12:14] sts at beg of next 2 rows. Leave rem 39[43:47] sts on a spare needle.

• on page 93

JUNIPER BERRIES

The chart grid shows row numbers on the left side: 50, 48, 46, 44, 42, 40, 38, 36, 34, 32, 30, 28, 26, 24, 22, 20, 18, 16, 14, 12, 10, 8, 6, 4, 2. On the right side: 49, 47, 45, 43, 41, 39, 37, 35, 33, 31, 29, 27, 25, 23, 21, 19, 17, 15, 13, 11, 9, 7, 5, 3, 1.

Chart annotations:
K2 ROWS D
K2 ROWS D
K2 ROWS D
K2 ROWS D
Rep 12 sts
BACK/FRONT/SLEEVES
2nd size sleeve ends here

FRONT

Work as given for back until 12 rows less than back have been worked to shoulder shaping, ending with a WS row.
Shape neck
Next row: Patt 40[44:48] sts, K2 tog and turn leaving rem sts on a spare needle.
Complete left side of neck first.
Dec 1 st at neck edge on every row until 32[36:40] sts rem.
Cont without further shaping until work measures same as back to shoulder shaping, ending at armhole edge.
Shape shoulder
Cast off 10[12:13] sts at beg of next and foll alt row. Work 1 row. Cast off rem 12[12:14] sts.
With RS of work facing return to sts on spare needle. Sl centre 19[23:27] sts onto a holder, rejoin yarn at neck edge, K2 tog and patt to end.
Complete as given for first side of neck.

SLEEVES

Using 3¼mm (US3) needles and A, cast on 45[51:57] sts.
Cont in K1, P1 rib as given for back for 7cm, 2¾ins ending with a RS row.
Inc row: Rib 4[3:1], ☆inc in next st, rib 3[4:5], rep from ☆ to last 5[3:2] sts, inc in next st, rib to end. 55[61:67] sts.
Change to 4mm (US6) needles. Cont in patt from chart inc 1 st at each end of every foll 4th row until there are 113[122:135] sts.
Cont without further shaping until work

Key
A □
B ×
C ○
D /

measures 46cm from beg, ending with a WS row.
Patt 10 rows. Cast off loosely.

TO MAKE UP/TO FINISH
Join right shoulder seam.

NECKBAND
With RS of work facing, using 3¼mm (US3) needles and A, K up 18 sts down left front neck, K across 19[23:27] sts at centre front neck, K up 19 sts up right side of neck, then K across 39[43:47] sts on back neck. 95[103:111] sts.
Beg with a WS row cont in K1, P1 rib as given for back for 6cm, 2½ins.
Leave sts on a length of contrast yarn.

Join left shoulder and neckband seam. Fold neckband in half onto WS and backstitch each st to corresponding st at base of neckband. Placing centre of cast off edge of sleeve to shoulder seam, set in sleeves, sewing 10 rows to cast off sts at underarm. Join side and sleeve seams.

HEDGEHOG

Patt instructions for sweater on pages 22-5
Patt instructions for hedgehog toy on page 147
Patt instructions for scarf and mittens on pages 140-1

THISTLE

Lady's Sweater with Matching Skirt

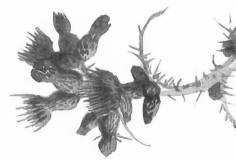

Sizes

To fit bust 81 – 86[91 – 97:102 – 107]cm,
32 – 34[36 – 38:40 – 42]ins
Actual bust 103[110:125]cm,
40½[43¼:49¼]ins
Length 68cm, 26¾ins
Sleeve seam 43[45:47]cm,
17[17¾:18½]ins

Materials

13[15:16] × 50g balls of Sunbeam Pure
Wool DK
One pair each 3¼mm (US3) and 4mm
(US6) knitting needles
3¼mm (US3) circular needle
Cable needle

Tension/Gauge

27 sts and 30 rows to 10cm, 4ins over patt
using 4mm (US6) needles

SWEATER

BACK

☆☆Using 3¼mm (US3) needles, cast on
118[130:146] sts.

Cont in K2, P2 rib as foll:
1st row: (RS) K2, ☆P2, K2, rep from ☆
to end.
2nd row: P2, ☆K2, P2, rep from ☆ to
end.
Rep these 2 rows for 10cm, 4ins ending
with a 1st row.
Inc row: Rib 9[11:7], ☆inc in next st, rib
4[5:5], rep from ☆ to last 9[11:7] sts, inc
in next st, rib to end. 139[149:169] sts.
Change to 4mm (US6) needles and cont
in patt as foll:
1st row: (RS) P6[11:6], ☆K7, P8, rep
from ☆ to last 13[18:13] sts, K7, P
end.
2nd row: K6[11:6], ☆P7, K8, rep from ☆
to last 13[18:13] sts, P7, K to end.
3rd row: P6[11:6], ☆sl next 4 sts onto
cable needle and hold at back of work,
K3 then K4 from cable needle – called
C7B, P8, rep from ☆ to last 13[18:13] sts,
C7B, P to end.
4th row: As 2nd row.
5th row: P6[11:6], ☆K7, P6, K3 tog,
yfwd, K1, yfwd, K2 tog, (yfwd, K1)
twice, yfwd, K3 tog tbl, P6, rep from ☆
to last 13[18:13] sts, K7, P to end.
6th row: K6[11:6], P7, ☆K6, P11, K6,
P7, rep from ☆ to last 6[11:6] sts, K to
end.
7th row: P6[11:6], ☆K7, P5, (K2 tog,
yfwd) 3 times, K1 tbl, (yfwd, sl 1, K1,
psso) 3 times, P5, rep from ☆ to last
13[18:13] sts, K7, P to end.
8th row: K6[11:6], P7, ☆K5, P13, K5,
P7, rep from ☆ to last 6[11:6] sts, K to
end.
9th row: P6[11:6], ☆K7, P3, K3 tog,
yfwd, (K2 tog, yfwd) twice, K1 tbl, yfwd,
K1, yfwd, K1 tbl, (yfwd, sl 1, K1, psso)
twice, yfwd, K3 tog tbl, P3, rep from ☆
to last 13[18:13] sts, K7, P to end.
10th row: K6[11:6], P7, ☆K3, P17, K3,
P7, rep from ☆ to last 6[11:6] sts, K to
end.
11th row: P6[11:6], ☆C7B, P4, (K2 tog
yfwd) 3 times, K1 tbl, K1, K1 tbl, (yfwd,
sl 1, K1, psso) 3 times, P4, rep from ☆ to
last 13[18:13] sts, C7B, P to end.

THISTLE

12th row: K6[11:6], P7, ☆K4, P15, K4, P7, rep from ☆ to last 6[11:6] sts, K to end.

13th row: P6[11:6], ☆K7, P5, (K2 tog, yfwd) twice, K1 tbl, K3, K1 tbl, (yfwd, sl 1, K1, psso) twice, P5, rep from ☆ to last 13[18:13] sts, K7, P to end.

14th row: As 8th row.

15th row: P6[11:6], ☆K7, P6, K2 tog, yfwd, K1 tbl, K5, K1 tbl, yfwd, sl 1, K1, psso, P6, rep from ☆ to last 13[18:13] sts, K7, P to end.

16th row: As 2nd row.

17th–20th rows: Rep 1st–4th rows.

21st row: P4[9:4], ☆K3 tog, yfwd, K1, yfwd, K2 tog, (yfwd, K1) twice, yfwd, K3 tog tbl, P6, K7, P6, rep from ☆ to last 15[20:15] sts, K3 tog, yfwd, K1, yfwd, K2 tog, (yfwd, K1) twice, yfwd, K3 tog tbl, P4[9:4].

22nd row: K4[9:4], ☆P11, K6, P7, K6, rep from ☆ to last 15[20:15] sts, P11, K to end.

23rd row: P3[8:3], ☆(K2 tog, yfwd) 3 times, K1 tbl, (yfwd, sl 1, K1, psso) 3 times, P5, K7, P5, rep from ☆ to last 16[21:16] sts, (K2 tog, yfwd) 3 times, K1 tbl, (yfwd, sl 1, K1, psso) 3 times, P3[8:3].

24th row: K3[8:3], ☆P13, K5, P7, K5, rep from ☆ to last 16[21:16] sts, P13, K to end.

25th row: P1[6:1], ☆K3 tog, yfwd, (K2 tog, yfwd) twice, K1 tbl, yfwd, K1, yfwd, K1 tbl, (yfwd, sl 1, K1, psso) twice, yfwd, K3 tog tbl, P3, K7, P3, rep from ☆ to last 18[23:18] sts, K3 tog, yfwd, (K2 tog, yfwd) twice, K1 tbl, yfwd, K1, yfwd, K1 tbl, (yfwd, sl 1, K1, psso) twice, yfwd, K3 tog tbl, P1[6:1].

26th row: K1[6:1], ☆P17, K3, P7, K3, rep from ☆ to last 18[23:18] sts, P17, K to end.

27th row: P2[7:2], ☆(K2 tog, yfwd) 3 times, K1 tbl, K1, K1 tbl, (yfwd, sl 1, K1, psso) 3 times, P4, C7B, P4, rep from ☆ to last 17[22:17] sts, (K2 tog, yfwd) 3 times, K1 tbl, K1, K1 tbl, (yfwd, sl 1, K1, psso) 3 times, P2[7:2].

28th row: K2[7:2], ☆P15, K4, P7, K4, rep from ☆ to last 17[22:17] sts, P15, K2[7:2].

29th row: P3[8:3], ☆(K2 tog, yfwd) twice, K1 tbl, K3, K1 tbl, (yfwd, sl 1, K1, psso) twice, P5, K7, P5, rep from ☆ to last 16[21:16] sts, (K2 tog, yfwd) twice, K1 tbl, K3, K1 tbl, (yfwd, sl 1, K1, psso) twice, P3[8:3].

30th row: As 24th row.

31st row: P4[9:4], ☆K2 tog, yfwd, K1 tbl, K5, K1 tbl, yfwd, sl 1, K1, psso, P6, K7, P6, rep from ☆ to last 15[20:15] sts, K2 tog, yfwd, K1 tbl, K5, K1 tbl, yfwd, sl 1, K1, psso, P4[9:4].

32nd row: As 22nd row.

These 32 rows form the patt.

Rep these 32 rows twice more, then work 1st–6th rows again.

Shape armholes

Cast off 10 sts at beg of next 2 rows. 119[129:149] sts.

Next row: P6[11:6], ☆K3 tog, yfwd, (K2 tog, yfwd) twice, K1 tbl, yfwd, K1, yfwd, K1 tbl, (yfwd, sl 1, K1, psso) twice, yfwd, K3 tog tbl, P3, K7, P3, rep from ☆ to last 23[28:23] sts, K3 tog, yfwd, (K2 tog, yfwd) twice, K1 tbl, yfwd, K1, yfwd, K1 tbl, (yfwd, sl 1, K1, psso) twice, yfwd, K3 tog tbl, P6[11:6]. ☆☆

Cont in this way with patt as set, working edge sts in rev st st until the 32 patt rows have been completed 5 times in all, then work 1st–14th rows again.

Shape shoulders

Cast off 36[41:51] sts at beg of next 2 rows. Leave rem 47 sts on a spare needle.

FRONT

Work as given for back from ☆☆ to ☆☆.

Divide for neck

Next row: (WS) Patt 59[64:74] sts and turn, leaving rem sts on a spare needle.

Complete right side of neck first.

Dec 1 st at neck edge on next and every foll 3rd row until 36[41:51] sts rem.

Cont without further shaping until work matches back to shoulder, ending with same patt row at armhole edge.

Shape shoulder

Cast off rem sts.

With WS of work facing return to sts on spare needle. Sl centre st onto a safety pin, rejoin yarn at neck edge, patt to end. Complete to match first side of neck, reversing all shapings.

SLEEVES

Using 3¼mm (US3) needles, cast on 50 sts.

Work in K2, P2 rib as given for back for 8cm, 3ins ending with a 1st row.

Inc row: Rib 6, ☆inc in next st, rep from ☆ to last 7 sts, rib to end. 87 sts.

Change to 4mm (US6) needles and commence patt as given for back as foll:

1st row: (RS) P10, ☆K7, P8, rep from ☆ to last 17 sts, K7, P10.

This row establishes the patt, cont in patt inc 1 st at each end of 2nd and every foll 4th row until there are 121 sts working extra sts in rev st st.

Cont without further shaping until work measures 47[49:51]cm, 18½[19¼:20]ins from beg, ending with a WS row. Cast off fairly loosely.

TO MAKE UP/TO FINISH

Join right shoulder seam.

NECKBAND

With RS of work facing, using 3¼mm (US3) circular needle, K up 70 sts down left side of neck, K 1 st from safety pin and mark this st with a coloured thread, K up 71 sts up right side of neck, then K across 47 sts on back neck. 189 sts.

Work in rows.

1st row: (WS) ☆P2, K2, rep from ☆ to within 2 sts of marked st, P2 tog, P1, P2 tog tbl, work in rib to end.

2nd row: Work in rib to within 2 sts of marked st, sl 1, K1, psso, K1, K2 tog, work in rib to end.

Rep these 2 rows twice more, then the 1st row again.

Cast off in rib, dec on this row as before.

Join left shoulder and neckband seam.

Set in sleeves, placing centre of cast off edge to shoulder seams and sewing final rows to cast off sts at underarm. Join side and sleeve seams.

RIBBED SKIRT

Sizes

To fit hips 86[91:97:102]cm, 34[36:38:40]ins

Length to waistband 74cm, 29¼ins

Materials

11[11:12:12] × 50g balls of double knitting yarn

One pair 3¼mm (US3) knitting needles 3¾mm (US5) and 4mm (US6) circular needles

2.5cm, 1in wide elastic for waistband

Tension/Gauge

32 sts and 28 rows to 10cm, 4ins over rib slightly stretched using 4mm (US6) needles

BACK

Using 4mm (US6) circular needle, cast

BLACKBERRY *Lady's Sweater*

on 153[163:173:183] sts.

Work in rows in rib as foll:

1st row: (RS) K3, ☆P2, K3, rep from ☆ to end.

2nd row: K1, P2, ☆K2, P3, rep from ☆ to last 5 sts, K2, P2, K1.

These 2 rows form the rib.

Cont in rib until work measures 56cm, 22ins from beg, ending with a WS row.

Change to 3¾mm (US5) circular needle and cont in rib until work measures 61cm, 24ins from beg, ending with a WS row.

Commence shaping.

Next row: K3, ☆P2 tog, K3, rep from ☆ to end. 123[131:139:147] sts.

Next row: K1, P2, ☆K1, P3, rep from ☆ to last 4 sts, K1, P2, K1.

Next row: K3, ☆P1, K3, rep from ☆ to end.

Rep the last 2 rows until work measures 66cm, 26ins, from beg, ending with a WS row.

Next row: K3, ☆K2 tog, K2, rep from ☆ to end. 93[99:105:111] sts.

Beg with a P row, cont in st st until work measures 74cm, 29¼ins from beg, ending with a K row.

Dec row: P11[10:13:13], ☆P2 tog, P8[9:9:10], rep from ☆ to last 12[12:15:14] sts, P2 tog, P to end. 85[91:97:103] sts.

Change to 3¼mm (US3) needles.

Cont in waist rib as foll:

1st row: K2, ☆P1, K1, rep from ☆ to last st, K1.

2nd row: K1, ☆P1, K1, rep from ☆ to end.

Rep these 2 rows 3 times more. Cast off very loosely in rib.

FRONT

Work as given for back.

TO MAKE UP/TO FINISH

Join side seams. Cut elastic to fit waist, join in a ring. Attach to WS of waist rib using a herringbone casing.

Sizes

To fit bust 81[86:91:97]cm, 32[34:36:38]ins

Actual bust 100[105:111:116.5]cm, 39½[41¼:43¾:45¾]ins

Length 60cm, 23¾ins

Sleeve seam 44cm, 17¼ins

Materials

6[7:7:8] × 50g balls of Argyll Chameleon

One pair each 3¾mm (US5) and 5mm (US8) knitting needles

Tension/Gauge

24 sts and 24 rows to 11cm, 4¼ins over patt using 5mm (US8) needles

BACK

Using 3¾mm (US5) needles, cast on 83[87:91:97] sts.

Cont in K1, P1 rib as foll:

1st row: (RS) K1, ☆P1, K1, rep from ☆ to end.

2nd row: P1, ☆K1, P1, rep from ☆ to end.

Rep these 2 rows for 8cm, 3ins ending with a 1st row.

Inc row: Rib 3[2:1:4], inc in next st, ☆rib 2, inc in next st, rep from ☆ to last 4[3:2:5] sts, rib to end. 109[115:121:127] sts.

Change to 5mm (US8) needles.

Commence patt.

1st row: (RS) P3, ☆K1, P5, rep from ☆ to last 4 sts, K1, P3.

2nd row: K3 tog, ☆yfwd, (K1, yfwd, K1) all into next st, yfwd, K2 tog tbl, K3 tog, pass 2nd st on right hand needle over last st, rep from ☆ to last 4 sts, yfwd, (K1, yfwd, K1) all into next st, yfwd, K3 tog tbl.

3rd row: K1, ☆P5, K1, rep from ☆ to end.

4th row: P1, ☆K5, P1, rep from ☆ to end.

5th row: As 3rd row.

6th row: K into front and back of first st, ☆yfwd, K2 tog tbl, K3 tog, pass 2nd st on right hand needle over last st, yfwd, (K1, yfwd, K1) all into next st, rep from ☆ to last 6 sts, yfwd, K2 tog tbl, K3 tog, pass 2nd st on right hand needle over last st, yfwd, K into front and back of last st.

7th row: As 1st.

8th row: K3, ☆P1, K5, rep from ☆ to last 4 sts, P1, K3.

These 8 rows form the patt.

Cont in patt until work measures approximately 30cm, 11¾ins from beg, ending with a 4th or 8th patt row.

Shape armholes

Cast off 12 sts at beg of next 2 rows. 85[91:97:103] sts.

Cont in patt until work measures approximately 60cm, 23¾ins from beg, ending with a 4th or 8th patt row.

Cast off loosely.

FRONT

Work as given for back.

SLEEVES

Using 3¾mm (US5) needles, cast on 37 sts.

Work in K1, P1 rib as given for back for 6cm, 2½ins ending with a 1st row.

Inc row: ☆K twice into next st, rep from ☆ to end. 74 sts.

Change to 5mm (US8) needles.

Beg with a P row, cont in rev st st inc 1st at each end of 3rd and every foll 4th row until there are 98 sts. Now inc 1 st at each end of every foll alt row until there are 120 sts.

Cont without shaping until work measures 44cm, 17¼ins from beg, ending with a K row.

Mark each end of last row to denote underarm.

Beg with a K row, cont in st st until work measures 5.5cm, 2¼ins from markers, ending with a P row.

Cast off loosely.

TO MAKE UP/TO FINISH

Do not press.

Join shoulder seams for 11[12:12:13]cm,

BLACKBERRY

HAZEL NUTS and ACORNS

$4\frac{1}{4}[4\frac{3}{4}:4\frac{3}{4}:5\frac{1}{4}]$ins, leaving centre open for neck. Placing centre of cast off edge to shoulder seam, set in sleeves, joining rows after marker to cast off sts at underarm. Join side and sleeve seams.

HAZEL NUTS AND ACORNS

Lady's Sweater

Sizes

To fit bust 76 – 81[86 – 91:97 – 102:107 – 112)cm, 30 – 32[34 – 36:38 – 40:42 – 44]ins
Actual bust 93[102:111:120]cm, $36\frac{3}{4}[40:43\frac{3}{4}:47\frac{1}{4}]$ins
Length 62[64:66:68]cm, $24\frac{1}{2}[25\frac{1}{4}:26:26\frac{3}{4}]$ins
Sleeve seam 47[48:49:50]cm, $18\frac{1}{2}[19:19\frac{1}{4}:19\frac{3}{4}]$ins

Materials

18[19:20:21] × 50g balls of Sunbeam Aran Tweed
One pair each 4mm (US6) and 5mm (US8) knitting needles
Cable needle

Tension/Gauge

18 sts and 24 rows to 10cm, 4ins over st st using 5mm (US8) needles

PATT PANEL A

(worked over 10 sts)
1st row: (WS) K2, P6, K2.
2nd row: P2, K6, P2.
3rd row: K2, P2, keeping yarn at front, sl 2 P-wise, P2, K2.
4th row: P2, sl next 2 sts onto cable needle and hold at back of work, K1 then K2 from cable needle – called Cr3R, sl next st onto cable needle and hold at front of work, K2 then K1 from cable needle – called Cr3L, P2.
5th–8th rows: Rep 3rd–4th rows twice.
9th–12th rows: Rep 1st–2nd rows twice.
These 12 rows form patt panel A.

PATT PANEL B

(worked over 9 sts)
1st row: (WS) K4, P1, K4.
2nd row: P4, yon, K1, yrn, P4.
3rd row: K4, P3, K4.
4th row: P4, K1, yfwd, K1, yfwd, K1, P4.
5th row: K4, P5, K4.
6th row: P4, K2, yfwd, K1, yfwd, K2, P4.
7th row: K4, P7, K4.
8th row: P4, K1, sl 1, K1, psso, yfwd, K1, yfwd, K3, P4.
9th row: K4, P8, K4.
10th row: P4, K1, sl 1, K1, psso, K5, P4.
11th row: K4, P7, K4.
12th row: P4, K1, sl 1, K1, psso, K4, P4.
13th row: K4, P6, K4.
14th row: P4, K1, sl 1, K1, psso, K3, P4.
15th row: K4, P5, K4.
16th row: P4, K1, sl 1, K1, psso, K2, P4.
17th row: K4, P4, K4.
18th row: P4, K1, sl 1, K1, psso, K1, P4.
19th row: K4, P3, K4.
20th row: P4, K1, sl 1, K1, psso, P4.
21st row: K4, P2, K4.
22nd row: P4, K2 tog, P4.
These 22 rows form patt panel B.

PATT PANEL C

(worked over 18 sts)
1st row: (WS) K8, P2, K8.
2nd row: P7, sl next st onto cable needle and hold at back of work, K1 then K1 from cable needle – called Cr2b(K), sl next st onto cable needle and hold at front of work, K1, then K1 from cable needle – called Cr2f(K), P7.
3rd row: K6, sl next st onto cable needle and hold at front of work, P1 then K1 from cable needle – called Cr2f(P), P2, sl next st onto cable needle and hold at back of work, K1 then P1 from cable needle – called Cr2b(P), K6.
4th row: P5, Cr2b(P), Cr2b(K), Cr2f(K), Cr2f(P), P5.
5th row: K4, Cr2f(P), K1, P4, K1, Cr2b(P), K4.
6th row: P3, Cr2b(P), P1, Cr2b(P), K2, Cr2f(P), P1, Cr2f(P), P3.
7th row: K1, (K2, P1) twice, K1, P2, K1, (P1, K2) twice, K1.
8th row: P3, (K1, P1) twice into next st, turn P4, turn K4, turn P2 tog twice, turn K2 tog – called MB, P1, Cr2b(P), P1, K2, P1, Cr2f(P), P1, MB, P3.
9th row: K5, P1, K2, P2, K2, P1, K5.
10th row: P5, MB, P2, K2, P2, MB, P5.
These 10 rows form patt panel C.

BACK

☆☆Using 4mm (US6) needles, cast on 102[112:117:127] sts.

Cont in cable rib as foll:

1st row: (RS) ☆P3, insert needle from back of work through 1st and 2nd sts on left hand needle, K 2nd st, K 1st st and sl both from needle tog, rep from ☆ to last 2 sts, P2.

2nd row: ☆K3, P 2nd st on left hand needle, then P 1st st and sl both from needle tog, rep from ☆ to last 2sts, K2.

Rep these 2 rows for 10cm, 4ins, ending with a WS row.

Inc row: K to end, inc 2[0:3:1] sts evenly. 104[112:120:128] sts.

Change to 5mm (US8) needles and commence patt.

1st row: (WS) (K1, P1) 3[5:7:9] times, P2, work 1st row patt panel A, P2, work 1st row patt panel B, P2, work 1st row patt panel A, P2, work 1st row patt panel C, P2, work 1st row patt panel A, P2, work 1st row patt panel B, P2, work 1st row patt panel A, P2, (P1, K1) 3[5:7:9] times.

2nd row: (P1, K1) 3[5:7:9] times, K 2nd st on left hand needle, then K 1st st and sl both off needle tog – called Tw2, work 2nd row patt panel A, Tw2, work 2nd row patt panel B, Tw2, work 2nd row patt panel A, Tw2, work 2nd row patt panel C, Tw2, work 2nd row patt panel A, Tw2, work 2nd row patt panel B, Tw2, work 2nd row patt panel A, Tw2, (K1, P1) 3[5:7:9] times.

3rd row: (P1, K1) 3[5:7:9] times, P2, work 3rd row patt panel A, P2, work 3rd row patt panel B, P2, work 3rd row patt panel A, P2, work 3rd row patt panel C, P2, work 3rd row patt panel A, P2, work 3rd row patt panel B, P2, work 3rd row patt panel A, P2, (K1, P1) 3[5:7:9] times.

4th row: (K1, P1) 3[5:7:9] times, Tw2, work 4th row patt panel A, P2, work 4th row patt panel B, Tw2, work 4th row patt panel A, Tw2, work 4th row patt panel C, Tw2, work 4th row patt panel A, Tw2, work 4th row patt panel B, Tw2, work 4th row patt panel A, Tw2, (P1, K1) 3[5:7:9] times.

These 4 rows establish the patt, placing the patt panels and setting the twists and moss st edge sts. ☆☆

Cont in patt until work measures 62[64:66:68]cm, 24½[25¼:26:26¾]ins from beg, ending with a WS row.

Shape shoulders

Cast off 33[37:41:45] sts at beg of next 2 rows.

Leave rem 38 sts on a holder.

FRONT

Work as given for back from ☆☆ to ☆☆.

Cont in patt until work measures 56[58:60:62]cm, 22[22¾:23¾:24½]ins, from beg, ending with a WS row.

Shape neck

Next row: Patt 44[48:52:56] sts and turn, leaving rem sts on a spare needle.

Complete left side of neck first.

Cast off 4 sts at beg of next row and 3 sts at beg of foll alt row, then 2 sts at beg of next alt row. Dec 1 st at beg of foll 2 alt rows. 33[37:41:45] sts.

Cont without shaping until work matches back to shoulder, ending at armhole edge.

Shape shoulder

Cast off rem sts.

With RS of work facing, sl centre 16 sts onto a holder, rejoin yarn at neck edge and patt to end.

Patt 1 row. Complete as given for left side of neck.

SLEEVES

Using 4mm (US6) needles, cast on 42 sts. Cont in cable rib as given for back for 8cm, 3ins, ending with a WS row.

Inc row: K11[9:7:5], ☆K twice into next st, rep from ☆ to last 11[9:7:5] sts, K to end. 62[66:70:74] sts.

Change to 5mm (US8) needles and commence patt.

1st row: (WS) (K1, P1) 4[5:6:7] times, P2, work 1st row patt panel A, P2, work 1st row patt panel C, P2, work 1st row patt panel A, P2, (P1, K1) 4[5:6:7] times.

2nd row: (P1, K1) 4[5:6:7] times, Tw2, work 2nd row patt panel A, Tw2, work 2nd row patt panel C, Tw2, work 1st row patt panel A, Tw2, (K1, P1) 4[5:6:7] times.

These 2 rows form the twist patt, setting the patt panels with edge sts in moss st.

Cont in patt *at the same time*, inc and work into moss st 1 st at each end of 8th and every foll 7th row until there are 86[90:94:98] sts.

Cont without further shaping until work measures 47[48:49:50]cm, 18½[19:19¼:19¾]ins from beg, ending with a WS row.

Cast off fairly loosely.

TO MAKE UP/TO FINISH

Join right shoulder seam.

NECKBAND

With RS of work facing, using 4mm (US6) needles, K up 21 sts down left side of neck, K across 16 sts at centre front, K up 22 sts up right side of neck then K across 38 sts of back neck. 97 sts.

Beg with 2nd row work in cable rib as given for back for 5cm, 2ins, ending with a 2nd row.

Cast off in patt.

Join left shoulder and neckband seam. Fold neckband in half onto WS and slip stitch down.

Placing centre of cast off edge of sleeves to shoulder seams, set in sleeves.

Join side and sleeve seams.

YELLOW-HAMMERS

Child's Sweater

Sizes

To fit chest 56 – 61[61 – 66]cm, 22 – 24[24 – 26]ins

Actual chest 63[71]cm, 24¾[28]ins

Length 35[40]cm, 13¾[15¾]ins

Sleeve seam 28[32]cm, 11[12½]ins

Materials

2[2] × 50g balls of Poppletons Emmerdale DK in main colour (A)

cont'd page 104

YELLOW-HAMMERS

AUTUMN LEAVES

1[2] balls in contrast colour (B)
1 ball each in contrast colours (C and D)
One pair each 3¼mm (US3) and 4mm (US6) knitting needles

Tension/Gauge
25 sts and 26 rows to 10cm, 4ins over patt using 4mm (US6) needles

BACK
Using 3¼mm (US3) needles, cast on 67[77] sts.
Cont in K1, P1 rib as foll:
1st row: (RS) K1, ☆P1, K1, rep from ☆ to end.
2nd row: P1, ☆K1, P1, rep from ☆ to end.
Rep these 2 rows for 5cm, 2ins ending with a 1st row.
Inc row: Rib 6[5], ☆inc in next st, rib 4[5], rep from ☆ to last 6 sts, inc in next st, rib to end. 79[89] sts.
Change to 4mm (US6) needles.
Beg with a K row, cont in st st working colour patt from chart. Read odd numbered rows (K) from right to left and even numbered rows (P) from left to right. Strand yarn not in use loosely across WS of work. Cont in patt until work measures 22[25]cm, 8¾[9¾]ins from beg, ending with a P row.
Shape armholes
Cast off 10 sts at beg of next 2 rows. 59[69] sts.
Cont without further shaping until work measures 35[40]cm, 13¾[15¾]ins from beg, ending with a P row.
Shape shoulders
Cast off 16[19] sts at beg of next 2 rows.
Leave rem 27[31] sts on a spare needle.

FRONT
Work as given for back until 12[16] rows less than back to shoulder shaping have been worked, ending with a P row.
Shape neck
Next row: Patt 23[26] and turn, leaving rem sts on a spare needle.
Complete left side of neck first.
Dec 1 st at neck edge on every row until 16[19] sts rem.
Cont without further shaping until work measures same as back to shoulder shaping, ending at armhole edge.
Shape shoulder
Cast off rem sts.
With RS of work facing, return to sts on spare needle, sl centre 13[17] sts onto a holder, rejoin yarn to next st and patt to end.
Complete as given for first side of neck.

SLEEVES
Using 3¼mm (US3) needles, cast on 35[39] sts.
Cont in K1, P1 rib as given for back for 5cm, 2ins ending with a 1st row.
Inc row: Rib 4[0], ☆inc in next st, rib 1, rep from ☆ to last 5[1] sts, inc in next st, rib 4[0]. 49[59] sts.
Change to 4mm (US6) needles.
Beg with a K row, cont in st st working colour patt from chart. Inc and work into patt 1 st at each end of 3rd and every foll 6th row until there are 65[75] sts.
Cont without further shaping until work measures 28[32]cm, 11[12½]ins from beg, ending with a P row.
Patt 10 more rows. Cast off loosely.

TO MAKE UP/TO FINISH
Join right shoulder seam.

NECKBAND
With RS of work facing, using 3¼mm (US3) needles and A, K up 16[18] sts down left side of neck, K13[17] sts at centre front, K up 15[17] sts up right side of neck then K across 27[31] sts on back neck. 71[83] sts.
Beg with a 2nd row, cont in K1, P1 rib as given for back for 5cm, 2ins.
Cast off loosely in rib.

Fold neckband in half onto WS and slip stitch in place. Placing centre of cast off edge of sleeves to shoulder seam and sewing final rows to cast off sts at underarm, set in sleeves. Join side and sleeve seams.

Key
A □
B ×
C /
D ○

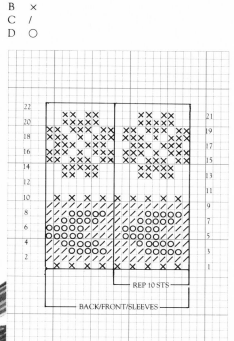

Autumn Leaves *Lady's Mohair Jacket*

Sizes
To fit bust 76 – 81[86 – 91:97 – 102]cm,
30 – 32[34 – 36:38 – 40]ins
Actual bust 99[109:119]cm, 39[43:47]ins
Length 58.5, 23ins
Sleeve seam 41cm, 16ins

Materials
9[10:11] × 50g balls of Patons Mohair in
main colour (A)
1 × 50g ball of Patons Beehive DK in
each of contrast colours (B, C and D)
Oddment (odds and ends) for embroidery
(E)
One pair each 4mm (US6) and 5½mm
(US9) knitting needles
3.50mm (USE/4) crochet hook
8 buttons
Pair of shoulder pads

Tension/Gauge
16 sts and 22 rows to 10cm, 4ins over st st
using 5½mm (US9) needles

BACK
Using 4mm (US6) needles and A, cast
on 70[78:86] sts.
Cont in K1, P1 rib for 8cm, 3ins ending
with a RS row.
Inc row: P3[7:11], inc in next st, ☆P8,
inc in next st, rep from ☆ to last 3[7:11]
sts, P to end. 78[86:94] sts.
Change to 5½mm (US9) needles. Beg
with a K row cont in st st until work
measures 34cm, 13½ins from beg, ending
with a P row.
Shape armholes
Cast off 3 sts at beg of next 2 rows and 2
sts at beg of foll 4 rows.
Dec 1 st at each end of next and every foll
10th row until 56[64:72] sts rem.
Cont without further shaping until work

measures 58.5cm, 23ins from beg, ending
with a P row.
Shape shoulders
Cast off 5[6:7] sts at beg of next 4 rows.
Shape back neck
Next row: Cast off 4[5:6] sts, work to
end.
Next row: Cast off 4[5:6], work 4[5:6] sts
including st used to cast off and turn
leaving rem sts on a spare needle.
Complete left side of neck first.
Next row: Work to end.
Cast off rem 4[5:6] sts.
With WS of work facing, return to sts on
spare needle, rejoin yarn, cast off centre
20 sts, work to end.
Cast off rem 4[5:6] sts.

LEFT FRONT
Using 4mm (US6) needles and A, cast
on 34[38:42] sts.
Cont in K1, P1 rib for 8cm, 3ins ending
with a RS row.
Inc row: P8[8:9], inc in next st,
☆P5[6:7], inc in next st, rep from ☆ to
last 7[8:8] sts, P to end. 38[42:46] sts.
Change to 5½mm (US9) needles. Beg
with a K row cont in st st until work
measures 34cm, 13½ins from beg, ending
with a P row.
Shape armhole
Cast off 3 sts at beg of next row and 2 sts
at beg of 2 foll alt rows.
Dec 1 st at armhole edge on next and
every foll 10th row until 27[31:35] sts
rem.
Cont without further shaping until work
measures 53cm, 21ins from beg, ending
with a K row.
Shape neck
Cast off 5 sts at beg of next row and 2 sts
at beg of 2 foll alt rows. 18[22:26] sts.
Cont without further shaping until work
measures same as back to shoulder
shaping, ending with a P row.
Shape shoulder
Cast off 5[6:7] sts at beg of next and foll
alt row, then 4[5:6] sts at beg of next alt
row. Work 1 row. Cast off rem 4[5:6] sts.

RIGHT FRONT
Work as given for left front, reversing all
shapings.

SLEEVES
Using 4mm (US6) needles and A, cast
on 34 sts.
Cont in K1, P1 rib for 8cm, 3ins ending
with a RS row.

Inc row: P to end, working twice into
every st. 68 sts.
Change to 5½mm (US9) needles. Beg
with a K row cont in st st inc 1 st at each
end of 5th and every foll 6th row until
there are 88 sts.
Cont without further shaping until work
measures 41cm, 16ins from beg, ending
with a P row.
Shape sleeve top
Cast off 3 sts at beg of next 2 rows. Dec 1
st at each end of next and 3 foll alt rows
then at each end of every foll 4th row
until 68 sts rem. Dec 1 st at each end of 2
foll alt rows. Work 1 row. Cast off 4 sts at
beg of foll 4 rows. Work 1 row. Cast off
rem 48 sts.

BUTTONBAND
Using 4mm (US6) needles and A, cast
on 8 sts.
Cont in K1, P1 rib until band is long
enough, when slightly stretched, to fit up
left front to neck, ending at inner neck
edge. Cut yarn and leave sts on a safety
pin.

TO MAKE UP/TO FINISH
Sew on button band. Mark the position
of 8 buttons. The first 2cm, ¾in above
cast on edge, the last 2 rows below neck
edge, with the other 6 evenly spaced
between.

BUTTONHOLE BAND
Work as given for buttonband but end at
outer neck edge, do not cut yarn and
make buttonholes opposite markers as
foll:
1st row: (RS) Rib 2, cast off 4, rib to end.
2nd row: Rib to end, casting on 4 sts over
those cast off in previous row.

Sew on buttonhole band. Join shoulder
seams.

NECKBAND
With RS of work facing, using 4mm
(US6) needles and A, rib across 8 sts of
buttonhole band, K up 58 sts evenly
around neck edge, rib across 8 sts on
buttonband. 74 sts.
Cont in K1, P1 rib for 4cm, 1½ins. Cast
off very loosely in rib.

Fold neckband in half onto WS and
catch down. Set in sleeves, gathering top
over shoulder section. Join side and
sleeve seams. Sew on buttons.

CROCHET INSTRUCTIONS
LEAVES (make 8)
Upper part
Using 3.50mm (USE/4) crochet hook and B, make 12 ch.
Foundation row: Work 1 dc (sc) into 3rd ch from hook, ☆2 dc (sc) into next ch, 1 dc (sc) into next ch, rep from ☆ to last ch, 2 dc (sc) in last ch, turn.
Next row: 2 ch, 1 dc (sc) into each dc (sc) to end, 1 dc (sc) in 2nd of 2 ch.
Cut yarn and fasten off.
Centre part
Using 3.50mm (USE/4) crochet hook and B, make 13 ch.
Foundation row: Work 1 tr(dc) into 4th ch from hook, ☆2 tr(dc) into next ch, 1 tr(dc) into next ch, rep from ☆ to last ch, 2 tr(dc) into last ch, turn.
Next row: 3 ch, miss 1st tr, 1 tr(dc) into each tr(dc) to end, 1 tr(dc) in 3rd of 3 ch.
Cut yarn and fasten off.
Lower part
Using 3.50mm (USE/4) crochet hook and B, make 9 ch.
Foundation row: Work 1 tr(dc) into 4th ch from hook, 1 tr(dc) into each ch to end, turn.
Next row: 1 ch, ss into each tr(dc) to end, ss into 3rd of 3 ch.
Cut yarn and fasten off.
These 3 parts make 1 leaf.
Make 8 more leaves in C and 8 in D.
Sew the 3 parts of each leaf together, joining the fastened off ends then catching the long edges to form the flat leaf shape.
Using E embroider in chain stitch 'a stem' on each front and sleeve top with 'twigs' for 5 leaves on each sleeve and 7 on each front. Sew leaves to ends of 'twigs'.
Sew in shoulder pads.

CRIMSON TOADSTOOLS

Children's Sweater and Cardigan

Sizes
To fit chest/bust 51 – 56[61 – 66:71 – 76:81 – 86]cm, 20 – 22[24 – 26:28 – 30:32 – 34]ins
Actual chest/bust 64[72.5:81:89]cm, 25¼[29½:32:35]ins
Length 36[40:44:50]cm, 14¼[15¾:17¼:19¾]ins
Sleeve seam 28[31:38:42]cm, 11[12¼:15:16½]ins

Materials
CARDIGAN
2[2:3:3] × 50g balls of Sunbeam Paris Mohair in main colour (A)
1[1:1:1] ball each in contrast colours (B, C, D, E and F)

SWEATER
1[1:2:2] × 50g balls of Sunbeam Paris Mohair in main colour (A)
2[2:2:2] balls in contrast colour (B)
1[1:1:1] ball each in contrast colours (C, D, E and F)

One pair each 4½mm (US7) and 5½mm (US9) knitting needles
6 'Pikaby' buttons for cardigan *or*

CARDIGAN
4[4:5:5] × 25g balls of Sunbeam Sumatra in main colour (A)
2[2:2:2] balls each in contrast colours (B and C)
1[1:1:1] ball each in contrast colours, (D, E and F)

SWEATER
2[2:3:3] × 25g balls of Sunbeam Sumatra in main colour (A)
3[3:3:3] balls in contrast colour (B)
2[2:2:2] balls in contrast colour (C)
1[1:1:1] ball each in contrast colours (D, E and F)

One pair each 4mm (US6) and 5mm (US8) knitting needles
6 'Pikaby' buttons for cardigan

Tension/Gauge
19 sts and 19 rows to 10cm, 4ins over patt using 5½mm (US9) needles and Paris Mohair OR 5mm (US8) needles and Sumatra

CARDIGAN
BACK
Using smaller needles and A, cast on 51[57:63:69] sts.
☆☆Cont in K1, P1 rib as foll:
1st row: (RS) K1, ☆P1, K1, rep from ☆ to end.
2nd row: P1, ☆K1, P1, rep from ☆ to end.
Rep these 2 rows for 6cm, 2½ins ending with a 1st row.
Inc row: Rib 7[6:5:4], ☆inc in next st, rib 3, rep from ☆ to last 8[7:6:5] sts, inc in next st, rib to end. 61[69:77:85] sts.
Change to larger needles and beg with a K row cont in st st working patt from chart. Read odd numbered rows (K) from

right to left and even numbered rows (P) from left to right. Strand yarn not in use loosely across back of work.
Cont in patt until work measures 20.5[23:24:27] cm, 8¼[9:9½:10¾]ins from beg, ending with a WS row.
Shape armholes
Cast off 8 sts at beg of next 2 rows. 45[53:61:69] sts. ☆☆
Cont without further shaping until work measures 36[40:44:50]cm, 14¼[15¾:17¼:19¾]ins from beg, ending with a WS row.
Shape shoulders
Cast off 9[13:17:21] sts at beg of next 2 rows. Leave rem 27 sts on a spare needle.

LEFT FRONT
Using smaller needles and A, cast on 31[33:37:39] sts.
Work in K1, P1 rib as given for back for 6cm, 2½ins ending with a 1st row.
Next row: Rib 6 and sl sts onto a safety pin, rib 5[6:5:6], ☆inc in next st, rib 4[2:3:2], rep from ☆ to last 5[6:6:6] sts, inc in next st, rib to end. 29[33:37:41] sts.
Change to larger needles and beg with a K row cont in st st working patt from chart.
Cont in patt until work measures 20.5[23:24:27]cm, 8¼[9:9½:10¾]ins from beg, ending with a WS row.
Shape armhole
Cast off 8 sts at beg of next row. 21[25:29:33] sts.
Cont without further shaping until work measures 30[34:38:44]cm, 11¾[13½:15:17¼]ins from beg, ending with a RS row.
Shape neck
Cast off 4 sts at beg of next row, 3 sts at beg of foll alt row and 2 sts at beg of next 2 alt rows. Dec 1 st at neck edge on foll alt row. 9[13:17:21] sts.
Cont without further shaping until work matches back to shoulder, ending with a WS row.
Shape shoulder
Cast off rem sts.

RIGHT FRONT
Using smaller needles and A, cast on 31[33:37:39] sts.
Work 2 rows in K1, P1 rib as given for back.
1st buttonhole row: Rib 2, cast off 2, rib to end.

CRIMSON TOADSTOOLS

2nd buttonhole row: Rib to end, casting on 2 sts over those cast off in previous row.

Cont in rib until work measures 6cm, 2½ins ending with a 1st row.

Next row: Rib 4[5:5:5], ☆inc in next st, rib 4[2:3:2], rep from ☆ to last 12[13:12:13] sts, inc in last st, rib 5[6:5:6] turn and leave rem 6 sts on a safety pin. 29[33:37:41] sts.

Complete to match left front, reversing all shapings.

SLEEVES

Using smaller needles and A, cast on 35[37:39:41] sts.

Work in K1, P1 rib as given for back for 6cm, 2½ins, ending with a 1st row.

Inc row: Rib 4[3:2:11], ☆inc in next st, rib 1[1:1:0], rep from ☆ to last 5[4:3:11] sts, inc in next st, rib to end. 49[53:57:61] sts.

Change to larger needles and beg with a K row cont in st st working patt from chart. Inc and work into patt 1 st at each end of 5th and every foll 8th[6th:5th:4th] row until there are 57[65:77:85] sts. Cont without further shaping until work measures 32[35:42:46]cm, 12½[13¾: 16½:18¼]ins from beg, ending with a WS row. Cast off loosely.

BUTTONBAND

With RS of work facing, rejoin A to sts on safety pin on left front.

Using smaller needles cont in K1, P1 rib until band, when slightly stretched, fits up front edge to neck shaping, ending at inner neck edge. Cut yarn and leave sts on safety pin.

Mark the positions of 4 buttons on this band, evenly spaced between one worked in welt and another to be worked on neckband.

BUTTONHOLE BAND

With WS of work facing, rejoin A to sts on safety pin on right front.

Using smaller needles cont in K1, P1 rib until band, when slightly stretched, fits up front edge to neck shaping, ending at outer edge without cutting yarn, *at the same time*, making buttonholes opposite markers as foll:

1st buttonhole row: (RS) Rib 2, cast off 2, rib to end.

2nd buttonhole row: Rib to end, casting on 2 sts over those cast off in previous row.

TO MAKE UP/TO FINISH

Join shoulder seams. Sew on button and buttonhole bands.

NECKBAND

With RS of work facing, using smaller needles and A, rib across 6 sts of buttonhole band, K up 18 sts up right front neck, K across 27 sts on back neck, K up 18 sts down left front neck, then rib across 6 sts on buttonband. 75 sts.

Beg with a 2nd row, work 1 row rib as given for back.

Rep 1st and 2nd buttonhole rows as given for front band.

Work 4 rows rib.

Rep 1st and 2nd buttonhole rows as given for front band.

Work 2 rows rib. Cast off very loosely in rib.

Fold neckband in half onto WS and catch down, oversewing around buttonhole.

Placing centre of cast off edge of sleeve to shoulder seams, set in sleeves joining final rows to cast off sts at underarm.

Join side and sleeve seams. Sew on buttons.

SWEATER
BACK

Using smaller needles and B, cast on 51[57:63:69] sts.

Complete as given for back of cardigan.

FRONT

Using smaller needles and B, cast on 51[57:63:69] sts.

Work as given for back of cardigan from ☆☆ to ☆☆.

Cont without further shaping until work measures 30[34:38:44]cm, 11¾[13½: 15:17¼]ins from beg, ending with a WS row.

Shape neck

Next row: Patt 17[21:25:29] sts and turn leaving rem sts on a spare needle.

Complete left side of neck first.

☆☆☆Cast off 3 sts at beg of next row and 2 sts at beg of foll 2 alt rows.

Dec 1 st at neck edge on foll alt row. 9[13:17:21] sts.

Cont without further shaping until work matches back to shoulder shaping,

ending at armhole edge.

Shape shoulder

Cast off rem sts.

With RS of work facing return to sts on spare needle. Sl centre 11 sts onto a holder, rejoin yarn at neck edge and patt to end.

Patt 1 row. Complete as given for first side of neck from ☆☆☆ to end.

SLEEVES

Using smaller needles and B, cast on 35[37:39:41] sts.

Complete as given for sleeves of cardigan.

TO MAKE UP/TO FINISH

Join right shoulder seam.

With RS of work facing, using smaller needles and B, K up 15 sts down left side of neck, K across 11 sts at centre front, K up 16 sts up right side of neck, then K across 27 sts on back neck. 69 sts.

Beg with a 2nd row, work 10 rows K1, P1 rib as given for back of cardigan.

Cast off very loosely in rib.

Fold neckband in half onto WS and catch down. Placing centre of cast off edge to shoulder seam, set in sleeves, joining final rows to cast off sts at underarm.

Join side and sleeve seams.

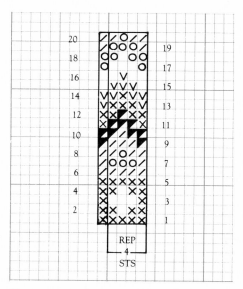

Key
A ×
B □
C ╱
D ○
E V
F ▶

Winter

SEED-VESSELS

SEED-VESSELS *Lady's Sweater and Waistcoat with Matching Hood and Mittens*

Sizes
To fit bust 81[86:91:97]cm, 32[34:36:38]ins
Sweater
Actual bust 97[102:108:113]cm, 38[40:42½:44½]ins
Length 66[67:68:69]cm, 26[26½:26¾:27¼]ins
Sleeve seam 45[45:46:46]cm, 17¾[17¾:18¼:18¼]ins
Waistcoat
Actual bust 104[109:115:120]cm, 41[43:45¼:47¼]ins
Length 70[71:72:73]cm, 27½[28:28¼:28¾]ins
Cowl
Length 50cm, 19¾ins
Mittens
To fit an average hand

Materials

Sweater
11[12:13:14] × 50g balls of Scotnord Wollspass

Waistcoat
9[10:10:11] × 50g balls of Scotnord Wollspass
4 'Pikaby' buttons

Mittens and Cowl
5 × 50g balls of Scotnord Wollspass

One pair each 3¼mm (US3), 3¾mm (US5) and 4mm (US6) knitting needles
3¼mm (US3) circular needle
Set of four 3¼mm (US3) double pointed needles
Cable needle

Tension/Gauge
22 sts and 30 rows to 10cm, 4ins over st st using 4mm (US6) needles
34 sts and 30 rows to 10cm, 4ins over cowl patt using 4mm (US6) needles

SWEATER

BACK
☆☆Using 3¼mm (US3) needles, cast on 86[92:98:104] sts.
Cont in K2, P2 rib as foll:
1st row: (RS) K2[1:2:1], P2[0:2:0], ☆K2, P2, rep from ☆ to last 2[3:2:3] sts, K2[3:2:3].
2nd row: P2[3:2:3], ☆K2, P2, rep from ☆ to last 4[1:4:1] sts, K2[0:2:0], P2[1:2:1].
Rep these 2 rows for 8cm, 3ins ending with a RS row.
Inc row: Rib 7[2:5:8], ☆inc in next st, rib

1[2:2:2], inc in next st, rib 2, rep from ☆ to last 4[0:3:6] sts, rib to end. 116[122:128:134] sts.
Change to 4mm (US6) needles and commence patt:
1st row: (RS) K20[22:23:25], ☆P2, K8, P2, K20[21:23:24], rep from ☆ to last 0[1:0:1] sts, K0[1:0:1].
2nd and every foll alt row: P20[22:23:25], ☆K2, P8, K2, P20[21:23:24], rep from ☆ to last 0[1:0:1] sts, P0[1:0:1].
3rd row: As 1st row.
5th row: K20[22:23:25], ☆P2, sl next 4 sts onto cable needle and hold at front of work, K4 then K4 from cable needle – called C8F, P2, K20[21:23:24], rep from ☆ to last 0[1:0:1] sts, K0[1:0:1].
7th–10th rows: Rep 1st and 2nd rows twice.
These 10 rows form the patt. Cont in patt until work measures 42cm, 16½ins from beg, ending with a WS row.
Shape armholes
Dec 1 st at each end of next 10 rows. 96[102:108:114] sts.☆☆
Cont without further shaping until work measures 66[67:68:69]cm, 26[26½: 26¾:27¼]ins from beg, ending with a WS row.
Shape shoulders
Cast off 14[15:16:17] sts at beg of next 4 rows. Leave rem 40[42:44:46] sts on a spare needle.

FRONT
Work as given for back from ☆☆ to ☆☆.
Cont without further shaping until work measures 58[59:60:61]cm, 22¾[23¼: 23¾:24]ins from beg, ending with a WS row.
Shape neck
Next row: Patt 38[40:42:44] sts and turn, leaving rem sts on a spare needle.
Complete left side of neck first.
Dec 1 st at neck edge on next 4 rows, then on every foll alt row until 28[30:32:34] sts rem.
Cont without further shaping until work measures same as back to shoulder shaping, ending at armhole edge.
Shape shoulder
Cast off 14[15:16:17] sts at beg of next row. Work 1 row. Cast off rem sts.
With RS of work facing, return to sts on spare needle. Sl centre 20[22:24:26] sts onto a holder, rejoin yarn and patt to end.
Complete to match first side of neck.

SLEEVES
Using 3¼mm (US3) needles, cast on 44[48:52:56] sts.
Cont in K2, P2 rib for 8cm, 3ins ending with a RS row.
Inc row: Rib 3[5:2:4], ☆inc in next st, rib 1, inc in next st, rib 1[1:2:2], rep from ☆ to last 1[3:0:2] sts, rib 1[3:0:2]. 64[68:72:76] sts.
Change to 4mm (US6) needles and commence patt:
1st row: (RS) K26[28:30:32], P2, K8, P2, K26[28:30:32].
2nd and every foll alt row: P26[28:30:32], K2, P8, K2, P26[28:30:32].
3rd row: As 1st row.
5th row: K26[28:30:32], P2, C8F, P2, K26[28:30:32].
7th–10th rows: Rep 1st and 2nd rows twice.
These 10 rows form the patt. Cont in patt, inc 1 st at each end of next and every foll 4th row until there are 108[112:116:120] sts, working inc sts in st st.
Cont without further shaping until work measures 45[45:46:46]cm, 17¾[17¾: 18¼:18¼]ins from beg, ending with a WS row.
Shape top
Dec 1 st at each end of next 10 rows. 88[92:96:100] sts.
Cast off.

TO MAKE UP/TO FINISH
Join right shoulder seam.

NECKBAND
Using 3¼mm (US3) needles, with RS of work facing, K up 22 sts down left side of neck, K across 20[22:24:26] sts at centre front neck, K up 22 sts up right side of neck and K across 40[42:44:46] sts on back neck. 104[108:112:116] sts. Cont in K2, P2 rib for 6cm, 2½ins.
Cast off in rib.

Join left shoulder and neckband seam. Fold neckband in half onto WS and catch down. Set in sleeves. Join side and sleeve seams.

WAISTCOAT

BACK
Using 3¼mm (US3) needles, cast on 102[108:114:120] sts.
Work in K2, P2 rib as given for sweater back for 8cm, 3ins ending with a RS row.

Inc row: Rib 2[5:4:7], ☆inc in next st, rib 4[4:5:5], inc in next st, rib 4, rep from ☆ to last 0[3:0:3] sts, rib 0[3:0:3]. 122[128:134:140] sts.

Change to 4mm (US6) needles and cont in patt:

1st row: (RS) K22[23:25:26], ☆P2, K8, P2, K21[23:24:26], rep from ☆ to last 1[0:1:0] sts, K1[0:1:0].

2nd and every foll alt row: P22[23:25:26], ☆K2, P8, P21[23:24:26], rep from ☆ to last 1[0:1:0] sts, P1[0:1:0].

3rd row: As 1st row.

5th row: K22[23:25:26], ☆P2, C8F, P2, K21[23:24:26], rep from ☆ to last 1[0:1:0] sts, K1[0:1:0].

7th–10th rows: Rep 1st and 2nd rows twice.

These 10 rows form the patt. Cont in patt until work measures 44cm, 17¼ins from beg, ending with a WS row.

Shape armholes
Dec 1 st at each end of next 12 rows. 98[104:110:116] sts.

Cont without further shaping until work measures 70[71:72:73]cm, 27½[28:28¼:28¾]ins from beg, ending with a WS row.

Shape shoulders
Cast off 14[15:16:17] sts at beg of next 4 rows. Leave rem 42[44:46:48] sts on a spare needle.

LEFT FRONT

☆☆☆Using 3¼mm (US3) needles, cast on 48[50:54:56] sts.

Cont in K2, P2 rib as given for 2nd[1st:1st:2nd] size of sweater back for 8cm, 3ins ending with a RS row.

Inc row: Rib 6[5:9:8], ☆inc in next st, rib 3, rep from ☆ to last 6[5:9:8] sts, inc in next st, rib 5[4:8:7]. 58[61:64:67] sts.☆☆☆

Change to 4mm (US6) needles and commence patt:

1st row: (RS) K22[23:25:26], P2, K8, P2, K24[26:27:29].

2nd and every foll alt row: P24[26:27:29], K2, P8, K2, P22[23:25:26].

3rd row: As 1st row.

5th row: K22[23:25:26], P2, C8F, P2, K24[26:27:29].

7th–10th rows: Rep 1st and 2nd rows twice.

These 10 rows form the patt. Cont in patt until work measures 30[31:32:33]cm, 11¾[12¼:12½:13]ins from beg, ending at front edge,

Shape neck
Dec 1 st at beg of next and every foll 6th[6th:6th:5th] row, *at the same time,* when work measures same as back to armhole shaping, ending at side edge,

Shape armhole
Still dec at front edge as before, dec 1 st at armhole edge on next 12 rows.

Keeping armhole edge straight, cont to dec at front edge only until 28[30:32:34] sts rem.

Cont without further shaping until work measures same as back to shoulder shaping, ending at armhole edge.

Shape shoulder
Cast off 14[15:16:17] sts at beg of next row. Work 1 row. Cast off rem sts.

RIGHT FRONT

Work as given for left front from ☆☆☆ to ☆☆☆.

Change to 4mm (US6) needles and commence patt:

1st row: (RS) K24[26:27:29], P2, K8, P2, K22[23:25:26].

2nd and every foll alt row: P22[23:25:26], K2, P8, K2, P24[26:27:29].

3rd row: As 1st row.

5th row: K24[26:27:29], P2, C8F, P2, K22[23:25:26].

7th–10th rows: Rep 1st and 2nd rows twice.

These 10 rows form the patt. Complete to match left front.

TO MAKE UP/TO FINISH

Join shoulder seams.

BUTTONHOLE BAND

Using 3¼mm (US3) circular needle, with RS of work facing, K up 84[86:88:90] sts up right front to beg of neck shaping, 115[116:117:118] sts to shoulder then K across 21[22:23:24] sts from back neck. 220[224:228:232] sts.

Work in rows. Work 5 rows K2, P2 rib.

Buttonhole row: Rib 4[6:2:4], (cast off 2 sts, rib 24[24:26:26] including st used to cast off) 3 times, cast off 2 sts, rib to end.

Next row: Rib to end casting on 2 sts over those cast off in previous row.

Work 2 rows in rib.

Cast off in rib.

BUTTONBAND

Using 3¼mm (US3) circular needle, with RS of work facing, K across 21[22:23:24] sts on back neck, K up

115[116:117:118] sts, down front neck to beg of shaping, and 84[86:88:90] sts down left front. 220[224:228:232] sts.

Work in rows to match buttonhole band, omitting buttonholes.

ARMBANDS

Using 3¼mm (US3) needles and with RS of work facing, K up 144[148:152:156] sts evenly from armhole edge.

Work in K2, P2 rib for 3cm, 1¼ins, dec 1 st at each end of every 3rd row.

Cast off in rib.

Join front bands at centre back neck. Join side seams. Sew on buttons.

COWL

Using 4mm (US6) needles, cast on 182 sts.

Cont in K2, P2 rib as foll:

1st row: (RS) K2, ☆P2, K2, rep from ☆ to end.

2nd row: P2, ☆K2, P2, rep from ☆ to end.

Rep these 2 rows for 3cm, 1¼ins ending with a WS row.

Commence patt:

1st row: (RS) K3, P2, ☆K8, (P2, K2) twice, P2, rep from ☆ to last 15 sts, K8, P2, K2, P2, K1.

2nd and every foll alt row: K3, P2, K2, ☆P8, (K2, P2) twice, K2, rep from ☆ to last 13 sts, P8, K2, P2, K1.

3rd row: As 1st row.

5th row: K3, P2, ☆C8F, (P2, K2) twice, P2, rep from ☆ to last 15 sts, C8F, P2, K2, P2, K1.

7th–10th rows: Rep 1st and 2nd rows twice.

These 10 rows form the patt. Cont in patt until work measures 47cm, 18½ins from beg, ending with a WS row.

Work in K2, P2 rib for 3cm, 1¼ins. Cast off in rib.

TO MAKE UP/TO FINISH

Join side seam.

MITTENS

RIGHT MITTEN

☆☆Using 3¼mm (US3) needles, cast on 36 sts.

Cont in K2, P2 rib for 8cm, 3ins ending with a WS row.☆☆

Next row: K24, (inc in next st) 5 times, K7. 41 sts.

SONG THRUSH *His & Her Cardigans*

Next row: P.
Commence patt.
1st row: K23, P2, K8, P2, K6.
2nd and every foll alt row: P6, K2, P8, K2, P23.
3rd row: As 1st row.
5th row: K23, P2, C8F, P2, K6.
7th–10th rows: Rep 1st and 2nd rows twice.
These 10 rows form the patt. Cont in patt until work measures 14cm, 5½ins from beg, ending with a WS row.
Divide for thumb
Next row: K3, sl next 6 sts onto a safety pin, cast on 6 sts, patt to end. Now cont in patt until work measures 23cm, 9ins from beg, ending with a WS row.
Shape top
Next row: K1, sl 1, K1, psso, patt to last 3 sts, K2 tog, K1.
Next row: Patt to end.
Rep these 2 rows until 31 sts rem.
Cast off.
Complete thumb
Using set of four double pointed needles, with RS of work facing, K across 6 sts on safety pin, K up 1 st, then K up 6 sts across cast on sts of palm. 13 sts.
Cont in rounds of st st (every round K) for 5cm, 2ins.
Shape top
Next row: ☆K2 tog, rep from ☆ to last st, K1. 7 sts.
Cut yarn, thread through rem sts, draw up and fasten off securely.

LEFT MITTEN

Work as given for right mitten from ☆☆ to ☆☆.
Next row: K7, (inc in next st) 5 times, K24. 41 sts.
Next row: P.
Complete to match right mitten, reversing patt and thumb as foll:
Commence patt.
1st row: K6, P2, K8, P2, K23.
Divide for thumb
Next row: Patt 32, sl next 6 sts onto a safety pin, cast on 6 sts, patt to end.

TO MAKE UP/TO FINISH

Join side seam.

Sizes
To fit bust/chest 86[97:107:117]cm, 34[38:42:46]ins
Actual bust/chest 96[107:118:129]cm, 37¾[42:46½:50¾]ins
Length 61[64:67:70]cm, 24[25¼:26½:27½]ins
Sleeve seam 43[43:48:48]cm, 17[17:19:19]ins

Materials
11[11:12:13] × 50g balls of Phildar Sagittaire
One pair each 3mm (US3) and 3¾mm (US5) knitting needles
5 'Pikaby' buttons

Tension/Gauge
25 sts and 36 rows to 10cm, 4ins over patt using 3¾mm (US5) needles

BACK
Using 3mm (US3) needles, cast on 90[100:110:120] sts.

Cont in K1, P1 rib for 9cm, 3½ins, ending with a RS row.
Inc row: Rib 7[6:5:4], ☆inc in next st, rib 2, rep from ☆ to last 5[4:3:2] sts, rib to end. 116[130:144:158] sts.
Change to 3¾mm (US5) needles and commence patt.
1st row: (RS) ☆(K1, P1) 4[5:6:7] times, (P2, K2) twice, P2, rep from ☆ to last 8[10:12:14] sts, (K1, P1) 4[5:6:7] times.
2nd row: ☆(P1, K1) 4[5:6:7] times, (K2, P2) twice, K2, rep from ☆ to last 8[10:12:14] sts, (P1, K1) 4[5:6:7] times.
These 2 rows form the patt. Cont in patt until work measures 42cm, 16½ins from beg, ending with a WS row.
Shape raglan armholes
Cast off 2[3:4:5] sts at beg of next 2 rows.
Dec 1 st at each end of next and every foll alt row until 44[46:48:50] sts rem.
Cast off.

POCKET LININGS
(make 2)
Using 3mm (US3) needles, cast on 28[30:32:34] sts. Beg with a K row cont in st st for 8cm, 3ins, ending with a P row. Leave sts on a spare needle.

LEFT FRONT
☆☆Using 3mm (US3) needles, cast on 46[50:56:60] sts.
Cont in K1, P1 rib for 9cm, 3½ins ending with a RS row.
Inc row: Rib 1[4:5:3], ☆inc in next st, rib 3[2:2:2], rep from ☆ to last 1[4:6:3] sts, inc in next st, rib to end. 58[65:72:79] sts.☆☆
Change to 3¾mm (US5) needles and commence patt.
1st row: (RS) ☆(K1, P1) 4[5:6:7] times, (P2, K2) twice, P2, rep from ☆ to last 4[5:6:7] sts, (K1, P1) 2[2:3:3] times, K0[1:0:1].
2nd row: K0[1:0:1], (P1, K1) 2[2:3:3] times, ☆(K2, P2) twice, K2, (P1, K1) 4[5:6:7] times.
These 2 rows form the patt. Cont in patt until work measures 17cm, 6¾ins from beg, ending with a WS row.
Place pocket
Next row: Patt 8[10:12:14], sl next 28[30:32:34] sts on a holder, patt across sts of first pocket lining, patt to end.
Cont in patt until work measures 36 rows less than back to armhole shaping, ending with a WS row.
Shape neck

Dec 1 st at end of next row and at same edge on every foll 4th row until work measures same as back to armhole shaping, ending at side edge.
Shape armhole
Still dec at neck edge as before, cast off 2[3:4:5] sts at beg of next row, then dec 1 st at armhole edge on every foll alt row until 16[19:22:25] sts rem.
Keeping neck edge straight, cont to dec at armhole edge only until 2 sts rem.
Work 2 tog and fasten off.

RIGHT FRONT

Work as given for left front from ☆☆ to ☆☆.
Change to 3¾mm (US5) needles and commence patt.
1st row: (RS) K0[1:0:1], (P1, K1) 2[2: 3:3] times, ☆(P2, K2) twice, P2, (P1, K1) 4[5:6:7] times, rep from ☆ to end.
2nd row: ☆(K1, P1) 4[5:6:7] times, (K2, P2) twice, K2, rep from ☆ to last 4[5:6:7] sts, (K1, P1) 2[2:3:3] times, K0[1:0:1].
These 2 rows form the patt. Cont in patt until work measures 17cm, 6½ins from beg, ending with a WS row.
Place pocket
Next row: Patt 22[25:28:31], sl next 28[30:32:34] sts on a holder, patt across sts of second pocket lining, patt to end.
Complete to match left front, reversing all shapings.

SLEEVES

Using 3mm (US3) needles, cast on 54[62:70:78] sts.
Cont in K1, P1 rib for 9cm, 3½ins, ending with a WS row.
Change to 3¾mm (US5) needles and commence patt.
1st row: (RS) (K1, P1) 2[3:4:5] times, ☆(P2, K2) twice, P2, (K1, P1) 4[5:6:7] times, rep from ☆ to last 14[16:18:20] sts, (P2, K2) twice, P2, (K1, P1) 2[3:4:5] times.
2nd row: (P1, K1) 2[3:4:5] times, ☆(K2, P2) twice, K2, (P1, K1) 4[5:6:7] times, rep from ☆ to last 14[16:18:20] sts, (K2, P2) twice, K2, (P1, K1) 2[3:4:5] times.
These 2 rows form the patt. Cont in patt, inc 1 st at each end of every foll 7th[6th:6th:6th] row until there are 82[94:106:118] sts.
Cont without further shaping until work measures 43[43:48:48]cm, 17[17:19: 19]ins from beg, ending with a WS row.
Shape raglan top

Cast off 2[3:4:5] sts at beg of next 2 rows.
Dec 1 st at each end of next and every foll alt row until 10 sts rem. Cast off.

BUTTONBAND

With 3mm (US3) needles, cast on 11 sts.
Cont in K1, P1 rib as foll:
1st row: (RS) K2, ☆P1, K1, rep from ☆ to last st, K1.
2nd row: ☆K1, P1, rep from ☆ to last st, K1.
Rep these 2 rows once more.
Buttonhole row: K2, P1, K1, P1, yon, K2 tog, K1, P1, K2.
Cont in rib, making 4 more buttonholes 7cm, 2¾ins apart, until band is long enough, when slightly stretched, to fit, front edges, across sleeve tops and back neck.
Cast off in rib.

POCKET TOPS

With RS of work facing, using 3mm (US3) needles, rejoin yarn to sts on holder. Work 10 rows K1, P1 rib.
Cast off in rib.

TO MAKE UP/TO FINISH

Join raglan armholes. Sew on button-band. Catch down pocket linings on WS and pocket tops on RS of work. Join side and sleeve seams. Sew on buttons.

PARSNIP AND PARSLEY *Lady's Coat*

Size

To fit bust 81–107cm, 32–42ins
Actual bust 129cm, 50¾ins

Length 98.5cm, 38¾ins
Sleeve seam with cuff unfolded 45cm, 17¾ins

Materials

26 × 50g balls of Sunbeam Aran Knit OR Aran Tweed
One pair each 4mm (US6) and 5mm (US8) knitting needles
4mm (US6) and 5mm (US8) short double pointed needles
Cable needle
11 'Pikaby' buttons

Tension/Gauge

16 sts and 28 rows to 10cm, 4ins over patt using 5mm (US8) needles

BACK

Using 4mm (US6) needles, cast on 100 sts. Cont in moss st as foll:
1st row: (RS) ☆K1, P1, rep from ☆ to end.
2nd row: ☆P1, K1, rep from ☆ to end.
These 2 rows form moss st. Rep these 2 rows 3 times more.
Change to 5mm (US8) needles. Commence patt.
1st row: (RS) ☆K5, (P1, K1) twice, P1, rep from ☆ to end.
2nd row: ☆(P1, K1) 3 times, P4, rep from ☆ to end.
3rd row: ☆K3, (P1, K1) twice, P1, K2, rep from ☆ to end.
4th row: ☆P3, (K1, P1) twice, K1, P2, rep from ☆ to end.
5th row: ☆(K1, P1) 3 times, K4, rep from ☆ to end.
6th row: ☆P5, (K1, P1) twice, K1, rep from ☆ to end.
7th row: As 5th row.
8th row: As 4th row.
9th row: As 3rd row.
10th row: As 2nd row.
These 10 rows form the patt. Cont in patt until work measures 70cm, 27½ins from beg, ending with a WS row.
Shape raglan armholes
Keeping patt correct, dec 1 st at each end of next and every foll alt row until 20 sts rem, ending with a WS row.
Cast off.

LEFT FRONT

Using 4mm (US6) needles, cast on 50 sts.
☆☆Cont in moss st as given for back.
Work 8 rows.

SONG THRUSH

PARSNIP AND PARSLEY

Change to 5mm (US8) needles. Cont in patt as given for back until work measures 70cm, 27½ins from beg, ending with a WS row. ☆☆

Shape raglan armhole

Dec 1 st at beg of next and every foll alt row until 20 sts rem, ending with a RS row.

Shape neck

Still dec at armhole edge as before, cast off 10 sts at beg of next row then dec 1 st at neck edge on every row until 1 st rem. Fasten off.

RIGHT FRONT

Using 4mm (US6) needles, cast on 40 sts. Work as given for left front from ☆☆ to ☆☆.

Shape raglan armhole

Dec 1 st at end of next and every foll alt row until 10 sts rem, ending with a WS row.

Shape neck

Still dec at armhole edge as before, dec 1 st at beg of next and every foll alt row until 1 st rem. Fasten off.

SLEEVES

Using 4mm (US6) needles, cast on 38 sts. Work in K1, P1 rib for 15cm, 6ins ending with a RS row.

Inc row: Rib 8, ☆inc in next st, rib 1, rep from ☆ to last 8 sts, inc in next st rib to end. 50 sts.

Change to 5mm (US8) needles. Cont in patt as given for back, inc and work into patt 1 st at each end of 3rd and every foll 4th row until there are 70 sts.

Cont without further shaping until work measures 45cm, 17¾ins from beg, ending with a WS row.

Shape raglan sleeve top

Dec 1 st at each end of next and every foll 3rd row until 32 sts rem, then at each end of every foll alt row until 10 sts rem. Work 1 row.

Cast off.

RIGHT BACK RAGLAN INSET

Using 4mm (US6) needles, cast on 8 sts. Cont in rib patt as foll:

1st row: (RS) K1, P2, K2, P2, K1.

2nd row: P1, K2, P2, K2, P1.

These 2 rows form the rib patt. Cont in rib patt until band is long enough, when slightly stretched, to fit back sleeve raglan edge, ending with a RS row.

Shape top

Cast off 4 sts at beg of next row. Work 1 row. Cast off rem 4 sts.

LEFT BACK RAGLAN INSET

Work as given for right back raglan inset, reversing shaping.

RIGHT FRONT RAGLAN INSET

Using 4mm (US6) needles, cast on 8 sts. Cont in rib patt as given for right back raglan inset until band, when slightly stretched, fits up front raglan edge, ending with a WS row.

Shape top

Dec 1 st at beg of next and every foll alt row until 3 sts rem.

Work 1 row. Cast off.

LEFT FRONT RAGLAN INSET

Work as given for right front raglan inset, reversing shaping.

BUTTONBAND

Using 4mm (US6) needles, cast on 28 sts. Cont in K2, P2 rib until band is long enough, when slightly stretched, to fit up left front to neck, ending at inner edge. Cut yarn and leave sts on a holder.

TO MAKE UP/TO FINISH

Sew on buttonband. Mark the position of 10 buttons, the first in 3rd row from cast on edge, the last 4 rows below neck edge with the others evenly spaced between.

BUTTONHOLE BAND

Using 4mm (US6) needles, cast on 28 sts. Work 2 rows K2, P2 rib.

1st buttonhole row: (RS) Rib 4, cast off 3 sts, work to end.

2nd buttonhole row: Work to end, casting on 3 sts over those cast off in previous row.

Work 2 rows K2, P2 rib.

Change to 4mm (US6) and 5mm (US8) double pointed needles and cont in rib and cable panel as foll, *at the same time*, making buttonhole opposite markers as before.

1st row: (RS) Using 4mm (US6) needles, rib 8, using 5mm (US8) needles, K2, P2, sl next 3 sts onto cable needle and hold at back of work, K3 then K3 from cable needle, sl next 3 sts onto cable needle and hold at front of work, K3 then K3 from cable needle, P2, K2.

2nd row: Using 5mm (US8) needles, P2, K2, P12, K2, P2, using 4mm (US6) needles, rib to end.

3rd row: Using 4mm (US6) needles, rib 8, using 5mm (US8) needles, K2, P2, K12, P2, K2.

4th row: As 2nd row.

5th row: As 3rd row.

6th row: As 2nd row.

These 6 rows form the rib and cable panel patt. Cont as set until band is long enough, when slightly stretched, to fit up right front to neck, ending at outer edge. Do not cut yarn.

Sew raglan insets in place. Sew on buttonhole band.

NECKBAND

With RS of work facing, work across 28 sts of buttonhole band, using 4mm (US6) needles, K up 82 sts evenly around neck edge, rib across 8 sts on buttonband. 118 sts.

1st row: (WS) Work in K2, P2 rib to last 28 sts, patt to end.

Cont in this way until collar measures 9cm, 3½ins ending with a WS row.

Work 1st and 2nd buttonhole rows again.

Cont as set until collar measures 12.5cm, 5ins ending with a WS row.

Cast off, in rib over ribbed sections.

HALF POCKET LINING
(make 2)

Using 5mm (US8) needles, cast on 24 sts.

Beg with a K row cont in st st until work measures 5cm, 2ins from beg, ending with a P row.

Shape side

Cast on 2 sts at beg of next row. 26 sts.

Cont without further shaping until work measures 15cm, 6ins from beg, ending with a P row.

Cast off 2 sts at beg of every row until 12 sts rem. Work 1 row. Cast off.

UNDER LINING
(make 2)

Work as given for half pocket lining reversing side shaping.

Sew linings tog, RS facing, leaving unshaped short end free for opening. With cast on edge uppermost, sew opening edges to back and fronts at desired position at sides.

Join sleeve seams and side seams above and below pockets. Sew on buttons.

CHRISTMAS *Child's Sweater with Lace Collar*

Sizes
To fit chest 56[61:66]cm, 22[24:26]ins
Actual chest 62[65:71]cm,
24½[25½:28]ins
Length 31[36:41]cm, 12¼[14¼:16]ins
Sleeve seam 27[31:35]cm,
10¾[12¼:13¾]ins

Materials
4[5:5] × 50g balls of Pingouin Confort
OR Pingouin 4 Pingouins
One pair each 3¼mm (US3) and 4mm
(US6) knitting needles

Tension/Gauge
22 sts and 28 rows to 10cm, 4ins over st st
using 4mm (US6) needles

BACK
☆☆Using 3¼mm (US3) needles, cast on
63[67:73] sts.
Cont in K1, P1 rib as foll:
1st row: (RS) K1, ☆P1, K1, rep from ☆
to end.
2nd row: P1, ☆K1, P1, rep from ☆ to
end.
Rep these 2 rows for 5cm, 2ins ending
with a 1st row.
Inc row: Rib 1[6:5], ☆inc in next st, rib
14[13:15], rep from ☆ to last 2[5:4] sts,
inc in next st, rib to end. 68[72:78] sts.
Change to 4mm (US6) needles. Beg with
a K row cont in st st until work measures
20[24:28]cm, 8[9½:11]ins from beg,
ending with a P row.
Shape armholes
Cast off 5[5:6] sts at beg of next 2 rows. .
58[62:66] sts.☆☆
Cont without further shaping until work

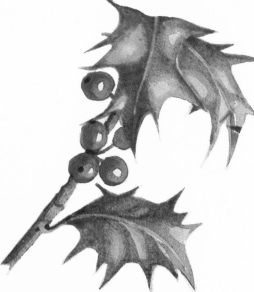

measures 31[36:41]cm, 12¼[14¼:16]ins
from beg, ending with a P row.
Shape shoulders
Cast off 18[19:20] sts at beg of next 2
rows. Leave rem 22[24:26] sts on a spare
needle.

FRONT
Work as given for back from ☆☆ to ☆☆.
Cont without further shaping until work
measures 12[14:16] rows less than back to
shoulder shaping, ending with a P row.
Divide for neck
Next row: K25[26:27] and turn, leaving
rem sts on a spare needle.
Complete left side of neck first.
Dec 1 st at neck edge on every row until
18[19:20] sts rem.
Cont without further shaping until work
measures same as back to shoulder,
ending at armhole edge.
Shape shoulder
Cast off rem sts.
With RS of work facing, return to sts on
spare needle. Sl centre 8[10:12] sts onto a
holder, rejoin yarn to next st, K to end.
Complete to match first side of neck.

SLEEVES
Using 3¼mm (US3) needles, cast on
31[33:37] sts.
Cont in K1, P1 rib as given for back for
5cm, 2ins ending with a 1st row.
Inc row: Rib 4[6:8], ☆inc in next st, rib
10, rep from ☆ to last 5[5:7] sts, inc in
next st, rib to end. 34[36:40] sts.
Change to 4mm (US6) needles. Beg with
a K row, cont in st st inc 1 st at each end
of 5th and every foll 6th[7th:8th] row
until there are 50[54:58] sts.
Cont without further shaping until work
measures 27[31:35]cm, 10¾[12¼:
13¾]ins from beg, ending with a P row.
Place a marker at each end of last row.
Work 6[6:8] rows. Cast off loosely.

TO MAKE UP/TO FINISH
Join right shoulder seam.

NECKBAND
With RS of work facing, using 3¼mm
(US3) needles, K up 13[15:17] sts down
left side of neck, K across 8[10:12] sts at
centre front, K up 13[15:17] sts up right
side of neck, then K across 22[24:26] sts
on back neck, inc 1 st at centre.
57[65:73] sts.
Beg with 2nd row, work 2cm, ¾in K1,

P1 rib as given for back.
Cast off loosely in rib.

Join left shoulder and neckband seam.
Placing centre of cast off edge of sleeve to
shoulder seams and sewing final rows
after markers to cast off sts at underarm,
set in sleeves. Join side and sleeve seams.

COLLAR

Size
To fit neckband 33cm, 13ins
Depth 5cm, 2ins

Materials
10g Coats Anchor Mercer-Crochet
Cotton No 20
One pair 2¼mm (US1) knitting needles
1 'Pikaby' button

Tension/Gauge
36 sts and 40 rows to 10cm, 4ins over patt
using 2¼mm (US1) needles

COLLAR
Cast on 82 sts, very loosely.
K 2 rows.
Next row: K1 tbl, ☆yfwd, sl 1, K1, psso,
yfwd, K1 tbl, rep from ☆ to end. 109 sts.
Next row: P.
Next row: K1 tbl, ☆yfwd, sl 1, K2 tog,
psso, yfwd, K1 tbl, rep from ☆ to end.
Next row: P.
Rep last 2 rows 5 times more.
Next row: K1 tbl, ☆yfwd, sl 1, K2 tog,
psso *at the same time* K tbl sl st, yfwd, K1
tbl, rep from ☆ to end. 136 sts.
Next row: P.
Cut yarn.

EDGING
With RS of work facing, K up 12 sts from
row ends, K across 136 sts on needle, K
up 12 sts from row ends. 160 sts.
Beg with a P row, work 11 rows st st.
Cast off very loosely.

TO MAKE UP/TO FINISH
Carefully pin out, press and starch. Fold
edging in half to WS and catch down.
Sew button at one neck edge. Make a
button loop to correspond on the other.

CHRISTMAS HOLLY

Holly *Child's Sweater*

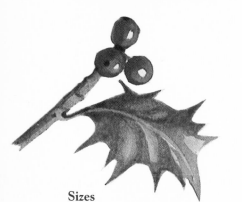

Sizes
To fit chest 51[56:61:66]cm,
20[22:24:26]ins
Actual chest 56.5[60:66.5:70]cm,
22¼[23¾:26¼:27½]ins
Length 36[38:40:42]cm,
14¼[15:15¾:16½]ins
Sleeve seam 30[33:33:36]cm,
11¾[13:13:14¼]ins

Materials
3[4:4:5] × 50g balls of Emu Superwash
OR Supermatch DK in main colour (A)
1 ball each in 2 contrast colours (B and C)
One pair each 3¼mm (US3) and 4mm
(US6) knitting needles

Tension/Gauge
23 sts and 26 rows to 10cm, 4ins over st st
using 4mm (US6) needles

BACK
☆☆Using 3¼mm (US3) needles and A,
cast on 61[65:69:73] sts.
Cont in K1, P1 rib as foll:
1st row: K1, ☆P1, K1, rep from ☆ to end.

2nd row: P1, ☆K1, P1, rep from ☆ to end.
Rep these 2 rows for 5cm, 2ins, ending
with a 2nd row.
Inc row: Rib 12[13:9:8], ☆inc in next st,
rib 11[12:6:7], rep from ☆ to last
13[13:11:9] sts, inc in next st, rib to end.
65[69:77:81] sts.
Change to 4mm (US6) needles and beg
with a P row, work 7[3:9:7] rows st st.
Commence patt.
1st row: (RS) K1B, ☆3A, 1B, rep from ☆
to end.
2nd row: P1A, ☆1B, 3A, rep from ☆ to
end.
3rd row: ☆K2A, 1B, 1A, rep from ☆ to
last st, 1A.
4th row: P1A, ☆2A, 1B, 1A, rep from ☆
to end.
5th row: ☆K1C, 3A, rep from ☆ to last
st, 1C.
6th row: P1A, ☆1A, 1C, 2A, rep from ☆
to end.
7th row: ☆K2A, with C, cast on 2 sts,
cast off 2 sts to make bobble, 1A, rep
from ☆ to last st, 1A.
8th row: P1C, ☆3A, 1C, rep from ☆ to
end.
9th row: ☆K1A, 1B, 2A, rep from ☆ to
last st, 1A.
10th row: P1A, ☆1A, 1B, 2A, rep from
☆ to end.
11th row: ☆K3A, 1B, rep from ☆ to last
st, 1A.
12th row: P1B, ☆3A, 1B, rep from ☆ to
end.
Cont in A only. Work 6[8:8:12] rows st st.
These 18[20:20:24] rows form the patt.
Cont in patt until work measures 21cm,
8½ins from beg, ending with a WS row.
Shape armholes
Cast off 4 sts at beg of next 2 rows.
57[61:69:73] sts. ☆☆
Cont in patt until work measures
36[38:40:42]cm,   14¼[15:15¾:16½]ins
from beg, ending with a WS row.
Shape shoulders
Cast off 14[16:18:20] sts at beg of next 2
rows. Leave rem 29[29:33:33] sts on a
spare needle.

FRONT
Work as given for back from ☆☆ to ☆☆.
Cont in patt until work measures
30[32:34:36]cm,   11¾[12½:13½:14¼]
ins from beg, ending with a WS row.
Shape neck
Next row: Patt 24[26:29:31] sts and turn
leaving rem sts on a spare needle.

Complete left side of neck first.
Cast off 4 sts at beg of next row, 3 sts at
beg of foll alt row, then 2 sts at beg of
next alt row. Dec 1 st at neck edge on foll
1[1:2:2] alt rows. 14[16:18:20] sts.
Cont without further shaping until work
measures same as back to shoulder
shaping, ending at armhole edge.
Shape shoulder
Cast off rem sts.
With RS of work facing, return to sts on
spare needle. Sl centre 9[9:11:11] sts onto
a holder, rejoin yarn at neck edge, patt to
end.
Patt 1 row. Complete as given for first
side of neck.

SLEEVES
Using 3¼mm (US3) needles and A, cast
on 33[37:43:47] sts.
Work in K1, P1 rib as given for back for
5cm, 2ins, ending with a 1st row.
P 1 row.
Now cont in patt as given for back.
Inc and work into patt 1 st at each end
of every 3rd row until there are 69[77:87:
97] sts.
Cont without shaping until work
measures   32[35:35:38]cm,   12½[13¾:
13¾:15]ins from beg, ending with a WS
row. Cast off loosely.

TO MAKE UP/TO FINISH
Join right shoulder seam.

NECKBAND
With RS of work facing, using 3¼mm
(US3) needles and A, K up 22 sts down
left side of neck, K across 9[9:11:11] sts at
centre front, K up 23 sts up right side of
neck, then K across 29[29:33:33] sts on
back neck. 83[83:89:89] sts.
Beg with a 2nd row, work in K1, P1 rib as
given for back for 5cm, 2ins.
Cast off loosely in rib.

Join left shoulder and neckband seam,
fold neckband in half onto WS and slip
stitch in place. Placing centre of cast off
edge to shoulder seams, set in sleeves,
joining final rows to cast off sts at
underarms. Join side and sleeve seams.

Ivy *Lady's Mohair Jacket*

BACK

Using 5½mm (US9) needles and A, cast on 85[97] sts.

Cont in K1, P1 rib as foll:

1st row: (RS) K1, ☆P1, K1, rep from ☆ to end.

2nd row: P1, ☆K1, P1, rep from ☆ to end.

Rep these 2 rows for 2cm, ¾in ending with a WS row, inc 1 st in centre of last row. 86[98] sts.

Beg with a K row, commence working colour patt from chart. Working in st st unless otherwise indicated, reading odd numbered rows (K) from right to left and even numbered rows (P) from left to right. Use small separate balls of C for each area of colour. Twist yarns when changing colour to avoid a hole.

Cont in patt until work measures 68[70]cm, 26¾[27½]ins from beg, ending with a P row.

Shape shoulders

Cast off.

Key

A ☐
B •
■ Using C, (K1, P1) twice into st.
× Using C, ybk, sl 3, K1, p3sso.

RIGHT FRONT

Using 5½mm (US9) needles and A, cast on 39[45] sts.

Cont in K1, P1 rib as given for back for 2cm, ¾in ending with a WS row, inc 1 st in centre of last row. 40[46] sts.

Cont in colour patt from chart until work measures 62[63]cm, 24½[24¾]ins from beg, ending with a P row.

Shape neck

Cast off 9 sts at beg of next row. Dec 1 st at neck edge on every row until 26[31] sts rem.

Cont without further shaping until work measures same as back to shoulder, ending with a P row.

Shape shoulder

Cast off.

LEFT FRONT

Work as given for right front, reversing neck shaping.

SLEEVES

Using 5½mm (US9) needles and A, cast on 31[35] sts.

Cont in K1, P1 rib as given for back for 5cm, 2ins ending with a WS row, inc 1 st at end of last row. 32[36] sts.

Sizes

To fit bust 86[102]cm, 34[40]ins
Actual bust 110[125]cm, 43¼[49¼]ins
Length 68[70]cm, 26¾[27½]ins
Sleeve seam 42[46]cm, 16½[18¼]ins

Materials

6[7] × 50g balls of Sirdar Nocturne in main colour (A)
3[4] balls in contrast colour (B)
2[2] balls in contrast colour (C)
One pair each 4½mm (US7) and 5½mm (US9) knitting needles

Tension/Gauge

16 sts and 20 rows to 10cm, 4ins over st st using 5½mm (US9) needles

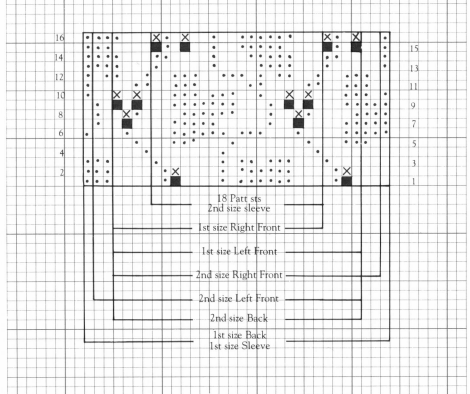

18 Patt sts
2nd size sleeve
1st size Right Front
1st size Left Front
2nd size Right Front
2nd size Left Front
2nd size Back
1st size Back
1st size Sleeve

IVY

ROBIN

ROBIN *Man's and Boy's Sweaters*

Cont in colour patt from chart, *at the same time*, inc 1 st at each end of 3rd and every foll alt row until there are 66[76] sts, then at each end of every foll 4th row until there are 80[90] sts, working extra sts in patt.

Cont without further shaping until work measures 42[46]cm, 16½[18¼]ins from beg, ending with a P row.

Cast off loosely.

TO MAKE UP/TO FINISH
Join shoulder seams.

NECKBAND
With RS of work facing, using 4½mm (US7) needles and A, K up 9 sts across front neck, K up 12 sts up right side of neck, 27[29] sts across back neck, 12 sts down left side of neck and 9 sts across front neck. 69[71] sts.

Beg with a WS row, cont in K1, P1 rib as given for back for 7cm, 2¾ins.

Cast off loosely in rib.

Fold neckband in half onto WS and catch down.

RIGHT FRONT BORDER
With RS of work facing, using 5½mm (US9) needles and A, K up 99[101] sts evenly up right front edge and end of neckband.

Beg with a 2nd row, work in K1, P1 rib as given for back for 7cm, 2¾ins.

Cast off loosely in rib.

LEFT FRONT BORDER
Work to match right front border.

Fold borders in half onto WS and catch down. Place centre of cast off edge of sleeve to shoulder seams and set in sleeves. Join side and sleeve seams.

Sizes
To fit chest 56 – 61[66 – 71:76 – 81:86 – 91:97 – 102:107 – 112]cm, 22 – 24[26 – 28:30 – 32:34 – 36:38 – 40:42 – 44]ins
Actual chest 69[80:91:102.5:114: 125]cm, 27¼[31½:36:40¼:45:49¼]ins
Length 38.5[46:54:61:64:68]cm, 15¼[18¼:21¼:24:25¼:26¾]ins
Sleeve seam 30[36:42:46:48:49]cm, 11¾[14¼:16½:18¼:19:19¼]ins

Materials
4[5:6:7:8:9] × 100g balls of Samband Lopi
One pair each 4½mm (US7) and 6½mm (US10½) knitting needles
Cable needle

Tension/Gauge
14 sts and 19 rows to 10cm, 4ins over st st using 6½mm (US10½) needles

BACK
☆☆Using 4½mm (US7) needles, cast on 42[52:56:64:72:80] sts.

Cont in K1, P1 rib for 5[5:7:7:7:7]cm, 2[2:2¾:2¾:2¾:2¾]ins, ending with a RS row.

Inc row: Rib 7[8:6:10:8:7], ☆inc in next st, rib 3[4:3:3:4:5], rep from ☆ to last 7[9:6:10:9:7] sts, inc in next st, rib to end. 50[60:68:76:84:92] sts.

Change to 6½mm (US10½) needles and commence patt.

1st size only
1st row: (RS) Sl 1, (K5, P2) 3 times, K6, (P2, K5) 3 times, K1 tbl.
2nd row: Sl 1, (P5, K2) 3 times, P6, (K2, P5) 3 times, K1 tbl.
3rd–6th rows: Rep 1st–2nd rows twice.
7th row: Sl 1, (K5, P2) 3 times, sl next 3 sts onto cable needle and hold at back of work, K3 then K3 from cable needle – called C6B, (P2, K5) 3 times, K1 tbl.
8th row: As 2nd row.
9th–12th rows: Rep 1st–2nd rows twice.
These 12 rows form the patt.

2nd, 3rd, 4th, 5th and 6th sizes only
1st row: (RS) Sl 1, K[2:6:10:14:18], P2, K6, (P2, K5) twice, P2, K6, P2, (K5, P2) twice, K6, P2, K[2:6:10:14:18], K1 tbl.
2nd row: Sl 1, P[2:6:10:14:18], K2, P6, (K2, P5) twice, K2, P6, K2, (P5, K2) twice, P6, K2, P[2:6:10:14:18], K1 tbl.
3rd–6th rows: Rep 1st–2nd rows twice.
7th row: Sl 1, K[2:6:10:14:18], P2, C6B – see 1st size, (P2, K5) twice, P2, C6B, P2, (K5, P2) twice, C6B, P2, K[2:6:10:14:18], K1 tbl.
8th row: As 2nd row.
9th–12th rows: Rep 1st–2nd rows twice.
These 12 rows form the patt.

All sizes
Cont in patt until work measures 24[30:35:39:41:43]cm, 9½[12:13¾: 15½:16:17]ins from beg, ending with a WS row.

Shape armholes
Dec 1 st at each end of every row until 38[48:54:62:68:76] sts rem.☆☆

Cont without further shaping until work measures 38.5[46:54:61:64:68]cm, 15¼ [18¼:21¼:24:25¼:26¾]ins from beg, ending with a WS row.

Shape shoulders
Cast off 5[6:8:9:9:11] sts at beg of next 2 rows, then 6[7:8:9:10:11] sts at beg of foll 2 rows. Leave rem 16[22:22:26:30:32] sts on a spare needle.

FRONT
Work as given for back from ☆☆ to ☆☆.

Cont without further shaping until work measures 33[41:47:55:58:61]cm, 13[16: 18½:21¾:22¾:24]ins from beg, ending with a WS row.

Shape neck
Next row: Patt 15[19:22:24:25:28] and turn, leaving rem sts on a spare needle.

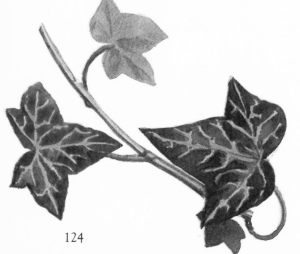

MISTLETOE *Lady's Sweater*

Complete left side of neck first.
Dec 1 st at neck edge on every row until 13[15:19:21:21:24] sts rem, then on every foll alt row until 11[13:16:18:19:22] sts rem. Cont without further shaping until work measures same as back to shoulder shaping, ending at armhole edge.
Shape shoulder
Cast off 5[6:8:9:9:11] sts at beg of next row. Work 1 row. Cast off rem 6[7:8:9:10:11] sts.
With RS of work facing, return to sts on spare needle. Sl centre 8[10:10:14:18:20] sts onto a holder, rejoin yarn at neck edge, patt to end.
Complete to match first side of neck.

SLEEVES

Using 4½mm (US7) needles, cast on 20[24:28:30:34:38] sts.
Cont in K1, P1 rib for 5[5:7:7:7:7]cm, 2[2:2¾:2¾:2¾:2¾]ins, ending with a RS row.
Inc row: Rib 5[4:3:6:3:5], ☆inc in next st, rib 1[2:2:1:2:2], rep from ☆ to last 5[5:4:6:4:6] sts, inc in next st, rib to end. 26[30:36:40:44:48] sts.
Change to 6½mm (US10½) needles. Beg with a K row, cont in st st, inc 1 st at each end of next and every foll 5th[5th:5th:5th:5th:6th] row until there are 44[50:58:66:70:74] sts.
Cont without further shaping until work measures 30[36:42:46:48:49]cm, 11¾ [14¼:16½:18¼:19:19¼]ins from beg, ending with a WS row.
Shape top
Dec 1 st at each end of every row until 32[38:44:52:54:58] sts rem.
Cast off loosely.

TO MAKE UP/TO FINISH

Join right shoulder seam.

NECKBAND

Using 4½mm (US7) needles, with RS of work facing, K up 14[14:16:16:18:18] sts down left side of neck, K across 8[10:10:14:18:20] sts at centre front, K up 14[14:16:16:18:18] sts up right side of neck, then K across 16[22:22:26:30:32] sts on back neck. 52[60:64:72:84:88] sts.
Cont in K1, P1 rib for 2[2:2.5:2.5:3:3]cm, ¾[¾:1:1:1¼:1¼]ins.
Cast off loosely in rib.

Join left shoulder and neckband seam. Set in sleeves. Join side and sleeve seams.

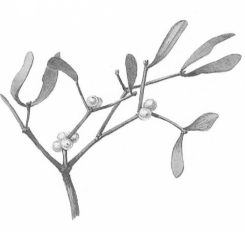

Sizes

To fit bust 71 – 76[81 – 86:91 – 97:102 – 107]cm, 28 – 30[32 – 34:36 – 38:40 – 42]ins
Actual bust 79[89.5:99.5:109]cm, 31¼[35¼:39¼:43]ins
Length 56[59:61.5:64]cm, 22[23¼:24¼:25¼]ins
Sleeve seam 37[38:39:40]cm, 14½[15:15½:15¾]ins

Materials

6[7:7:7] × 50g balls of Sunbeam Paris Mohair (A)
2[3:3:4] × 50g balls of Sunbeam Sapphire DK (B)
One pair each 3¾mm (US5), 4mm (US6) and 5½mm (US9) knitting needles

Tension/Gauge

16 sts and 22 rows to 10cm, 4ins over st st using 5½mm (US9) needles and A

RIGHT BACK

Using 5½mm (US9) needles and A, cast on 27[31:35:39] sts.
Beg with a K row, cont in st st until work measures 19cm, 7½ins from beg, ending with a P row.
Shape raglan armhole
Dec 1 st at beg of next and every foll alt row until 2[3:4:5] sts rem, ending with a P row. Leave sts on a spare needle.

LEFT BACK

Work as given for right back, reversing raglan shaping.

BACK PANEL

Using 4mm (US6) needles and B, cast on 13 sts.
1st row: P.
2nd row: (RS) K1, (yfwd, sl 1, K1, psso) twice, K3, (K2 tog, yfwd) twice, K1.
3rd and every foll alt row: P.
4th row: K2, (yfwd, sl 1, K1, psso) twice, K1, (K2 tog, yfwd) twice, K2.
6th row: K3, yfwd, sl 1, K1, psso, yfwd, sl 1, K2 tog, psso, yfwd, K2 tog, yfwd, K3.
8th row: K1, K2 tog, yfwd, K1, yfwd, sl 1, K1, psso, K1, K2 tog, yfwd, K1, yfwd, sl 1, K1, psso, K1.
10th row: K2 tog, yfwd, K3, yfwd, sl 1, K2 tog, psso, yfwd, K3, yfwd, sl 1, K1, psso.
12th row: K1, yfwd, sl 1, K1, psso, K7, K2 tog, yfwd, K1.
14th row: K2, yfwd, sl 1, K1, psso, K5, K2 tog, yfwd, K2.
These 14 rows form the lace patt. Cont in patt until panel is long enough, when slightly stretched, to fit along straight centre back edges, ending with a P row, dec 1 st at each end of last row. Leave sts on a holder. 11 sts.

LEFT FRONT

Work as given for right back.

RIGHT FRONT

Work as given for right back, reversing raglan shaping.

FRONT PANEL

Work as back panel.

SLEEVES
RIGHT HALF

Using 5½mm (US9) needles and A, cast on 27[30:33:36] sts.
Beg with a K row, cont in st st until

MISTLETOE   SNOWBIRDS

work measures 30[31:32:33]cm, 11¾ [12¼:12½:13]ins from beg, ending with a P row.
Shape raglan top
Dec 1 st at beg of next and every foll alt row until 2 sts rem, ending with a P row. Leave sts on a holder.

LEFT HALF
Work as given for right half, reversing raglan top shaping.

SLEEVE PANELS
(make 2)
Work as given for back panel until work is long enough, when slightly stretched, to fit along straight centre sleeve edge, ending with a P row, dec 1 st at each end of last row. Leave sts on a holder. 11 sts.

RAGLAN PANELS
(make 4)
Work as given for back panel until work is long enough, when slightly stretched, to fit armhole edge ending with a P row, dec 1 st at each end of last row. Leave sts on a holder. 11 sts.

TO MAKE UP/TO FINISH
Sew front and back panels in place having cast on edges level and sts on holder at neck.

BACK LOWER EDGE
With RS of work facing, using 4mm (US6) needles and A, K up 65[71:79:87] sts evenly along lower edge. Cont in K1, P1 rib as foll:
1st row: (WS) P1, ☆K1, P1, rep from ☆ to end.
2nd row: K1, ☆P1, K1, rep from ☆ to end.
Rep these 2 rows for 7cm, 2¾ins ending with a WS row. Cast off in rib.

FRONT LOWER EDGE
Work as given for back lower edge.

Sew sleeve panels in place, with cast on sts at cuff edges and sts on holder at top of sleeve.

CUFFS
With RS of work facing, using 4mm (US6) needles and A, K up 58[66:70:78] sts from cuff edge.
Dec row: ☆P2 tog, rep from ☆ to end. 29[33:35:39] sts.

Beg with a RS row, complete as given for lower edge.

Sew raglan panels in place, leaving left back raglan open.

NECKBAND
With RS of work facing, using 3¾mm (US5) needles and A, K11 sts of raglan panel, K2 sts of sleeve, K11 sts of sleeve panel, K2 sts of sleeve, K11 sts of raglan panel, K2[3:4:5] sts of front, K11 sts of centre panel, K2[3:4:5] sts of front, K11 sts of raglan panel, K2 sts of sleeve, K11 sts of sleeve panel, K2 sts of sleeve, K11 sts of raglan panel, K2[3:4:5] sts of back, K11 sts of centre panel, K2[3:4:5] sts of back. 104[108:112:116] sts.
Cont in K1, P1 rib for 3cm, 1¼ins ending with a WS row.
Change to B.
Next row: K.
Picot row: ☆Cast on 2 sts, cast off 6 sts, sl st on right hand needle back onto left needle, rep from ☆ to end.
Join left back raglan seam and neckband. Join side and sleeve seams.

SNOWBIRDS
Little Girl's Dress and Bolero

Sizes
To fit chest 56 – 61[61 – 66]cm, 22 – 24[24 – 26]ins
Dress actual chest 63[68]cm, 24¾[26¾]ins
Length 55[63]cm, 21¾[24¾]ins
Sleeve seam 7[9]cm, 2¾[3½]ins
Bolero actual chest 66[71]cm, 26[28]ins
Length 23.5[27]cm, 9¼[10¾]ins

Materials
Dress
6[8] × 50g balls of Patons Fairytale DK in main colour (A)
1 ball in contrast colour (B)
One pair each 3¼mm (US3) and 3¾mm (US5) knitting needles
1 'Pikaby' button
Ribbon for neck tie
Medium size crochet hook

Bolero
2[3] × 50g balls of Patons Fairytale DK
One pair each 3mm (US3) and 3¾mm (US5) knitting needles
Hook and eye fastener

Tension/Gauge
25 sts and 34 rows to 10cm, 4ins over st st using 3¾mm (US5) needles

DRESS
FRONT
☆☆Using 3¾mm (US5) needles and B, cast on 133[145] sts.
K 3 rows.
Commence patt.
1st row: Using A, K1, ☆(K2 tog) twice, (yfwd, K1) 3 times, yfwd, (sl 1, K1, psso) twice, K1, rep from ☆ to end.
2nd row: Using A, P.
3rd–8th rows: Rep 1st–2nd rows 3 times more.
9th–12th rows: Using B, K.
These 12 rows form the patt.
Work a further 12 rows in patt. Now beg with a K row, cont in st st until work measures 31[35]cm, 12¼[13¾]ins from beg, ending with a P row.
Dec row: K1, ☆K2 tog, rep from ☆ to end. 67[73] sts.
Change to 3¼mm (US3) needles.
Cont in K1, P1 rib as foll:
1st row: K1, ☆P1, K1, rep from ☆ to end.
2nd row: P1, ☆K1, P1, rep from ☆ to end.
Rep these 2 rows 3 times more, then work 1st row again.
Change to 3¾mm (US5) needles.
Inc row: K0[3], inc in next st, ☆K5, inc in next st, rep from ☆ to last 0[3] sts, K0[3]. 79[85] sts.
Beg with a P row, cont in st st until work measures 8[10]cm, 3[4]ins from top of ribbing, ending with a P row.
Shape armholes
Cast off 5 sts at beg of next 2 rows. Dec 1 st at each end of next and every foll alt row until 63[67] sts rem. ☆☆
Cont without further shaping until work measures 10[11]cm, 4[4¼]ins from beg of armhole shaping, ending with a P row.
Shape neck
Next row: K25[26] and turn, leaving rem sts on a spare needle.
Complete left side of neck first.
Dec 1 st at neck edge on every row until 17[18] sts rem. Cont without further shaping until work measures 14[16]cm, 5½[6¼]ins from beg of armhole shaping,

ending at armhole edge.
Shape shoulder
Cast off rem sts.
With RS of work facing, return to sts on spare needle. Sl centre 13[15] sts onto a holder, rejoin yarn to next st, K to end.
Complete to match first side of neck.

BACK

Work as given for front from ☆☆ to ☆☆.
Cont without further shaping until work measures 5[7]cm, 2[2¾]ins from beg of armhole shaping, ending with a P row.
Divide for back opening
Next row: K31[33] and turn, leaving rem sts on a spare needle.
Complete right side of neck first.
Cont without shaping until work measures same as front to shoulder shaping, ending at armhole edge.
Shape shoulder
Cast off 17[18] sts, work to end. Leave rem 14[15] sts on a holder.
With RS of work facing, return to sts on spare needle. Rejoin yarn, K2 tog, K to end. 31[33] sts.
Complete to match first side of neck.

SLEEVES

Using 3¼mm (US3) needles and A, cast on 45[49] sts.
Beg with a K row work 4 rows st st.
Picot hem row: K1, ☆yfwd, K2 tog, rep from ☆ to end.
Beg with a P row work 5 rows st st.
Change to 3¾mm (US5) needles.
Inc row: K1, ☆inc in next st, K1, rep from ☆ to end. 69[73] sts.
Beg with a P row cont in st st until work measures 7[9]cm, 2¾[3½]ins from picot hem row, ending with a P row.
Shape top
Cast off 5 sts at beg of next 2 rows. Dec 1 st at each end of next and every foll alt row until 29[31] sts rem, ending with a P row.
Work 4[6] rows. Cast off.

TO MAKE UP/TO FINISH

Join shoulder seams.

COLLAR

With RS of work facing, using 3¼mm (US3) needles and A, K across 14[15] sts on left back, K up 14[17] sts down left front neck, K across 6[7] sts from centre front sts. 34[39] sts.
K 9 rows, ending at back opening edge.

Dec 1 st at end of next and 2 foll alt rows.
Cast off, dec as before.
With RS of work facing, return to sts on front neck holder. Rejoin yarn, K2 tog, K5[6] sts of centre front, K up 14[17] sts up right side of neck, then K across 14[15] sts on right back. 34[39] sts.
Complete as given for first side of collar, reversing shaping.

Set in sleeves, gathering top to fit. Join side and sleeve seams. Fold picot hem on sleeves to WS and catch down.

With RS of work facing, using crochet hook and A, work a row of dc (sc) crochet around back opening. Make a 4 ch button loop at neck edge. Sew on button. Cut a length of ribbon, tie in a bow and sew to front neck.

BOLERO

BACK

Using 3mm (US3) needles, cast on 83[89] sts.
Beg with a K row, work 4 rows st st.
Picot hem row: K1, ☆yfwd, K2 tog, rep from ☆ to end.
Beg with a P row, work 5 rows st st.
Change to 3¾mm (US5) needles.
Beg with a K row, cont in st st until work measures 8[9.5], 3[3¾]ins from picot hem row, ending with a P row.
Shape armholes
Cast off 6 sts at beg of next 2 rows. Dec 1 st at each end of next and every foll alt row until 61[65] sts rem.
Cont without further shaping until work measures 23.5[27]cm, 9¼[10¾]ins from picot hem row, ending with a P row.
Shape shoulders
Cast off 15[16] sts at beg of next 2 rows.
Leave rem 31[33] sts on a spare needle.

LEFT FRONT

Using 3mm (US3) needles, cast on 41[45] sts.
Beg with a K row, work 4 rows st st.
Picot hem row: K1, ☆yfwd, K2 tog, rep from ☆ to end.
Beg with a P row, work 5 rows st st.
Change to 3¾mm (US5) needles.
Beg with a K row, cont in st st until work measures same as back to armhole shaping, ending at side edge.
Shape armhole
Cast off 6 sts at beg of next row. Dec 1 st

at armhole edge on every foll alt row until 30[33] sts rem.
Cont without further shaping until work measures 17[21] rows less than back to shoulder shaping, ending at front edge.
Shape neck
Cast off 5 sts at beg of next row. Dec 1 st at neck edge on every row until 15[16] sts rem. Cont without further shaping until work measures same as back to shoulder shaping, ending at armhole edge.
Shape shoulder
Cast off rem sts.

RIGHT FRONT

Work as given for left front, reversing shapings, working 1 more row before neck shaping.

TO MAKE UP/TO FINISH

Join shoulder seams.

ARMBANDS

With RS of work facing, using 3mm (US3) needles, K up 97[105] sts evenly around armhole edge.
Beg with a P row, work 3 rows st st.
Picot hem row: K1, ☆yfwd, K2 tog, rep from ☆ to end.
Beg with a P row, work 3 rows st st. Cast off loosely.

FRONT EDGINGS

With RS of work facing, using 3mm (US3) needles, K up 47[53] sts from front edge.
Complete as given for armbands.

NECK EDGING

With RS of work facing, using 3mm (US3) needles, beg at picot row of right front edging, K up 25[29] sts up right side of neck, K across 31[33] sts on back neck, K up 25[29] sts down left side of neck to picot row of left front edging. 81[91] sts.
Complete as given for armbands.

Join side seams. Fold all picot hems to WS and catch down. Sew hook and eye fastener to front neck.

SNOWFLAKES *Children's Sweater and Cardigan*

Sizes

To fit chest 51[56:61:66:71]cm,
20[22:24:26:28]ins
Sweater actual chest 56[60:66:70:75]cm,
22[23¾:26:27½:29½]ins
Cardigan actual chest
58[61.5:67:71:77]cm,
22¾[24¼:26½:28:30½]ins
Length 36[38:40:42:44]cm,
14¼[15:15¾:16½:17¼]ins
Sleeve seam 25[26:27:28:30]cm,
9¾[10¼:10¾:11:11¾]ins

Materials

Sweater
4[4:5:5:6] × 50g balls of Sunbeam Aran
Knit in main colour (A)
3[3:3:4:4] balls in contrast colour (B)

Cardigan
4[5:5:5:6] × 50g balls of Sunbeam Aran
Knit in main colour (A)
3[3:3:4:4] balls in contrast colour (B)
5 'Pikaby' toggles

Both versions
One pair each 4mm (US6) and 5mm
(US8) knitting needles

Tension/Gauge

21 sts and 21 rows to 10cm, 4ins over patt
using 5mm (US8) needles

Key
A ☐
B ✕

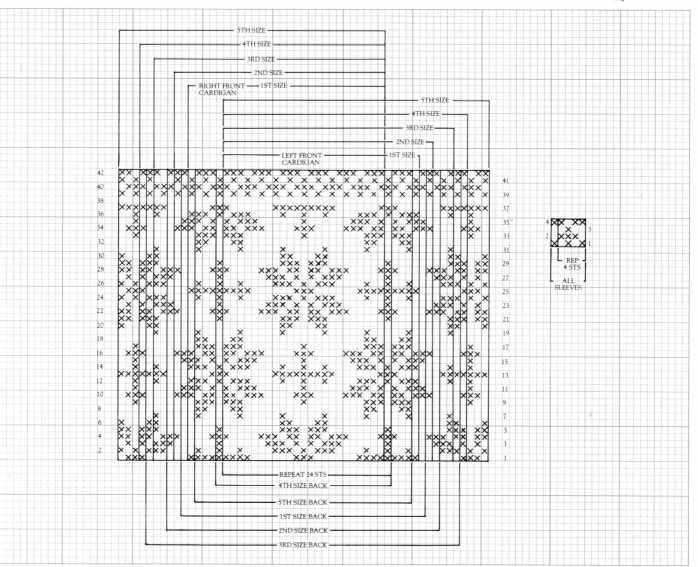

SNOWFLAKES

SWEATER

BACK

☆☆Using 4mm (US6) needles and A, cast on 53[57:61:65:69] sts.

Cont in K1, P1 rib as foll:

1st row: (RS) K1, ☆P1, K1, rep from ☆ to end.

2nd row: P1, ☆K1, P1, rep from ☆ to end.

Rep these 2 rows for 5[5:6:6:7]cm, 2[2:2½:2½:2¾]ins, ending with a RS row.

Inc row: Rib 9[8:9:8:7], ☆inc in next st, rib 6[7:5:6:5], rep from ☆ to last 9[9:10:8:8] sts, inc in next st, rib to end. 59[63:69:73:79] sts.

Change to 5mm (US8) needles. Beg with a K row cont in st st working colour patt from chart.• Read odd numbered rows (K) from right to left and even numbered rows (P) from left to right. Strand yarn not in use loosely across WS of work, twisting yarns when changing colour to avoid a hole. Work 42 rows, then rep 39th–42nd rows inclusive only until work measures 22[23:24:25:26]cm, 8¾[9:9½: 9¾:10¼]ins from beg, ending with a P row.

Shape armholes

Cast off 6 sts at beg of next 2 rows. 47[51:57:61:67] sts. ☆☆

Cont without further shaping until work measures 36[38:40:42:44]cm, 14¼[15: 15¾:16½:17¼]ins from beg, ending with a P row.

Shape shoulders

Cast off 7[9:12:14:17] sts at beg of next 2 rows. Leave rem 33 sts on a spare needle.

FRONT

Work as given for back from ☆☆ to ☆☆. Cont without further shaping until work measures 12 rows less than back to shoulder shaping, ending with a P row.

Shape neck

Next row: Patt 18[20:23:25:28] sts and turn leaving rem sts on a spare needle. Complete left side of neck first.

Cast off 4 sts at beg of next row, 3 sts at beg of next alt row and 2 sts at beg of foll alt row. Dec 1 st at neck edge on every foll alt row until 7[9:12:14:17] sts rem.

Cont without further shaping until work measures same as back to shoulder shaping, ending at armhole edge.

Shape shoulder

Cast off rem sts.

With RS of work facing, return to sts on

spare needle. Sl centre 11 sts onto a holder, rejoin yarn at neck edge and patt to end.

Work 1 row. Complete as given for first side of neck.

SLEEVES

Using 4mm (US6) needles and A, cast on 29[29:31:31:33] sts.

Cont in K1, P1 rib as given for back for 5cm, 2ins ending with a RS row.

Inc row: Rib 3[7:7:5:5], ☆inc in next st, rib 1[0:0:0:0], rep from ☆ to last 4[7:7:5:5] sts, inc in next st, rib to end. 41[45:49:53:57] sts.

Change to 5mm (US8) needles. Beg with a K row cont in st st working colour patt from chart,† *at the same time*, inc and work into patt, 1 st at each end of 3rd and every foll 4th row until there are 61[65:69:73:77] sts.

Cont without further shaping until work measures 28[29:30:31:33]cm, 11[11½: 11¾:12¼:13]ins from beg, ending with a P row.

Cast off loosely.

TO MAKE UP/TO FINISH

Join right shoulder seam.

NECKBAND

With RS of work facing, using 4mm (US6) needles and A, K up 18 sts down left side of neck, K across 11 sts at centre front, K up 17 sts up right side of neck, then K across 33 sts on back neck. 79 sts. Beg with a WS row, cont in K1, P1 rib as given for back for 5cm, 2ins.

Cast off in rib.

Join left shoulder and neckband seam. Fold neckband in half onto WS and catch down. Placing centre of cast off edge of sleeve to shoulder seam, set in sleeves, sewing final rows to cast off sts at underarm. Join side and sleeve seams.

CARDIGAN

BACK

Work as given for back of sweater.

LEFT FRONT

Using 4mm (US6) needles and A, cast on 25[27:29:31:33] sts.

Cont in K1, P1 rib as given for back for 5[5:6:6:7]cm, 2[2:2½:2½:2¾]ins ending with a RS row.

Inc row: Rib 6[7:7:6:6], ☆inc in next st,

rib 5[5:4:5:4], rep from ☆ to last 7[8:7:7:7] sts, inc in next st, rib to end. 28[30:33:35:38] sts.

Change to 5mm (US8) needles and beg with a K row cont in st st working colour patt from chart.

Work 42 rows, then rep 39th–42nd rows inclusive only until work measures same as back to armhole shaping, ending with a P row.

Shape armhole

Cast off 6 sts at beg of next row. 22[24:27:29:32] sts.

Cont without further shaping until work measures 30[32:34:36:38]cm, 11¾[12½: 13½:14¼:15]ins from beg, ending with a K row.

Shape neck

Cast off 5 sts at beg of next row, 4 sts at beg of foll alt row and 3 sts at beg of next alt row. Cast off 2 sts at beg of next alt row then dec 1 st at neck edge on foll alt row. 7[9:12:14:17] sts.

Cont without further shaping until work measures same as back to shoulder shaping, ending with a P row.

Shape shoulder

Cast off rem sts.

RIGHT FRONT

Work as given for left front, reversing all shapings.

SLEEVES

Work as given for sleeves of sweater.

LEFT FRONT BAND

Using 4mm (US6) needles and A, cast on 6 sts.

Cont in K1, P1 rib until band, when slightly stretched, fits up left front to neck edge, ending with a WS row. Cut yarn and leave sts on a spare needle.

RIGHT FRONT BAND

Work as given for left front band but do not cut yarn.

TOGGLE LOOPS

(make 5)

Using 4mm (US6) needles and A, cast on 18 sts. Cast off.

TO MAKE UP/TO FINISH

Sew on front bands. Join shoulder seams.

NECKBAND

With RS of work facing, using 4mm (US6) needles and A, rib across 6 sts of right front band, K up 22 sts up right side of neck, K across 33 sts on back neck, K up 22 sts down left side of neck, then rib across 6 sts on left frontband. 89 sts.

Cont in K1, P1 rib as given for sweater back for 5cm, 2ins. Cast off loosely in rib.

Fold neckband in half onto WS and catch down. Placing centre of cast off edge of sleeve to shoulder seam, set in sleeves, sewing final rows to cast off sts at underarm. Join side and sleeve seams.

Fold toggle loops in half and sew to right frontband. Sew on toggles.

FROST AND ICE

His & Her Sweaters

Sizes

To fit chest/bust 81[91:102:112]cm, 32[36:40:44]ins

Actual chest/bust 92[101:111:121]cm, 36¼[39¾:43¾:47¾]ins

Length 68[70:72:74]cm, 26¾[27½:28¼:29¼]ins

Sleeve seam 45[45:48:48]cm, 17¾[17¾:19:19]ins

Scarf length 140cm, 55¼ins

Materials

Sweater

18[19:20:21] × 50g balls of Sunbeam Aran Knit in main colour (A)

2[2:2:2] balls in contrast colour (B)

Scarf

5 × 50g balls of Sunbeam Aran Knit

One pair each 3¾mm (US5) and 4½mm (US7) knitting needles

Cable needle

Set of four 3¾mm (US5) double pointed needles

Tension/Gauge

25 sts and 25 rows to 10cm, 4ins over patt using 4½mm (US7) needles

CABLE 1

(worked over 10 sts using B)

1st row: (WS) P.

2nd row: K.

3rd–4th rows: Rep 1st–2nd rows once.

5th row: K.

6th row: Sl next 5 sts onto cable needle and hold at front of work, K5, then K5 from cable needle – called C10F.

7th–14th rows: Rep 1st–2nd rows 4 times more.

These 14 rows form cable 1.

CABLE 2

(worked over 10 sts using B)

1st row: (WS) P.

2nd row: K.

3rd–10th rows: Rep 1st–2nd rows 4 times more.

11th row: P.

12th row: Sl next 5 sts onto cable needle and hold at back of work, K5, then K5, from cable needle – called C10B.

13th–14th rows: Rep 1st–2nd rows.

These 14 rows form cable 2.

CABLE 3

(worked over 10 sts using B)

Work as given for cable 2, but on 12th row work C10F instead of C10B.

CABLE 4

Work as given for cable 1, but on 6th row work C10B instead of C10F.

CENTRE PANEL

(worked over 49[61:73:85] sts using A)

1st row: (WS) (P2, K3[5:7:9]) 3 times, P2, K15, (P2, K3[5:7:9]) 3 times, P2.

2nd row: (Sl next 2 sts onto cable needle and hold at front of work, P1 then K2 from cable needle – called T3F, P2[4:6:8]) 3 times, T3F, P13, (sl next st onto cable needle and hold at back of work, K2 then P1 from cable needle – called T3B, P2[4:6:8]) 3 times, T3B.

3rd and foll alt rows: K the P sts and P the K sts of previous row.

4th row: P1, (T3F, P2[4:6:8]) 3 times, T3F, P11, (T3B, P2[4:6:8]) 3 times, T3B, P1.

6th row: P2, (T3F, P2[4:6:8]) 3 times, T3F, P9, T3B, P2[4:6:8]) 3 times, T3B, P2.

8th row: P3, (T3F, P2[4:6:8]) 3 times, T3F, P7, (T3B, P2[4:6:8]) 3 times, T3B, P3.

10th row: P4, (T3F, P2[4:6:8]) 3 times, T3F, P5, (T3B, P2[4:6:8]) 3 times, T3B, P4.

12th row: P5, (T3F, P2[4:6:8]) 3 times, T3F, P3, (T3B, P2[4:6:8]) 3 times, T3B, P5.

14th row: P6, (T3F, P2[4:6:8]) 3 times, T3F, P1, (T3B, P2[4:6:8]) 3 times, T3B, P6.

16th row: P6, (T3B, P2[4:6:8]) 3 times, T3B, P1, (T3F, P2[4:6:8]) 3 times, T3F, P6.

FROST AND ICE

18th row: P5, (T3B, P2[4:6:8]) 3 times, T3B, P3, (T3F, P2[4:6:8]) 3 times, T3F, P5.
20th row: P4, (T3B, P2[4:6:8]) 3 times, T3B, P5, (T3F, P2[4:6:8]) 3 times, T3F, P4.
22nd row: P3, (T3B, P2[4:6:8]) 3 times, T3B, P7, (T3F, P2[4:6:8]) 3 times, T3F, P3.
24th row: P2, (T3B, P2[4:6:8]) 3 times, T3B, P9, (T3F, P2[4:6:8]) 3 times, T3F, P2.
26th row: P1, (T3B, P2[4:6:8]) 3 times, T3B, P11, (T3F, P2[4:6:8]) 3 times, T3F, P1.
28th row: (T3B, P2[4:6:8]) 3 times, T3B, P13, (T3F, P2[4:6:8]) 3 times, T3F.
These 28 rows form the centre panel.

BACK

Using 3¾mm (US5) needles and A, cast on 90[100:110:120] sts.
Cont in K1, P1 rib for 10cm, 4ins ending with a WS row.
Inc row: K9[11:13:15], ☆inc in next st, K2, rep from ☆ to last 9[11:13:15] sts, inc in next st, K to end. 115[127:139: 151] sts.
Change to 4½mm (US7) needles and commence patt. Use small separate balls of yarn for each area of colour, twist yarn on WS of work when changing colour to avoid a hole.
1st row: (WS) (P1A, K2A) 3 times, work 1st row of cable 4, K2A, work 1st row of cable 3, K2A, work 1st row of centre panel, K2A, work 1st row of cable 2, K2A, work 1st row of cable 1, (K2A, P1A) 3 times.
2nd row: (K1A, P2A) 3 times, work 2nd row of cable 1, P2A, work 2nd row of cable 2, P2A, work 2nd row of centre panel, P2A, work 2nd row of cable 3, P2A, work 2nd row of cable 4, (P2A, K1A) 3 times.
These 2 rows establish the position of cables and centre panel with rev st st between and ribbing at side edges.
Cont in patt as set, keeping cables and centre panel correct until work measures 60[62:62:64]cm, 23¾[24½:24½:25¼]ins from beg, ending with a WS row. Cast off. Mark centre back with a coloured thread.

FRONT

Work as given for back, omit coloured marker thread.

LEFT SLEEVE

Using 3¾mm (US5) needles and A, cast on 40[44:48:52] sts.
Cont in K1, P1 rib for 8[8:9:9]cm, 3[3:3½:3½]ins ending with a WS row, inc 1 st at end of last row. 41[45:49: 53] sts.
Change to 4½mm (US7) needles and cont in rib patt as foll:
1st row: (RS) P2, ☆K1, P3, rep from ☆ to last 3 sts, K1, P2.
2nd row: K2, ☆P1, K3, rep from ☆ to last 3 sts, P1, K2.
These 2 rows form the rib patt. Cont in patt, inc 1 st at each end of next and every foll alt row until there are 129[133:141:145] sts.
Cont without further shaping until work measures 45[45:48:48]cm, 17¾[17¾:19: 19]ins from beg, ending with a WS row.
Shape saddle
Cast off 45[45:47:47] sts at beg of next 2 rows. 39[43:47:51] sts.
Cont in patt for a further 13[16: 17.5:20]cm, 5¼[6¼:6¾:8]ins, ending with a WS row.
Shape neck
Next row: Patt 19[21:23:25] and turn, leaving rem sts on a spare needle.
Complete back neck first.
Cont in patt until saddle fits along cast off edge of back to coloured marker, ending with a WS row. Cut yarn and leave sts on a holder.
With RS of work facing, return to sts on spare needle. Rejoin yarn, cast off centre 6[7:8:9] sts, patt to end. 14[15:16:17] sts.
Dec 1 st at neck edge of next 12[13:14:15] rows, then dec 1 st at neck edge on every row until 2 sts rem, then on every foll alt row until 1 st rem.
Fasten off.

RIGHT SLEEVE

Work as given for left sleeve reversing shapings.

TO MAKE UP/TO FINISH

Graft sts of back neck sections of sleeves tog. Sew cast off edges of back and front to saddle of sleeve.

NECKBAND

Using set of four 3¾mm (US5) double pointed needles and A, beg at centre back, K up 10[12:14:16] sts across back, 48[52:56:60] sts from front neck, then

10[12:14:16] sts to centre back. 68[76:84:92] sts.
Work 8 rounds K1, P1 rib. Cast off in rib.

Sew cast off edges of sleeves to back and front. Join side and sleeve seams.

SCARF

Using 4½mm (US7) needles, cast on 47 sts. Cont in rib patt as foll:
1st row: (RS) K2, ☆P3, K1, rep from ☆ to last st, K1.
2nd row: K1, P1, ☆K3, P1, rep from ☆ to last st, K1.
Rep the last 2 rows until work measures 140cm, 55ins from beg, ending with a WS row. Cast off in rib.

WINTER LEAVES
Lady's Jacket

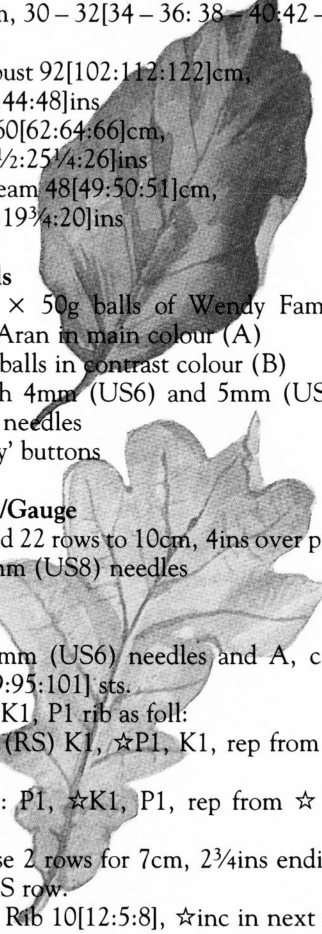

Sizes
To fit bust 76 – 81[86 – 91: 97 – 102:107 – 112]cm, 30 – 32[34 – 36: 38 – 40:42 – 44]ins
Actual bust 92[102:112:122]cm, 36¼[40:44:48]ins
Length 60[62:64:66]cm, 23¾[24½:25¼:26]ins
Sleeve seam 48[49:50:51]cm, 19[19¼:19¾:20]ins

Materials
8[8:9:9] × 50g balls of Wendy Family Choice Aran in main colour (A)
5[5:6:6] balls in contrast colour (B)
Pair each 4mm (US6) and 5mm (US8) knitting needles
9 'Pikaby' buttons

Tension/Gauge
20 sts and 22 rows to 10cm, 4ins over patt using 5mm (US8) needles

BACK
Using 4mm (US6) needles and A, cast on 83[89:95:101] sts.
Cont in K1, P1 rib as foll:
1st row: (RS) K1, ☆P1, K1, rep from ☆ to end.
2nd row: P1, ☆K1, P1, rep from ☆ to end.
Rep these 2 rows for 7cm, 2¾ins ending with a RS row.
Inc row: Rib 10[12:5:8], ☆inc in next st, rib 6[4:4:3], rep from ☆ to last 10[12:5:9] sts, inc in next st, rib to end.

WINTER LEAVES

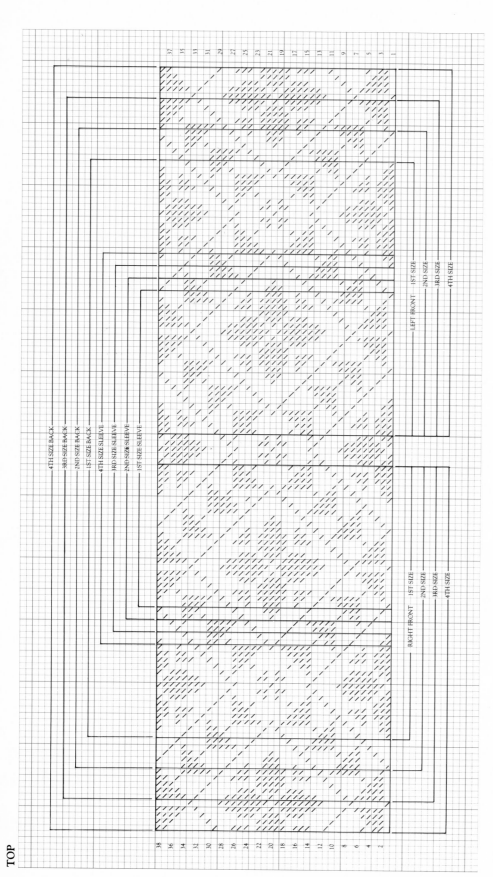

93[103:113:123] sts.
Change to 5mm (US8) needles. Beg with a K row cont in st st working colour patt from chart. Read odd numbered rows (K) from right to left and even numbered rows (P) from left to right. Strand yarn not in use loosely across WS of work and twist yarns tog when changing colour to avoid a hole.
Cont working from chart until work measures 37[38:39:40]cm, 14½[15:15½: 15¾]ins from beg, ending with a P row.
Shape armholes
Cast off 10 sts at beg of next 2 rows. 73[83:93:103] sts.
Cont without further shaping until work measures 60[62:64:66]cm, 23¾[24½ 25¼:26]ins from beg, ending with a P row.
Shape shoulders
Cast off 19[23:27:31] sts at beg of next 2 rows. Leave rem 35[37:39:41] sts on a spare needle.

LEFT FRONT
Using 4mm (US6) needles and A, cast on 41[45:49:53] sts.
Cont in K1, P1 rib as given for back for 7cm, 2¾ins ending with a WS row.
Inc row: Rib 10[9:8:9], ☆inc in next st, rib 9[8:7:6], rep from ☆ to last 11[9:9: 9] sts, inc in next st, rib to end. 44[49:54:59] sts.
Change to 5mm (US8) needles. Beg with a K row cont in st st working colour patt from chart.
Cont working from chart until work measures same as back to armhole shaping, ending with a P row.
Shape armhole
Cast off 10 sts at beg of next row. 34[39:44:49] sts.
Cont without further shaping until work measures 52[54:56:58]cm, 20½[21¼:22: 22¾]ins from beg, ending with a K row.
Shape neck
Cast off 5 sts at beg of next row, 4 sts at beg of next alt row and 3 sts at beg of foll alt row. Cast off 2 sts at beg of foll 1[1:2:2] alt rows then dec 1 st at neck edge on every foll alt row until 19[23:27:31] sts rem.

Cont without further shaping until work measures same as back to shoulder shaping, ending with a P row.
Shape shoulder
Cast off rem sts.

RIGHT FRONT

Work as given for left front, reversing all shapings.

SLEEVES

Using 4mm (US6) needles and A, cast on 41[45:49:53] sts.
Cont in K1, P1 rib as given for back for 6cm, 2½ins ending with a RS row.
Inc row: Rib 7[4:6:8], ☆inc in next st, rib 2[3:3:3], rep from ☆ to last 7[5:7:9] sts, inc in next st, rib to end. 51[55:59:63] sts.
Change to 5mm (US8) needles. Beg with a K row cont in st st working colour patt from chart, *at the same time*, inc and work into patt 1 st at each end of 3rd and every foll 4th row until there are 93[97:101:105] sts.
Cont without further shaping until work measures 53[54:55:56]cm, 21[21¼:21¾: 22]ins from beg, ending with a P row.
Cast off loosely.

BUTTONBAND

Using 4mm (US6) needles and A, cast on 9 sts.
Cont in K1, P1 rib as given for back until band is long enough, when slightly stretched, to fit up left front edge, ending at inner edge. Cut yarn and leave sts on a safety pin.

TO MAKE UP/TO FINISH

Join shoulder seams. Sew on button-band.
Mark the position of 8 buttons on the band, the first in the 3rd row from cast on edge, the last 3cm, 1¼ins below neck edge with the others evenly spaced between.

BUTTONHOLE BAND

Work as given for buttonband but end at outer edge, do not cut yarn and make buttonholes opposite markers as foll:
1st buttonhole row: (RS) Rib 4, cast off 2, rib to end.
2nd buttonhole row: Rib to end, casting on 2 sts over those cast off in previous row.

NECKBAND

With RS facing, using 4mm (US6) needles and A, rib across 9 sts of buttonhole band, K up 25 sts up right front neck, K across 35[37:39:41] sts on back neck, K up 25 sts down left front neck, then rib across 9 sts of buttonband. 103[105:107:109] sts.
Beg with a 2nd row, cont in K1, P1 rib as given for back. Work 1 row then rep 1st and 2nd buttonhole rows.
Work 6 rows in rib, rep 1st and 2nd buttonhole rows again.
Work 1 row in rib. Cast off loosely in rib. Sew on buttonhole band.
Fold neckband in half onto WS and catch down, neaten double buttonhole. Placing centre of cast off edge of sleeve to shoulder seam, set in sleeves sewing final rows to cast off sts at underarm. Join side and sleeve seams. Sew on buttons.

DAISY *Child's Sweater with Matching Beret, Mittens and Scarf*

Sizes
Sweater
To fit chest 51 – 56[61 – 66]cm, 20 – 22[24 – 26]ins
Actual chest 60[66]cm, 23¾[26]ins
Length 34[38]cm, 13½[15]ins
Sleeve seam 32[36]cm, 12½[14¼]ins
Mitts
Round hand 17.5[20.5]cm, 6¾[8¼]ins
Beret
Diameter of crown 23cm, 9ins
Scarf
Length 110[116.5]cm, 43¼[45¾]ins

Materials
For set
4[5] × 100g balls of Twilleys Capricorn in main colour (A)
1 ball in each of 2 contrast colours (B and C)
One pair each 4½mm (US7), 5mm (US8) and 6mm (US10) knitting needles

Tension/Gauge
13 sts and 22 rows to 10cm, 4ins over moss st using 6mm (US10) needles

SWEATER

BACK

Using 5mm (US8) needles and A, cast on 37[43] sts.
Cont in K1, P1 rib as foll:
1st row: (RS) K1, ☆P1, K1, rep from ☆ to end.
2nd row: P1, ☆K1, P1, rep from ☆ to end.
Rep these 2 rows for 6cm, 2½ins ending with a WS row.
Change to 6mm (US10) needles. Cont in moss st as foll:
1st row: (RS) K1, ☆P1, K1, rep from ☆ to end.
This row forms moss st patt.
Cont in patt until work measures 12[15]cm, 4¾[6]ins from beg ending with a WS row.
Commence yoke.
With C, K 4 rows.
With A, beg with a K row, work 2 rows st st.
Cont in st st, working colour motifs from chart. Strand yarn not in use loosely across back of work and twist yarns when changing colour to avoid a hole.
Read odd numbered rows (K) from right to left and even numbered rows (P) from left to right.
1st row: K1[2]A, work 1st row of chart, (K1[3]A, work 1st row of chart) twice, K1[2]A.
2nd row: P1[2]A, work 2nd row of chart, (P1[3]A, work 2nd row of chart) twice, P1[2]A.
These 2 rows establish the position of the motifs with st st between. Keeping chart correct cont as set until the 11 rows of chart have been completed.
With A, P 1 row.
With C, K 4 rows.
With A, P 1 row.
Cont in A, working in moss st until work

measures 34[38]cm, 13½[15]ins from beg, ending with a WS row.
Shape shoulders
Cast off 11[13] sts at beg of next 2 rows.
Leave rem 15[17] sts on a spare needle.

FRONT

Work as given for back until work measures 8[10] rows less than back to shoulder shaping, ending with a WS row.
Shape neck
Next row: Patt 16[18] and turn leaving rem sts on a spare needle.
Complete left side of neck first.
Dec 1 st at neck edge on every row until 11[13] sts rem.
Cont without further shaping until work measures same as back to shoulder shaping, ending at armhole edge.
Shape shoulder
Cast off rem sts.
With RS of work facing, return to sts on spare needle. Sl centre 5[7] sts onto a holder, rejoin yarn to next st and patt to end.
Complete as given for first side of neck.

SLEEVES

Using 5mm (US8) needles and A, cast on 21[23] sts.
Cont in K1, P1 rib as given for back for 6cm, 2½ins ending with a WS row.
Change to 6mm (US10) needles. Cont in moss st as given for back, inc 1 st at each end of 3rd and every foll 4th row until there are 39[43] sts.
Cont without further shaping until work measures 32[36]cm, 12½[14¼]ins from beg, ending with a WS row.
Cast off loosely.

TO MAKE UP/TO FINISH

Join right shoulder seam.

NECKBAND

With RS of work facing, using 5mm (US8) needles and A, K up 8[10] sts down left side of neck, inc in first st, (K1, inc in next st) 2[3] times across 5[7] sts at centre front, K up 8[10] sts up right side of neck, then inc in first st, (K1, inc in next st) 7[8] times across 15[17] sts on back neck. 47[57] sts.
Beg with a WS row cont in K1, P1 rib as given for back for 5cm, 2ins. Cast off loosely in rib.

Join left shoulder and neckband seam.

Placing centre of cast off edge of sleeve to shoulder seam, set in sleeves. Join side and sleeve seams.
Fold neckband in half onto WS and catch down.

MITTS

RIGHT HAND

☆☆Using 4½mm (US7) needles and A, cast on 23[27] sts.
Cont in K1, P1 rib as given for sweater back for 4cm, 1½ins ending with a WS row.
Change to 6mm (US10) needles. Cont in moss st as given for sweater back.
Work 8[10] rows. ☆☆
Divide for thumb
Next row: Patt 17[19] sts and turn.
Next row: Patt 4, cast on 4 sts. 8 sts.
☆☆☆Work 8[10] rows.
Shape top of thumb
Next row: ☆K2 tog, rep from ☆ to end. 4 sts.
Cut off yarn, thread through rem sts, draw up and fasten off securely. Join thumb seam.
With RS of work facing rejoin yarn to inside edge, K up 4 sts from base of thumb, patt to end. 23[27] sts.
Cont in moss st until work measures 13[14]cm, 5¼[5½]ins from beg, ending with a WS row.
Shape top
Next row: Work 2 tog, ☆patt 2, work 2 tog, rep from ☆ to last st, patt 1.
Next row: Patt to end.
Next row: Work 2 tog, ☆patt 1, work 2 tog, rep from ☆ to end.
Next row: Patt to end.
Next row: ☆Work 2 tog, rep from ☆ to last st, patt 1.
Next row: Patt to end.
Cut yarn, thread through rem sts, draw up and fasten off securely. Join seam.

LEFT HAND

Work as given for right hand from ☆☆ to ☆☆.
Divide for thumb
Next row: Patt 13[15] sts and turn.
Next row: Cast off 4, patt these sts, patt 4 sts, turn. 8 sts.
Complete as given for right hand from ☆☆☆ to end.

BERET

Using 5mm (US8) needles and A, cast on 61 sts.

Work 5 rows K1, P1 rib as given for back of sweater.
Inc row: Rib 1, ☆inc in next st, rep from ☆ to end. 121 sts.
Change to 6mm (US10) needles. Cont in moss st as given for back of sweater.
Work 18 rows.
Shape crown
1st row: ☆Patt 12, sl 1, K2 tog, psso, rep from ☆ to last st, patt 1.
2nd and every foll alt row: Patt to end.
3rd row: ☆Patt 10, sl 1, K2 tog, psso, rep from ☆ to last st, patt 1.
5th row: ☆Patt 8, sl 1, K2 tog, psso, rep from ☆ to last st, patt 1.
7th row: ☆Patt 6, sl 1, K2 tog, psso, rep from ☆ to last st, patt 1.
9th row: ☆Patt 4, sl 1, K2 tog, psso, rep from ☆ to last st, patt 1.
11th row: ☆Patt 2, sl 1, K2 tog, psso, rep from ☆ to last st, patt 1.
13th row: ☆Patt 1, sl 1, K1, psso, rep from ☆ to last st, patt 1.
15th row: ☆K2 tog, rep from ☆ to last st, patt 1.
Cut yarn, thread through rem sts, draw up and fasten off securely.
Join seam. With B, make a pom-pon approximately 7cm, 2¾ins in diameter and sew to crown.

SCARF

Using 6mm (US10) needles and A, cast on 19 sts.
Cont in moss st as given for sweater until work measures 110[116.5]cm, 43¼[45¾]ins from beg. Cast off.
Make 2 pom-pons, one in B and one in C approximately 9cm, 3½ins in diameter. Gather cast on and cast off edges of scarf and finish with a pom-pon.

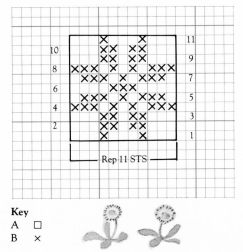

Key
A □
B ×

DAISY

ACCESSORIES

CHILD'S RIBBED POM-PON HAT

featured in 'Song Thrush and Young', 'Mouse and Hare', 'Hedgehog' and 'Snowflakes'.

Sizes
To fit ages 3 to 6 years

Materials
2 × 50g balls double knitting yarn.
Oddment (odds and ends) of contrast colour for pom-pon.
One pair 3¾mm (US5) knitting needles.

Tension/Gauge
28 sts and 30 rows to 10cm, 4ins over rib using 3¾mm (US5) needles.

HAT
Using 3¾mm (US5) needles cast on 109 sts.
1st row: (RS) K1, ☆P1, K1, rep from ☆ to end.
2nd row: P1, ☆K1, P1, rep from ☆ to end.
Rep these 2 rows until work measures 21cm, 8¼ins from beg, ending with a WS row.
Shape top
1st row: ☆Rib 7, K2 tog, rep from ☆ to last st, rib 1.
2nd and every foll alt row: Rib to end.
3rd row: ☆Rib 6, K2 tog, rep from ☆ to last st, rib 1.
5th row: ☆Rib 5, K2 tog, rep from ☆ to last st, rib 1.
Cont to dec in this way on every alt row until 25 sts rem, ending with a WS row.
Next row: ☆K2 tog, rep from ☆ to last st, K1.
Break off yarn and thread through rem 13 sts and fasten off securely.

TO MAKE UP/TO FINISH
Join seam, reversing seam for turn back.
Make a pom-pon and sew in position.
Roll brim or turn back.

CHILDREN'S MOHAIR BERETS

featured in 'Purple Willow', 'Daffy-down-Dilly' and 'Crimson Toadstools'.

Sizes
Small [medium: large]
Approximate measurement across diameter 20[22:24]cm, 8[8¾:9½]ins.

Materials
50g of Sunbeam Paris Mohair OR Sumatra OR Aran; oddments (odds and ends) of contrast colour for pom-pon or embroidery if required.
One pair each 4½mm (US7) and 5mm (US8) knitting needles if using Sunbeam Sumatra or Aran OR one pair each 5mm (US8) and 5½mm (US9) knitting needles if using Sunbeam Paris Mohair.

Tension/Gauge
16 sts and 22 rows to 10cm, 4ins over st st using 5mm (US8) needles (for Sumatra or Aran) OR 5½mm (US9) needles (for Paris Mohair).
N.B. Needle sizes given are for Mohair, for Sumatra or Aran read sizes given in square brackets [ ].

BERET
Using 5mm (US8) [4½mm (US7)] needles cast on 63[69:75] sts.
1st row: (RS) K1, ☆P1, K1, rep from ☆ to end.
2nd row: P1, ☆K1, P1, rep from ☆ to end.
Rep these 2 rows for 2.5cm, 1in ending with a 2nd row, inc 33[43, 53]sts evenly across last row. 96[112:128]sts.
Change to 5½mm (US8) [5mm (US8)] needles and beg with a K row, work in st st until work measures 5.5[6:8]cm 2¼[2½:3]ins from beg, ending with a RS row. K 1 row.
Shape crown
1st row: K.
2nd row: P.

3rd row: ☆K2 tog, K8[10:12], K2 tog tbl, rep from ☆ to end. 80[96:112] sts.
Work 3 rows in st st.
Next row: (RS) ☆K2 tog, K6[8:10], K2 tog tbl, rep from ☆ to end. 64[80:96] sts.
Work 3 rows in st st.
Cont to work decs in this way on every 4th row, working 2 sts less between decs, each time until 32[48:64] sts rem.
Next row: 1st size only: ☆K2 tog, K2 tbl, rep from ☆ to end. 16 sts. P 1 row.
2nd size only: ☆K2 tog, K2, K2 tog tbl, rep from ☆ to end. 32 sts. P 1 row. Next row: ☆K2 tog, K2 tog tbl, rep from ☆ to end. 16 sts. P 1 row.
3rd size only: ☆K2 tog, K4, K2 tog tbl, rep from ☆ to end. 48 sts. P 1 row. Complete as for 2nd size. 16 sts.
All sizes: K2 tog, ☆K3 tog, rep from ☆ 3 times, K2 tog. 6 sts.
Break yarn and thread through rem sts, pull up tightly and secure firmly.

TO MAKE UP/TO FINISH
Join seam.
Make pom-pon and sew on top of crown (optional) or embroider French Knots.

CHILDREN'S RIBBED SCARVES

featured in 'Fair Maids of February', 'Purple Willow', 'Song Thrush and Young', 'Mouse and Hare', 'Lambs', 'Daffy-down-Dilly', 'Crimson Toadstools' and 'Snowflakes'.

Size
Approximately 102cm, 40ins long by 13cm, 5¼ins wide.

Materials
2 × 50g balls double knitting yarn OR 3 × 25g balls mohair type yarn.
One pair 4mm (US6) knitting needles for double knitting yarn OR one pair 5mm (US8) knitting needles for mohair type yarn

Tension/Gauge
31 sts and 26 rows to 10cm, 4ins over rib

using 4mm (US6) needles and double knitting yarn
24 sts and 26 rows to 10cm, 4ins over rib using 5mm (US8) needles and mohair type yarn
N.B. Figures in square brackets should be worked if using mohair type yarn.

SCARF

Using 4mm (US6) [5mm (US8)] needles cast on 44[32] sts.
Work in K1, P1 rib OR K2, P2 rib until work measures 102cm, 40ins or length required.
Cast off loosely in rib, BUT if adding pom-pons DO NOT cast off, break off yarn and thread through sts, pull up and fasten off securely. Make 2 pom-pons (approximately 5cm, 2ins in diameter). Stitch one pom-pon to each end of scarf.

CHILDREN'S MITTENS

featured in 'Fair Maids of February', 'Purple Willow', 'Song Thrush and Young', 'Mouse and Hare', 'Lambs', and 'Snowflakes'.

Sizes
To fit ages 2 to 6 years. Small [medium:large]

Materials
1 × 50g ball double knitting OR 1 × 50g ball chunky OR 1 × 50g ball mohair type yarn; oddments (odds and ends) of contrast colour for embroidery if required.
A set of four 3¼mm (US3) and a set of four 3¾mm (US5) double pointed knitting needles if using double knitting yarn, OR a set of four 4mm (US6) and a set of four 5mm (US8) double pointed knitting needles if using mohair or chunky yarns.

Tension/Gauge
24 sts and 32 rows to 10cm, 4ins over st st using 3¾mm (US5) needles and using double knitting yarn
16 sts and 22 rows to 10cm, 4ins over st st using 5mm (US8) needles and using mohair or chunky yarns
N.B. Needle sizes given are for double knitting yarns, for mohair or chunky yarns read sizes given in square brackets [ ].

MITTENS
Using set of four 3¼mm (US3) [4mm (US6)] needles cast on 30[34:38] sts.

Work in rounds of K1, P1 rib for 4[4:5]cm, 1½[1½:2]ins.
Change to set of four 3¾mm (US3) [5mm (US7)] needles, cont in rounds of st st, work 2[4:6] rounds.
Next round: K15[17:19], sl next 4[5:6] sts onto a holder, cast on 4[5:6], K to end.
Cont in rounds of st st until work measures 11[12:13]cm, 4¼[4¾:5¼]ins from cast on edge.
Next round: K1, sl 1, K1, psso, K9[11: 13], K2 tog, K2, sl 1, K1, psso, K9[11:13], K2 tog, K1.
Next round: K to end.
Next round: K1, sl 1, K1, psso, K7[9:11], K2 tog, K2, sl 1, K1, psso, K7[9:11], K2 tog, K1.
Cont to dec in this way on every alt round 1[2:3] times more, then sl sts onto 2 needles with the decs at each end and graft the sts together.
Work thumb
Sl the 4[5:6] sts from holder onto needle; pick up and K4[5:6] sts from the cast on sts. Cont in rounds of st st on these 8[10:12] sts for 3[4:5]cm, 1¼[1½:2]ins.
Next round: ☆K2 tog, rep from ☆ to end.
Break off yarn thread through rem sts and fasten off securely.
Make second mitt in the same way, reversing position of thumb as foll: K11[12:13], sl next 4[5:6] sts onto holder, cast on 4[5:6], K to end.

TO MAKE UP/TO FINISH
Embroider French Knots or add pom-pons if desired.

LADY'S BERET, SCARF AND GLOVES

featured in 'Gorse'.

Sizes
Beret
Small [medium: large]
Approximate measurement across diameter 20[22:24]cm, 8[8¾:9½]ins.
N.B. Larger size recommended for adult, small and medium for children.

Scarf
Approximately 141cm, 55½ins long by 21cm, 8½ins wide.

Gloves
To fit average lady's hand.

Materials
Beret
2 × 50g balls double knitting yarn (we

used Sunbeam Pure Wool DK)
One pair each 3¼mm (US3) and 4mm (US6) knitting needles

Scarf
5 × 50g balls double knitting yarn (we used Sunbeam Pure Wool DK)
One pair 3¾mm (US5) knitting needles.

Gloves
2 × 50g balls double knitting yarn (we used Sunbeam Pure Wool DK).
One pair each 3¾mm (US5) and 4mm (US6) knitting needles

Tension/Gauge
24 sts and 28 rows to 10cm, 4ins over st st using 4mm (US6) needles
33 sts to 10cm, 4ins over rib using 3¾mm (US5) needles

BERET

Using 3¼mm (US3) needles, cast on 89[97:105] sts.
1st row: (RS) K1, ☆P1, K1, rep from ☆ to end.
2nd row: P1, ☆K1, P1, rep from ☆ to end.
Rep these 2 rows for 2.5cm, 1in, ending with a WS row, inc 55[63:71] sts evenly across last row. 144[160:176] sts.
Change to 4mm (US6) needles and beg with a K row, work in st st until work measures 6[8:8.5]cm, 2½[3:3¼]ins ending with a RS row. K 1 row.
Work 2 rows in st st.
Next row: (RS) ☆K2 tog, K14[16:18], K2 tog tbl, rep from ☆ to end. 128[144:160] sts. Work 3 rows in st st.
Next row: (RS) ☆K2 tog, K12[14:16], K2 tog tbl, rep from ☆ to end. 112[128:144] sts. Work 3 rows in st st.
Cont to dec 16 sts on next and every foll 4th row as set, working 2 less sts between decs, until 80 sts rem, ending with a RS dec row. P 1 row.
Cont to dec as before on next and every alt row until 32 sts rem. P 1 row.
Next row: (RS) ☆K2 tog, K2 tog tbl, rep from ☆ to end. 16 sts. P 1 row.
Next row: (RS) ☆K2 tog, rep from ☆ to end. 8 sts.
Next row: (WS) ☆P2 tog, rep from ☆ to end. 4 sts. Break off yarn, thread through rem sts and fasten off securely.

TO MAKE UP/TO FINISH
Join seam. Make a pom-pon and secure to centre of beret.

SCARF

Using 3¾mm (US5) needles, cast on 69 sts.

1st row: (RS) K1, ☆P1, K1, rep from ☆ to end.

2nd row: P1, ☆K1, P1, rep from ☆ to end.

Rep these 2 rows until work measures approximately 141cm, 55½ins from cast-on edge, ending with a WS row. Cast off loosely in rib.

GLOVES

RIGHT HAND

Using 3¾mm (US5) needles, cast on 41 sts.

1st row: (RS) K1, ☆P1, K1, rep from ☆ to end.

2nd row: P1, ☆K1, P1; rep from ☆ to end.

Rep these 2 rows until work measures 6cm, 2½ins ending with a 2nd row.

Change to 4mm (US6) needles. ☆☆Beg with a K row work 2 rows in st st.

Shape thumb gusset

1st row: K21, P1, K2, P1, K to end.

2nd and every foll alt row: P.

3rd row: K21, P1, K into front, back, front of next st, K1, P1, K to end.

5th row: K21, P1, K4, P1, K to end.

7th row: K21, P1, ☆inc in next st, K1, rep from ☆ once, P1, K to end.

9th row: K21, P1, K6, P1, K to end.

11th row: K21, P1, inc in next st, K3, inc in next st, K1, P1, K to end.

Cont to inc 2 sts in thumb gusset on every foll 4th row until there are 51 sts. Keeping 1 purl st at each side of thumb gusset, work 5 rows in st st.

Divide for thumb

K34, turn.

Next row: K1, P11, cast on 4 sts, turn.

Work 14 rows in st st on these 16 sts.

Shape top

1st row: ☆K1, K2 tog, rep from ☆ to last st, K1.

2nd row: P.

3rd row: ☆K1, K2 tog, rep from ☆ to last 2 sts, K2.

☆☆☆Break yarn, thread through rem sts, pull up tightly and fasten off securely. Using a flat seam, join seam.☆☆☆

With RS facing rejoin yarn and K up 4 sts from cast on sts at base of thumb, K to end. 43 sts.

Next row: P.

Next row: K21, K2 tog, K1, K2 tog, K to end. 41 sts.

Beg with a P row, work 9 rows st st.

First finger

Next row: K27, turn.

Next row: P12, cast on 3 sts, turn.

Work 18 rows in st st on these 15 sts.

Shape top

1st row: ☆K1, K2 tog, rep from ☆ to end. 10 sts.

2nd row: P.

3rd row: ☆K1, K2 tog, rep from ☆ to last st, K1.

4th row: As 2nd.

Complete as thumb from ☆☆☆ to ☆☆☆.

Second finger

With RS facing join in yarn and K up 3 sts from cast on sts at base of first finger, K5, turn.

Next row: P13, cast on 2 sts, turn.

Work 20 rows in st st on these 15 sts.

Shape top as first finger. Finish as thumb from ☆☆☆ to ☆☆☆.

Third finger

With RS facing join in yarn and K up 2 sts from cast on sts at base of second finger, K5, turn.

Next row: P12, cast on 3 sts, turn.

Work as first finger.

Fourth finger

With RS facing join in yarn and K up 3 sts from cast on sts at base of third finger, K4, turn.

Next row: P12, turn.

Work 14 rows in st st on these 12 sts.

Shape top

1st row: ☆K1, K2 tog, rep from ☆ to end.

2nd row: P.

3rd row: ☆K1, K2 tog, rep from ☆ once, K2.

4th row: As 2nd.

Finish as thumb and join seam to end of cuff.

LEFT HAND

Work as right hand to ☆☆. Beg with a K row work 2 rows in st st.

Shape thumb gusset

1st row: K16, P1, K2, P1, K to end.

2nd and every foll alt row: P.

3rd row: K16, P1, K into front, back and front of next st, K1, P1, K to end.

5th row: K16, P1, K4, P1, K to end.

7th row: K16, P1, ☆inc in next st, K1, rep from ☆ once, P1, K to end.

9th row: K16, P1, K6, P1, K to end.

11th row: K16, P1, inc in next st, K3, inc

in next st, K1, P1, K to end.

Cont to inc 2 sts in thumb gusset on every foll 4th row until there are 51 sts, keeping 1 purl st at each side of thumb gusset, work 5 rows in st st.

Divide for thumb

K29, cast on 4 sts, turn.

Next row: K1, P14, K1, turn.

Complete as thumb for right hand. With RS facing join in yarn and K up 4 sts from cast on sts at base of thumb, K22. 43 sts.

Next row: P.

Next row: K16, K2 tog, K1, K2 tog, K to end. 41 sts.

Beg with a P row, work 9 rows st st.

First finger

Next row: K27, cast on 3 sts, turn.

Next row: P14, turn. Complete as first finger of right hand.

Second finger

With RS facing join in yarn and K up 3 sts from cast on sts at base of first finger, K5, cast on 2 sts, turn.

Next row: P15, turn. Complete as second finger of right hand.

Third finger

With RS facing join in yarn and K up 2 sts from base of second finger, K5, cast on 3 sts, turn.

Next row: P15, turn. Complete as third finger of right hand.

Fourth finger

Work as right hand.

ARAN SCARF

featured in 'Willow Catkins'.

Size

Approximately 164cm, 64½ins long by 24cm, 9½ins wide

Materials

6 × 50g balls Aran type yarn

One pair 4½mm (US7) knitting needles

Tension/Gauge

24 sts and 21 rows to 10cm, 4ins over rib using 4½mm (US7) needles

SCARF

Using 4½mm (US7) needles, cast on 59 sts.

1st row: (RS) K1, ☆P1, K1, rep from ☆ to end.

2nd row: P1, ☆K1, P1, rep from ☆ to end.

Rep these 2 rows until work measures approximately 164cm, 64½ins or length required. Cast off in rib.

Toys

TEDDY'S *FAIR MAIDS OF FEBRUARY SWEATER AND SCARF* *See picture on page 30*

Sizes
Sweater chest 31cm, 12¼ins
Scarf length 50cm, 19¾ins

Materials

Sweater
1 × 50g ball of brushed yarn (we used Wendy Dolce) (A)
1 ball each in 2 contrast colours (B and C)
2 small buttons

Scarf
1 × 50g ball of brushed yarn (we used Wendy Dolce) (C)
1 ball each in 2 contrast colours (A and B)
One pair each 3¼mm (US3) and 4mm (US6) knitting needles

Tension/Gauge
24 sts and 32 rows to 10cm, 4ins over st st using 4mm (US6) needles.

SWEATER

BACK
Using 3¼mm (US3) needles and A, cast on 37 sts.
Cont in K1, P1 rib as foll:
1st row: K1, ☆P1, K1, rep from ☆ to end.

2nd row: P1, ☆K1, P1, rep from ☆ to end.
Rep these 2 rows for 2cm, ¾in, ending with a 2nd row.
Change to 4mm (US6) needles and beg with a K row, work 6 rows st st.
Commence patt.
1st row: (RS) K1C, ☆3B, 1C, rep from ☆ to end.
2nd row: P1B, ☆1C, 3B, rep from ☆ to end.
3rd row: K2B, ☆1C, 3B, rep from ☆ to last 3 sts, 1C, 2B.
4th row: ☆P3B, 1C, rep from ☆ to last st, 1B.
5th row: K1A, ☆3B, 1A, rep from ☆ to end.
6th row: P2B, ☆1A, 3B, rep from ☆ to last 3 sts, 1A, 2B.
7th row: K2B, ☆ with A, cast on 2 sts, cast off 2 sts to make bobble, 3B, rep from ☆ to last 3 sts, make bobble, 2B.
8th row: P1A, ☆3B, 1A, rep from ☆ to end.
9th row: K1B, ☆1C, 3B, rep from ☆ to end.
10th row: P2B, ☆1C, 3B, rep from ☆ to last 3 sts, 1C, 2B.
11th row: ☆K3B, 1C, rep from ☆ to last st, 1B.
12th row: ☆P1C, 3B, rep from ☆ to last st, 1C.
Cont in A only, beg with a K row work 6 rows in st st.

Change to 3¼mm (US3) needles and work 4 rows in rib as set at beg. Cast off in rib.

FRONT
Work as given for back.

SLEEVES
Place a marker on back and front 9cm, 3½ins from shoulder. With RS of work facing, using 4mm (US6) needles and A, K up 22 sts from marker to shoulder, then 22 sts from shoulder to marker on back. 44 sts.
Beg with a P row work 12 rows st st.
Dec row: P5, ☆P2 tog, P2, rep from ☆ to last 7 sts, P2 tog, P5. 35 sts.
Work 6 rows in K1, P1 rib as given for back.
Cast off in rib.

TO MAKE UP/TO FINISH
Join side and sleeve seams. Sew one button to each shoulder front and make a button loop to correspond on back.

SCARF

Using 4mm (US6) needles and C, cast on 33 sts.
Beg with a K row, work 6 rows st st.
☆☆ Work 12 rows in patt as given for back of sweater. ☆☆
Cont in C only, beg with a K row cont in st st until work measures 42.5cm, 16¾ins from beg, ending with a P row.
Rep from ☆☆ to ☆☆ again.
Cont in C only, beg with a K row, work 6 rows st st. Cast off.

TO MAKE UP/TO FINISH
Fold scarf in half lengthwise, join seam. Fold flat with seam at centre back. Using strands of C, approximately 15cm, 6ins long, work a fringe along both short ends of scarf.

LADYBIRD BUG BAG

Featured on page 76

Size
Length 32cm, 12½ins
Width at base 26cm, 10¼ins

Materials
1 × 100g ball of Jarol Rambler Aran
One pair 5mm (US8) knitting needles
1m, 1 yard × 2.5cm, 1in wide black canvas tape
35cm, 14ins black zip fastener
Square of black felt for eyes and spots
2 blazer buttons for eyes
Black and red sewing thread

Tension/Gauge
17 sts and 24 rows to 10cm, 4ins over st st using 5mm (US8) needles

BACK
Using 5mm (US8) needles, cast on 44 sts.
Work 8 rows in st st.
Dec 1 st at each end of next row and

every foll 5th row until 16 sts rem.
Work 2 rows straight.
Cast off.

LEFT FRONT
Using 5mm (US8) needles, cast on 22 sts.
Work 8 rows in st st.
Dec 1 st at beg of next row and at this same edge on every foll 5th row until 8 sts rem.
Work 2 rows straight.
Cast off.

RIGHT FRONT
Work to match left front reversing shaping.

TO MAKE UP/TO FINISH
Allowing zip teeth to show on RS, sew zip fastener to straight row-ends of fronts. With RS tog, join front to back. Cut 2 eye shapes from felt and sew to top of

fronts. Cut 10 'spots' 2·5cm, 1in in diameter from felt. Position them in matching pairs on fronts and sew in place. Cut tape into 2 equal lengths for straps and sew 1 end of each strap to top of back and other ends to base corners of back. Sew buttons on to felt eyes.

EYE

TOY MOUSE WITH TROUSERS AND SWEATER

Size
Height 43cm, 17ins

Materials

Mouse
2 × 50g balls DK yarn in grey
Oddments (odds and ends) of DK yarn in black for features
One pair 4mm (US6) knitting needles
Washable stuffing

Trousers, Sweater and Scarf
1 × 50g ball DK yarn (A)
1 × 50g ball DK yarn (B)
One pair each 3¼mm (US3) and 4mm (US6) knitting needles

Tension/Gauge
22 sts and 30 rows to 10cm, 4ins over st st using 4mm (US6) needles.

MOUSE

BODY
(make 2)
Using 4mm (US6) needles cast on 13 sts. Work in st st for 12cm, 4¾ins, ending

with a P row. Leave sts on holder.
Using 4mm (US6) needles cast on another 13 sts. Work in st st for 12cm, 4¾ins, ending with a P row.
K 1 row, cast on 2 sts, K across 13 sts on holder. 28 sts.
Cont in st st until work measures 22cm, 8¾ins, ending with a P row. Mark each end of row with a coloured thread.
Cont in st st until work measures 30cm, 11¾ins, ending with a P row. Cast off.
Sew top of two body pieces tog.

ARMS
(make 2)
Using 4mm (US6) needles, K up 36 sts

evenly between coloured threads. Work in st st for 10cm, 4ins, ending with a P row.

Next row: (K2 tog) to end. 18 sts.

Next row: P.

Next row: (K2 tog) to end. 9 sts. Break off yarn, leaving a long end. Thread end through rem sts, draw up tightly and secure.

HEAD

Using 4mm (US6) needles, cast on 37 sts.

Foundation row: (WS) P.

1st row: (RS) ☆K1, pick up bar that lies between needles and K tbl – called M1, K8, M1, K1, M1, K8, M1, rep from ☆ once more, K1. 45 sts.

2nd, 4th, 6th, 8th, 10th, 12th, 14th and 16th rows: P.

3rd row: K22, M1, K1, M1, K22. 47 sts.

5th row: K1, M1, K10, (M1, K1, M1, K11) twice, M1, K1, M1, K10, M1, K1. 55 sts.

7th row: K27, M1, K1, M1, K27. 57 sts.

9th row: K1, M1, K12, (M1, K1, M1, K14) twice, M1, K1, M1, K12, M1, K1. 65 sts.

11th row: K32, M1, K1, M1, K32. 67 sts.

13th row: K.

15th row: K31, K2 tog, K1, sl 1, K1, psso, K31. 65 sts.

17th row: Sl 1, K1, psso, K11, (K2 tog, K1, sl 1, K1, psso, K12) twice, K2 tog, K1, sl 1, K1, psso, K11, K2 tog. 57 sts.

18th row: P26, P2 tog tbl, P1, P2 tog, P26. 55 sts.

19th row: K25, K2 tog, K1, sl 1, K1, psso, K25. 53 sts.

20th row: P24, P2 tog tbl, P1, P2 tog, P24. 51 sts.

21st row: Sl 1, K1, psso, K9, (K2 tog, K1, sl 1, K1, psso, K7) twice, K2 tog, K1, sl 1, K1, psso, K9, K2 tog. 43 sts.

22nd and every foll alt row: P.

23rd row: K19, K2 tog, K1, sl 1, K1, psso, K19. 41 sts.

25th row: Sl 1, K1, psso, K7, (K2 tog, K1, sl 1, K1, psso, K4) twice, K2 tog, K1, sl 1, K1, psso, K7, K2 tog. 33 sts.

27th row: Sl 1, K1, psso, K12, K2 tog, K1, sl 1, K1, psso, K12, K2 tog. 29 sts.

29th row: Sl 1, K1, psso, K10, K2 tog, K1, sl 1, K1, psso, K10, K2 tog. 25 sts.

31st row: Sl 1, K1, psso, K8, K2 tog, K1, sl 1, K1, psso, K8, K2 tog. 21 sts.

33rd row: Sl 1, K1, psso, K2, K2 tog, K1, K3 tog, K1, sl 1, K2 tog, psso, K1, sl 1,

K1, psso, K2, K2 tog. 13 sts.

34th row: P.

Cast off.

EARS

(make 4)

Using 4mm (US6) needles cast on 18 sts.

Work in st st for 12 rows.

Dec 1 st at each end of next row and foll 2 alt rows. 12 sts.

Dec 1 st at each end of next 3 rows.

Cast off rem 6 sts.

TO MAKE UP/TO FINISH

Sew back seam of head, leaving opening for stuffing. Stuff head firmly, then join opening, leaving 3cm, 1¼ins open in centre. Join seams of arms and body, leaving an opening for stuffing. Gather ends of legs slightly. Stuff body and arms firmly, leaving 3cm, 1¼ins open for head. Sew head to body, stuffing firmly so that head stands up. Sew pairs of ears together, gathering cast-on edge slightly. Sew to either side of head.

SWEATER

BACK

Using 4mm (US6) needles and A, cast on 30 sts.

K 2 rows.

Beg K, st st for 6cm, 2½ins, ending with a P row.

Shape for sleeves

Cast on 18 sts at beg of next 2 rows. 66 sts.

Next row: K to end.

Next row: K3, P60, K3.

Rep these 2 rows until work measures 15cm, 6ins from beg, ending with a WS row.

Shape shoulders

Cast off 23 sts at beg of next 2 rows.

Leave rem 20 sts on a holder.

FRONT

Work as given for back until work measures 12cm, 4¾ins, ending with a WS row.

Shape neck

Next row: K25 sts, turn.

Cont on these sts only and leave rem sts on a spare needle.

Dec 1 st at neck edge on next 2 rows.

Cont straight until front matches back to shoulder, ending at side edge.

Shape shoulder

Cast off rem 23 sts.

With RS facing, sl centre 16 sts on to a holder, rejoin yarn to inner end of rem sts and K to end. Complete to match first side.

NECKBAND

Join right shoulder seam. With RS facing, using 3¼mm (US3) needles and A, K up 10 sts down left front neck, K16 sts from centre front, K up 10 sts up right front neck and K20 sts across back neck. 56 sts.

K 2 rows. Cast off.

TO MAKE UP/TO FINISH

Join left shoulder and neckband seam. Join side and sleeve seams.

TROUSERS

FRONT

Using 4mm (US6) needles and B, cast on 15 sts.

Beg with a K row, cont in st st for 9cm, 3½ins, ending with a P row, leave sts on a holder.

Using 4mm (US6) needles and B, cast on another 15 sts.

K 2 rows.

Beg with a K row, cont in st st for 9cm, 3½ins, ending with a P row.

K 1 row.

Cast on 2 sts, K across 15 sts on holder. 32 sts.

Cont in st st until work measures 15cm, 6ins, ending with a K row.

K 2 rows.

Shape for braces (suspenders)

Next row: (RS) Cast off 8 sts, sl next 2 sts on to a safety pin, cast off 12 sts, sl next 2 sts on to a safety pin, cast off 8 sts.

Rejoin yarn to first set of 2 sts.

Cont in g st for 16cm, 6¼ins.

Cast off.

Rejoin yarn to rem 2 sts.

Work to match first set.

BACK

Work as front, omitting braces by casting off all 32 sts.

TO MAKE UP/TO FINISH

Join inner leg and side seams.

Sew ends of braces to back.

SCARF

Using 4mm (US6) needles and A, cast

on 12 sts.
Work in g st for 30cm, 11¾ins.
Cast off.

TOY HEDGEHOG

Size
Approximate length 30cm, 11¾ins

Materials
3 × 50g balls Emu Superwash DK in main colour (M)
1 ball contrast colour (C)
One pair 5mm (US8) knitting needles
Oddment (odds and ends) of black yarn for eyes and nose
Small piece of black felt for paws
Stuffing

Tension/Gauge
14 sts and 22 rows to 10cm, 4ins over fur stitch using 5mm (US8) needles and yarn double

N.B. USE YARN DOUBLE THROUGHOUT

FUR STITCH (Use yarn double.)
1st row: (RS) K1, ☆K1 but do not drop st off left needle, bring yarn forward between needles and wind over left thumb to form a loop approximately 4cm, 1½ins, take yarn between needles to back and K the same st again but this time drop st off left needle, bring yarn forward between needles then take it over right needle to make a loop, pass the 2 sts just knitted over this loop and off right needle, K next st☆, rep from ☆ to ☆ to last 2 sts, K2.
2nd row: K.
3rd row: K2, rep from ☆ to ☆ of 1st row to last st, K1.
4th row: K.
These 4 rows form fur stitch.

LEFT BACK
Beg at rear end. Use yarn double.
Using 5mm (US8) needles and M, cast on 7 sts.
Working in fur stitch throughout and taking care to keep patt correct, shape work thus:
1st row: Work to end.
2nd row: Inc 1 st at each end of row.
3rd row: Inc 1 st at beg of row.
4th row: Inc 1 st at beg of row.
5th row: Inc 1 st at each end of row.
6th row: Work to end.
7th and 8th rows: As 5th and 6th rows.
9th row: As 3rd row.
10th row: Work to end.
11th row: Inc 1 st at beg of row and dec 1 st at end of row.
12th–14th rows: Work to end.
15th–18th rows: As 11th–14th rows.
19th and 20th rows: As 11th and 12th rows.
21st row: Inc 1 st at end of row.
22nd row: Work to end.
23rd–26th rows: As 21st and 22nd rows.
27th row: As 21st row.
28th row: Inc 1 st at beg of row.
29th–34th rows: As 27th and 28th rows.
35th–37th rows: Work to end.

38th row: Cast on 2 sts at beg of row and dec 1 st at end of row.

39th–41st rows: Work to end.

42nd row: Dec 1 st at end of row.

43rd row: Work to end.

44th row: Cast off 8 sts at beg of row.

45th row: Work to end.

46th row: Dec 1 st at each end of row.

47th row: Dec 1 st at end of row.

48th row: As 46th row.

49th row: Work to end.

50th row: As 46th row.

51st row: As 47th row.

52nd row: As 46th row.

53rd row: Work to end.

54th row: As 47th row.

55th row: Dec 1 st at beg of row.

56th row: Inc 1 st at beg of row and dec 1 st at end of row.

57th row: Dec 1 st at beg of row.

58th – 59th rows: As 56th and 57th rows.

60th row: As 56th row.

61st row: Dec 1 st at each end of row.

Cast off rem 3 sts.

RIGHT BACK

Work as for left back reversing all shapings.

LEFT TUMMY

Beg at rear end. Use yarn double.

With 5mm (US8) needles and C, cast on 7 sts.

Working in st st throughout shape work thus:

1st–4th rows: Work to end.

5th row: Inc 1 st at end of row.

6th row: Work to end.

7th row: As 5th row.

8th row: Inc 1 st at beg of row.

9th row: Work to end.

10th row: Dec 1 st at beg of row.

11th–13th rows: Work to end.

14th row: As 10th row.

15th–17th rows: Work to end.

18th row: Dec 1 st at beg of row and inc 1 st at end of row.

19th–25th rows: Work to end.

26th row: Inc 1 st at end of row.

27th–29th rows: Work to end.

30th row: As 26th row.

31st row: Work to end.

32nd row: Inc 1 st at each end of row.

33rd–35th rows: Work to end.

36th row: Cast off 2 sts at beg of row and dec 1 st at end of row.

37th row: Dec 1 st at end of row.

38th row: Dec 1 st at beg of row.

39th row: As 37th row.

40th row: Dec 1 st at each end of row.

41st row: Work to end.

42nd row: As 40th row.

43rd row: K2 tog and fasten off.

RIGHT TUMMY

Work as left tummy reversing all shapings.

FACE (Use yarn double.)

With 5mm (US8) needles and C, cast on 18 sts.

Working in st st throughout shape work thus:

Work 1 row.

Inc 1 st at each end of every row until there are 38 sts.

Work 2 rows straight.

Inc 1 st at each end of every row until there are 54 sts.

Work 10 rows straight.

Cast off 2 sts at beg of next 2 rows.

Work 4 rows straight.

Cast off 2 sts at beg of next 2 rows.

Cast off rem 46 sts.

TO MAKE UP/TO FINISH

With RS tog, fold face in half along cast-off edge and sew cast-off edge. Sew shorter edges of tummy pieces tog. With centre of cast-on edge of face to centre tummy seam, sew cast-on edge of face to tummy (leave 'legs' free at each side of tummy). Join centre back seam. Matching feet, sew tummy/face to back leaving an opening for stuffing. Stuff hedgehog and close opening. Cut 4 paws from felt and sew to feet. With oddment (odds and ends) of black yarn, embroider eyes and nose. Cut through centre of each fur stitch loop.

SNOWBIRDS RAG DOLL

Size

Height 58cm, 22¾ins

Materials

Doll

2 × 50g balls of Patons Fairytale 4 ply DK yarn for hair

One pair 2¾mm (US2) knitting needles

Washable stuffing

Felt and 2 small buttons for shoes

Embroidery thread for features

Ribbon for hair bows

Dress and Hat

2 × 50g balls of Patons Fairytale DK in main colour (A)

1 ball contrast colour (B)

One pair each 3¼mm (US3) and 3¾mm (US5) knitting needles

Medium-sized crochet hook

1 small button for back opening and 1 round button for collar trim 75cm, 29½ins × 9cm, 3½ins wide broiderie anglais trim for petticoat

Ribbon for bow

Tension/Gauge

25 sts and 34 rows to 10cm, 4ins over st st using 3¾mm (US5) needles and DK yarn

DOLL

BODY AND HEAD

(make 2)

Using 2¾mm (US2) needles cast on 32 sts.

Work in st st and inc 1 st at beg of first 4 rows. 36 sts.

Work 58 rows straight.

Shape shoulders

Cast off 6 sts at beg of next 2 rows.

Dec 1 st at each end of next row. 22 sts.

Inc 1 st at each end of next 3 rows.

Inc 1 st at beg of next 8 rows. 36 sts.

Work 38 rows straight.

Dec 1 st at each end of next 9 rows.

Cast off rem 18 sts.

ARMS

(make 2)

Using 2¾mm (US2) needles cast on 11 sts.

Work in st st and inc 1 st at beg of first 6 rows. 17 sts.

Work 6 rows straight.

Dec 1 st at beg of next 4 rows. 13 sts.

Work 1 row, thus ending with a K row.

Cut off yarn and leave sts on a spare needle.

Make another piece in the same way but do not cut off yarn.

Joining row: P to end, then on to same needle, P across sts of first piece. 26 sts.

Work 8 rows.

Next row: K1, M1, K to last st, M1, K1. 28 sts.

Work 9 rows.

Next row: K1, M1, K to last st, M1, K1. 30 sts.

Work 42 rows straight.

Dec 1 st at each end of next 14 rows.

P2 tog and fasten off securely.

LEGS
(make 2)

Using 2¾mm (US2) needles cast on 32 sts.

Work in st st for 27cm, 10¾ins, ending with a P row.

Shape foot

Next row: K14, sl 1, K1, psso, K2 tog, K14.

P 1 row.

Next row: K13, sl 1, K1, psso, K2 tog, K13.

P 1 row.

Next row: K12, sl 1, K1, psso, K2 tog, K12.

P 1 row.

Cont to shape in this way, working 1 st less at each end of every RS row until 18 sts rem, ending with a P row.

Cut off yarn leaving a long end. Thread end through rem sts, draw up tightly and secure.

TO MAKE UP/TO FINISH

With RS tog, sew round outer edge of body and head pieces, leaving an opening for stuffing. Stuff firmly, then join opening. Join seams of arms and legs, leaving top edge open. Stuff firmly then join open edges. Work lines of back stitch along each hand to indicate fingers. Sew arms and legs in position. Cut DK yarn into 41cm, 16ins lengths for hair. Arrange hair centrally on top of head and back stitch along centre to join hair to head and to form the 'parting'. Tie a ribbon at each side to form bunches then catch ribbon to head under hair.

Trim ends of hair. Embroider features on face. Using template cut 2 shoe uppers with centre hole and 2 shoe soles without hole, from felt. Sew soles to uppers. Place shoes on feet and sew buttons in position securing shoes to feet.

DRESS

FRONT

Using 3¾mm (US5) needles and B, cast on 73 sts.

K 3 rows.

Cont in patt:

1st row: (RS) With A, K1, ☆(K2 tog) twice, (yfwd, K1) 3 times, yfwd, (sl 1, K1, psso) twice, K1, rep from ☆ to end.

2nd row: P with A.

3rd–8th rows: Work 1st and 2nd rows 3 times.

9th–12th rows: K with B.

Rep 1st–12th rows once.

Cut off B. Cont with A only in st st until work measures 21cm, 8½ins from cast-on edge, ending with a P row.

Dec row: ☆K2 tog, rep from ☆ to last 3 sts, K3 tog. 36 sts.

Cont straight until work measures 28cm, 11ins from cast-on edge, ending with a P row.

Shape neck

Next row: K11, turn.

Cont on these sts only and leave rem sts on a spare needle.

Dec 1 st at neck edge on next 5 rows.

Cast off rem 6 sts.

With RS of work facing, sl centre 14 sts on to a holder, rejoin yarn to inner end of rem sts and K to end.

Complete to match first side.

BACK

Work as given for front until dec row has been worked. 36 sts.

Work 11 rows, thus ending with a P row.

Divide for opening

Next row: K18, turn.

Cont on these sts only and leave rem sts on a spare needle.

Work straight until back matches front to shoulder, ending at side edge.

Shape shoulder

Cast off 6 sts at beg of next row. Leave rem 12 sts on a holder.

With RS of work facing rejoin yarn to inner end of sts on spare needle, K to end.

Complete to match first side.

SLEEVES

With 3¼mm (US3) needles and A, cast on 33 sts.

Work 4 rows st st for hem.

Picot row: K1, ☆yfwd, K2 tog, rep from☆ to end.

Beg with a P row, work 4 rows st st.

Inc row: ☆P twice in next st, P1, rep from☆ to last st, P twice in last st. 50 sts.

Work 20 rows st st. Cast off.

COLLAR

Join shoulder seams.

With RS of work facing, using 3¼mm (US3) needles and A, K across 12 sts of left back neck, K up 8 sts down left front neck then K across first 7 sts on front neck. 27 sts.

K 5 rows, thus ending at back neck.

Next row: K to last 2 sts, K2 tog.

Next row: K.

Rep last 2 rows twice.

Cast off, dec as before.

With RS of work facing, using 3¼mm (US3) needles and A, K across rem 7 sts of front neck, K up 8 sts up right front neck then K across 12 sts of back neck. 27 sts.

K 5 rows, thus ending at front neck.

Next row: Sl 1, Kl, psso, K to end.

Next row: K.

Rep last 2 rows twice.

Cast off, dec as before.

TO MAKE UP/TO FINISH

Mark depth of armholes 6cm, 2½ins from shoulder seams on back and front. Sew sleeves to armholes between markers making a pleat at top of sleeve with fullness. Join side and sleeve seams. Fold sleeve hems on to WS and catch stitch in place. With RS facing, using crochet hook and A, work a row dc (sc) evenly around back opening, turn. Work 4 ch for button loop, miss next 2 dc (sc), slip stitch in to next dc (sc). Fasten off. Sew on button to correspond with button loop. Sew the round button to front neck for decoration. Tie ribbon in to a bow and sew to front neck. Join ends of broiderie anglais trim then sew top edge to WS of dress along top B row gathering in fullness to fit and allowing trim to show below dress.

CAP

Using 3¼mm (US3) needles and A, cast on 150 sts for frill.

K 3 rows.

Cut off A; join on B.

K 6 rows.

Dec row: ☆K2 tog, rep from☆ to end. 75 sts.

Cast off.

Using 3¾mm (US5) needles and B, cast on 20 sts for crown.

Work in st st inc 1 st at each end of next 14 rows. 48 sts.

Inc 1 st at beg of next 22 rows. 70 sts.

Work 15 rows straight.

Dec 1 st at beg of next 22 rows. 48 sts.

Dec 1 st at each end of next 14 rows. 20 sts.

Cast off.

TO MAKE UP/TO FINISH

Run a gathering thread along cast-off edge of frill. Sew frill to outer edge of crown, gathering to fit. Place cap on head and secure with a few stitches.

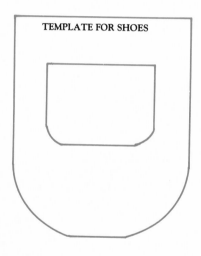

TEMPLATE FOR SHOES

MOTHER RABBIT'S OUTFIT

Also featured in 'Primroses and Snowdrops' on page 30

Size

To fit bunny 45cm, 17¾ins high (not including ears)

Cardigan
Actual chest measurement 36cm, 14¼ins
Length 12cm, 4¾ins
Sleeve seam 9cm, 3½ins

Skirt
Length 19cm, 7½ins

Materials

2 × 50g balls Wendy Dolce in main colour (A)

1 ball in each of 2 contrast colours (B and C)

One pair each 3¼mm (US3) and 4mm (US6) knitting needles

6 small buttons for cardigan

1m, 1yd × 2.5cm, 1in wide broiderie anglais trim for apron and mop cap

Ribbon for apron

Elastic for skirt and mop cap

Fabric flowers for trimming mop cap

Tension/Gauge

24 sts and 32 rows to 10cm, 4ins over st st using 4mm (US6) needles

SKIRT

Using 4mm (US6) needles and A, cast on 168 sts.

Work in K1, P1 rib for 2cm, ¾in.

Cont in st st until skirt measures 18cm, 7ins from beg, ending with a P row.

Change to 3¼mm (US3) needles.

Dec row: ☆P1, K2 tog, rep from ☆ to end. 112 sts.

Cont in K1, P1 rib for 2cm, ¾in.

Cast off.

TO MAKE UP/TO FINISH

Join side seam.

Fold ribbed waistband in half to inside and slip stitch loosely in place, leaving opening for elastic. Thread elastic through and sew opening.

CARDIGAN

BACK

Using 3¼mm (US3) needles and B, cast on 44 sts.

Work in K1, P1 rib for 2cm, ¾in.

Change to 4mm (US6) needles.

Cont in st st until back measures 4cm, 1½ins from beg, ending with a P row.

Shape armholes

Dec 1 st at each end of next 6 rows. 32 sts.

Mark each end of last row with a coloured thread.

Cont straight in st st until back measures 12cm, 4¾ins, ending with a P row.

Shape shoulders

Cast off 8 sts at beg of next 2 rows. Leave rem 16 sts on a holder.

LEFT FRONT

Using 3¼mm (US3) needles and B, cast on 22 sts.

Work in K1, P1 rib for 2cm, ¾in.

Work in K1, P1 rib for 2cm, ¾in.
Change to 4mm (US6) needles.
Cont in st st until sleeve seam measures 9cm, 3½ins, ending with a P row.
Shape top
Dec 1 st at each end of next 6 rows.
Cast off rem 26 sts, marking first and last sts with a coloured thread.

NECKBAND

Join shoulder seams.
Using 3¼mm (US3) needles and B, with RS facing, K up 12 sts up right front neck, K16 sts from back neck, K up 12 sts down left front neck. 40 sts.
Work in K1, P1 rib for 4 rows.
Cast off.

BUTTONHOLE BAND

Using 3¼mm (US3) needles and B, with RS facing, K up 36 sts up right front.
Work 1 row in K1, P1 rib.
Buttonhole row: K1, P1, (K2 tog, yrn, K1, P1, K1, P1) 5 times, K2 tog, yrn, K1, P1.
Work 2 rows in K1, P1 rib.
Cast off in rib

BUTTONBAND

Work as buttonhole band, omitting buttonholes.

TO MAKE UP/TO FINISH

Set in sleeves, placing top of sleeves to shoulder seam and matching coloured threads, making sure sleeve lies flat. Join side and sleeve seams. Sew on buttons to correspond with buttonholes.

APRON

Using 4mm (US6) needles and B, cast on 24 sts.
K 3 rows.
1st row: (RS) K.
2nd row: K2, P to last 2 sts, K2.
Rep these 2 rows until work measures 11cm, 4¼ins, ending with a 2nd row.
Next row: ☆K1, K2 tog, rep from ☆ to end.
K 2 rows.
Cast off.

TO MAKE UP/TO FINISH

Sew broderie anglais trim along side and cast-on edges. Gather top of apron to centre of length of ribbon and sew in place.

Change to 4mm (US6) needles.
Cont in st st until front measures 4cm, 1½ins from beg, ending at armhole edge.
Shape armhole
Dec 1 st at armhole edge on next 6 rows. 16 sts.
Mark end of last row with a coloured thread.
Cont straight in st st until front measures 10cm, 4ins, ending at neck edge.
Shape neck
Cast off 5 sts at beg of next row.

Dec 1 st at neck edge on next 3 rows.
Cont straight in st st until front matches back to shoulder, ending at side edge.
Shape shoulder
Cast off rem 8 sts.

RIGHT FRONT

Work as left front, reversing shapings.

SLEEVES

Using 3¼mm (US3) needles and B, cast on 38 sts.

MOP CAP

Using 4mm (US6) needles and C, cast on 8 sts.
Working in st st, cast on 4 sts at beg of next 4 rows.
Inc 1 st at each end of next 4 rows.
Inc 1 st at each end of every foll 4th row twice. 36 sts.

TO MAKE SPLIT FOR EARS

Next row: K10, cast off 16, K10.
Next row: P10, cast on 16, P10.
Work 14 rows straight in st st.
Cont in st st dec 1 st at each end of next and foll 4th row twice. 30 sts.
Dec 1 st at each end of next 3 rows. 24 sts.

Cast off 4 sts at beg of next 4 rows.
Cast off rem 8 sts.

TO MAKE UP/TO FINISH

Sew broderie anglais trim around mop cap. Using herringbone stitch, sew elastic to WS edge of mop cap. Trim with fabric flowers.

TEDDY'S *PURPLE WILLOW* SWEATER AND SCARF

TEDDY'S *CRIMSON TOADSTOOL* SWEATER, BERET AND SCARF

Size

Sweater chest 35cm, 13¾ins
Beret diameter across crown 18cm, 7ins
Scarf length 61cm, 24ins

Materials

Sweater
Oddments (odds and ends) from children's 'Purple Willow' or 'Crimson Toadstool' cardigan and sweater. See pages 19 and 106.
2 buttons

Beret and Scarf
1 × 50g ball of mohair
One pair each 4½mm (US7) and 5½mm (US9) OR 5mm (US8) knitting needles

Tension/Gauge

19 sts and 19 rows to 10cm, 4ins over patt using 5½mm (US9) needles and Paris Mohair OR 5mm (US8) needles and Sumatra

SWEATER

N.B. Use oddment (odds and ends) in largest quantity as A.

BACK

Using smaller needles and A, cast on 33 sts.
Work 4 rows K1, P1 rib.
Change to larger needles and beg with a K row cont in st st working patt from chart given on page 108.
Cont in patt until work measures 11.5cm, 4½ins from beg, ending with a WS row.
Change to smaller needles and cont in A.
Work 4 rows K1, P1 rib.
Cast off in rib.

FRONT

Work as given for back.

SLEEVES

Using smaller needles and A, cast on 25 sts.
Work 4 rows K1, P1 rib as given for back.
Inc row: Rib 1, ☆inc in next st, rib 1, rep from ☆ to end. 37 sts.
Change to larger needles and beg with a K row cont in st st working patt from chart.

Cont in patt until work measures 7cm, 2¾ins from beg, ending with a WS row. Cast off loosely.

TO MAKE UP/TO FINISH

Mark a point 9.5cm, 3¾ins down from shoulders on back and front. Sew sleeves in place between markers, without joining shoulder seams. Join side and sleeve seams. Sew one button to each shoulder front and make a button loop to correspond on back.

BERET

Using smaller needles, cast on 45 sts.
Work 3 rows K1, P1 rib.
Inc row: Rib 1, ☆inc in next st, rep from ☆ to last st, rib 1. 88 sts.
Change to larger needles and beg with a K row work 9 rows st st.
Next row: K.
Beg with a K row work 2 rows st st.
Commence shaping
Next row: ☆K2 tog, K7, K2 tog tbl, rep from ☆ to end. 72 sts.
Beg with a P row work 3 rows st st.
Next row: ☆K2 tog, K5, K2 tog tbl, rep from ☆ to end. 56 sts.
Beg with a P row, work 3 rows st st.
Cont to dec 16 sts in this way on next and every foll 4th row until 24 sts rem.
Next row: P.
Next row: K2 tog, ☆K1, K2 tog, rep from ☆ to last st, K1. 16 sts.
Next row: P.
Next row: ☆K2 tog, rep from ☆ to end.
Rep last 2 rows once more. 4 sts.
Cut off yarn, thread through rem sts, draw up and fasten off securely.

TO MAKE UP/TO FINISH

Join seam. Make a pom-pon approximately 4cm, 1½ins in diameter and sew to crown.

SCARF

Using smaller needles, cast on 8 sts.

Work in K1, P1 rib until scarf measures approx 61cm, 24ins.
Cast off in rib.

TEDDY'S *LADYBIRD* SWEATER

Size
Chest 32cm, 12½ins

Materials
1 × 50g ball of DK yarn (A)
1 small ball of DK yarn (B)
One pair each 3¼mm (US3) and 4mm (US6) knitting needles
2 small buttons

Tension/Gauge
23 sts and 26 rows to 10cm, 4ins over st st using 4mm (US6) needles

SWEATER
Work as given for 'Fair Maids of February' on page 143, omitting patt.
Swiss darn spots over sweater as shown in photograph using following chart.

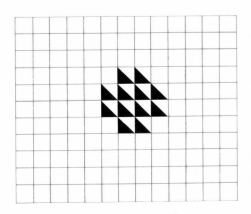

TEDDY'S *SNOWFLAKE* SWEATER, SCARF AND HAT

TEDDY'S *POPPY* SWEATER AND SCARF

Sizes
Sweaters: chest 34cm, 13½ins
Scarves: 46cm, 18ins

Materials
'Snowflake' outfit: 2 × 50g balls of Aran type yarn (A)
1 × 50g ball (B)
Small ball DK yarn for hat
'Poppy' outfit: 2 × 50g balls of Aran type yarn (A)
Oddments (odds and ends) in 2 contrast colours (B and C)
Pair each 4½mm (US7) and 5mm (US8)

knitting needles
2 small buttons for each of the sweaters

Tension/Gauge
18 sts and 24 rows to 10cm, 4ins over st st using 5mm (US8) needles

SWEATER
(Both 'Snowflake' and 'Poppy' sweaters are worked the same)

BACK
Using 4½mm (US7) needles and A, cast on 31 sts.
Work in K1, P1 rib as given for 'Fair Maids of February' sweater on page 143 for 2cm, ¾in.
Change to 5mm (US8) needles and beg with a K row, work in st st for 11cm, 4¼ins, ending with a P row.
Change to 4½mm (US7) needles and work 4 rows in K1, P1 rib as given for 'Fair Maids' sweater.
Cast off in rib.

FRONT
Work as given for back.

SLEEVES
Place a marker on back and front 9cm, 3½ins down from shoulder.
With RS of work facing, using 5mm (US8) needles and A, K up 17 sts from marker to shoulder on front, then 17 sts from shoulder to marker on back. 34 sts.
Beg with a P row work 12 rows st st.
Dec row: ☆P2 tog, P2, rep from ☆ to last 2 sts, P2 tog. 25 sts.
Work 6 rows K1, P1 rib as given on back.
Cast off in rib.

TO MAKE UP/TO FINISH
As given for 'Fair Maids' Sweater on page 143.
Then working from appropriate chart on page 156 Swiss Darn motif on front of sweater.

SCARF
Using 5mm (US8) needles cast on 8 sts.
Work in K1, P1 rib for 46cm, 18¼ins.
Cast off in rib.

BOBBLE HAT
('Snowflake' outfit)
Worked as given for 'Holly' hat on page 157.

TEDDY'S *PURPLE
WILLOW* SWEATER
AND SCARF

TEDDY'S *LADYBIRD*
SWEATER

TEDDY'S *POPPY*
SWEATER
AND SCARF

TEDDY'S *CRIMSON TOADSTOOL* SWEATER, BERET AND SCARF

TEDDY'S *HOLLY* SWEATER, SCARF AND BOBBLE HAT

TEDDY'S *SNOWFLAKE* SWEATER, SCARF AND HAT

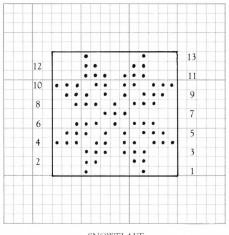

SNOWFLAKE

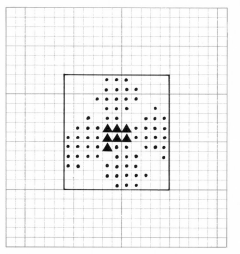

POPPY

TEDDY'S *HOLLY* SWEATER, SCARF AND BOBBLE HAT

Size

Sweater chest 32cm, 12½ins
Scarf length 50cm, 19¾ins

Materials

2 × 50g balls of DK yarn (A) (we used Emu Superwash)
2 × 50g balls of DK yarn (B)
One pair each 3¼mm (US3), 4mm (US6) knitting needles
2 small buttons for sweater

Tension/Gauge

23 sts and 26 rows to 10cm, 4ins over st st using 4mm (US6) needles.

SWEATER

This is worked as Teddy's 'Fair Maids of February' Sweater see page 143 BUT using A instead of B and C instead of A when working patt.

SCARF

This is worked as Teddy's 'Fair Maids of February' Scarf see page 143 BUT use B for main st st part and when working patt use A instead of C and B instead of A. Also use A for fringe.

BOBBLE HAT

Using 3¼mm (US3) needles and A, cast on 79 sts.
Work 2cm, ¾in in K1, P1 rib as given on back of sweater, ending with a 2nd row.
Change to 4mm (US6) needles and beg with a K row cont in st st as foll:
Next row: Cast off 7 sts, K33, turn, leave rem sts on a spare needle.
☆☆Dec 1 st at each end of next 11 rows. 11 sts.
Work 5 rows straight.
Cast off.
With RS of work facing, rejoin yarn to rem 39 sts on spare needle.
Cast off 6 sts, K to end. Complete to match first side from ☆☆ to ☆☆.

TO MAKE UP/TO FINISH

Join top of hat along cast-off edges. Join ribbed side seams. Make a small pom-pon and secure to top of hat.

Useful Addresses

Please send a stamped addressed envelope when contacting any of the following UK manufacturers. For US addresses and yarn equivalents see separate lists.

Spinners

Argyll Wools Ltd
PO Box 15,
Priestley Mills,
Pudsey,
W Yorkshire
LS28 9LT
Tel: 0532 558411

J & P Coats (UK) Ltd
39 Durham Street,
Glasgow
G41 1BS
Tel: 041 427 5311

Emu Wools Ltd
Leeds Road,
Greengates
Bradford,
W Yorks
Tel: 0274 614031

Hayfield Textiles Ltd
Hayfield Mills,
Glusburn,
Keighley,
W Yorks
BD20 6QP
Tel: 0535 33333

Jarol Ltd
White Rose Mills,
Cape Street,
Bradford
BD1 4RN
Tel: 0274 392274

Patons and Baldwins Ltd
PO Box,
McMullen Road,
Darlington,
Co Durham
DL1 1YQ
Tel: 0325 460133

Phildar (UK) Ltd
4 Gambrel Road,
Westgate Industrial Estate,
Northampton
NN5 5NF
Tel: 0604 583111

Pingouin
French Wools Ltd
7–11 Lexington Street,
London
W1R 4BY

Poppleton
Richard Poppleton and Sons Ltd
Albert Mills,
Horbury,
Wakefield,
W Yorks
WF4 5NJ
Tel: 0924 264141

Rowan Yarns
Green Lane Mill,
Washpit,
Holmfirth,
W Yorks
HD7 1RW
Tel: 0484 687715

Samband
Studio Yarns Ltd
The Citadel,
Blenheim Gardens,
London
SW2 5EQ
Tel: 01 671 7626

Scotnord Yarns Ltd
PO Box 27,
Athey St,
Macclesfield,
Cheshire
SK11 8EA
Tel: 0625 29436

Sirdar plc
PO Box 31,
Alverthorpe,
Wakefield,
W Yorks
WF2 9ND
Tel: 0924 371501

Sunbeam Knitting Wools
Crawshaw Mills,
Pudsey,
W Yorks
LS28 7BS
Tel: 0532 571871

HG Twilley Ltd
Roman Mill,
Little Casterton Road,
Stamford,
Lincolnshire
PE9 1BG
Tel: 0780 52661

Wendy Wools
Carter and Parker Ltd
Gordon Mills,
Guiseley,
Leeds
LS20 9PD
Tel: 0943 72264

Mailorder Addresses

Many yarns featured in this book are available by mail order (please send SAE), from the following.

Ries Wools at Holborn
242 High Holborn,
London WC1
Tel: 01 242 7721

Bishops of Ilford
Third Avenue,
Pioneer Market,
Ilford,
Essex
IG1 2RD
Tel: 01 478 0515

Useful Addresses for Readers in the United States and Canada

Argyll
Twilleys
Scotts Woolen Mill Inc
528 Jefferson Avenue,
Bristol, PA 19007

Emu
The Plymouth Yarn Co Inc
PO Box 28,
500 Lafayette St,
Bristol, PA 19007

Hayfield
Samband
Shepherd Wools Inc
711 Johnson Ave,
Blaine,
WA 98230

Patons
Susan Bates Inc
PO Box E,
RTE 9A,
Chester, CT 06412

Patons & Baldwins (Canada) Inc
1001 Roselawn Avenue,
Toronto, Ont

Phildar
6438 Dawson Boulevard,
85 North,
Norcross, GA 30093

Pingouin
PO Box 100,
Jamestown, SC 29453

Rowan
Westminster Trading Corp
5 Northern Boulevard,
Amherst, NH 03031

Sirdar
Kendex Corp
PO Box 1909,
616 Fitch Avenue,
Moor Park, CA 93021

Sunbeam
Estelle Designs & Sales Ltd
38 Continental Place,
Scarborough, Ont M1R 2T4

Equivalent Yarns

UK

Jarol Imps & Angels
Jarol Supersaver

Poppletons Emmerdale DK

4-ply
double knitting
Aran
chunky

US

Unger Baby Courtelle
Unger Britania

Unger roly Sport

sport
knitting worsted
fisherman
bulky

RETAIL AND MANUFACTURER CREDITS

Children's skirts and trousers made from a selection of patterns by:
McCall Pattern Distributors Ltd
London House,
42 Upper Richmond Road West,
London
SW14 8DD
Tel: 01 878 7916

Buttons by:
(i) Pikaby buttons available from haberdashery shops and departments
(ii) **The Button Box**
(personal callers and mailorder)
10 Bedford Street, Covent Garden,
London WC1

Beads by:
Creative Beadcraft Ltd
(personal callers)
Ells and Farrier Ltd
20 Princes Street
London W1
Tel: 01 629 9964
Creative Beadcraft Ltd
(mailorder)
Denmark Works,
Sheepcote Dell Road,
Beamond End,
Near Amersham,
Bucks
HP7 0RX
Tel: 0494 715606

Soft toy materials and handicraft supplies from:
Swancraft
(personal callers and mailorder brochure)
Westminster Road,
Vauxhall Industrial Estate,
Canterbury,
Kent
CT1 1YY
Tel: 0227 69888

Dried flowers from:
Winter Flora
Hall Farm,
Weston,
Beccles,
Suffolk

Garden equipment and baskets from a selection at:
Camden Garden Centre
66 Kentish Town Road,
London

Country Diary fabric and curtains by
Dorma
Further fabric supplied by:
Viyella

Children's shoes and boots by:
Start-rite
Norfolk

Toy chicks and Buffy O'Hare by:
Department 56
Showroom
1200 Second Avenue South,
Minneapolis
MN 55403/2523
USA
James Winchester Ltd
Dept 56,
38 Savile Row,
London W1X 2ET
Tel: 01 734 9421

Period clothing from a selection to buy at:
Gallery of Antique Textile and Costume
2 Church Street,
London NW8
or to hire from:
Jo Dalby
4 Ravey Street,
London EC2

Antique petticoats and lace from a selection at:
Lunn Antiques
86 New King's Road,
London SW6

Hats from a selection at:
The Hat Shop,
9 Gee's Court,
London W1

Ribbons throughout by:
CM Offray and Son Ltd
Fir Tree Place,
Church Road,
Ashford,
Middx
TW15 2PH

HAND-KNITTING DESIGNER CREDITS

Jane Blagden for:
'May'.

Pam Boon for:
'Fair Maids of February', 'Song Thrush and Young', 'Lambs', Toy Lamb.

Lynne Davies for:
'Buttercups and Daisies', 'Wild Pear', 'Honeysuckle', 'Willow Herb', 'Kingfisher', 'Hawthorn Blossom', 'Wild Hyacinths', 'Ladybirds', 'Red Berries', 'Yellow-Hammers', 'Blackberry', 'Christmas' (Note: knitted collar by designers at J and P Coats (UK) Ltd), 'Snowbirds' (including doll), 'Daisy'.

Jonathan Mitchell for:
'Mouse and Hare', 'Hedgehog'.

Brenda Morris for:
'Lady's Smock', 'Speedwell', 'Red Poppy', 'Robin'.

Debbie Scott for:
'Meadows', 'Poppies', 'Seed-vessels', Toy Hedgehog, Toy Mouse, Mother Rabbit's outfits worn by Buffy O'Hare, Ladybird bug bag.

Frances Smith for:
'Daffy-down-dilly', 'Wild Guelder Rose', 'Sparrow', 'Autumn Leaves', 'Parsnip and Parsley'.

Sue Smith for:
'Dog Roses', 'Ivy'.

Brenda Sparkes for:
'Snowdrops', 'Trailing Rose', 'Cornfield', 'Song Thrush', 'Frost and Ice'.

Rosy Tucker for:
'Swallows', 'Purple Willow', 'Willow Catkins', 'Forget-me-not', 'Thistle', 'Hazel Nuts and Acorns', 'Crimson Toadstools', 'Holly', 'Winter Leaves', Teddy's outfits.

Thanks to Lynne Davies, Rosy Tucker and Brenda Morris with regard to: 'Butterfly' and 'Mistletoe'.

Author Credits

Designers
Lynne Davies, Rosy Tucker, Brenda Sparkes,
Pam Boon, Frances Smith, Debbie Scott,
Brenda Morris, Sue Smith and Jane Blagden
Photographer
Belinda, assisted by Sara. *The Country Diary
Book of Knitting* was shot on location at Fawke
House.
Stylist
Annie Munro (represented by Pin-up)
Models
Vanessa Spiro (represented by Bookings)
Nicholas Pritchard
Billie and Jessie Lever Taylor
Simon Lloyd

Acknowledgements

The Country Diary Book of Knitting would not
have been possible without the enthusiasm
and help of many friends and colleagues.
Their names are too numerous to mention in
full and I sincerely apologise for any
omissions.

I would like to give special and sincere thanks
to Belinda for her superb photography and
kindness and to Marilyn Wilson for her
patience and hard work; to John Agar; Joan
Harris; Amanda Cooke; Daniela Felber;
Barbara Kramer; Claire Jarvis; Alison Procter;
Kay Dick; Jackie Owen; Sue Horen; Heather,
Colin and Judy; Mrs Miller; Rosy and Debbie
for their great help; Peter Tucker for kindly
lending Teddy, and, as always, to my dear
friend Kate and my son Jonathan for putting
up with me.